The Rural Architecture of Scotland

The Rural Architecture of Scotland

ALEXANDER FENTON
Director, National Museum of Antiquities of Scotland

BRUCE WALKER
Lecturer in Architecture,
Duncan of Jordanstone College of Art,
University of Dundee

JOHN DONALD PUBLISHERS LTD
EDINBURGH

ISBN 0 85976 020 0

The publishers acknowledge the financial assistance of the Scottish Arts Council in the publication of this volume.

Printed in Great Britain by Bell & Bain Ltd., Glasgow.

Contents

Figures

Introduction

FARM buildings are not static. Once erected, they are like other mortal things subject to change and decay. As farming techniques alter, as new equipment comes into play, buildings are adapted, extensions are added, and buildings that were perfectly adequate when originally built, may become forlorn and fragmentary elements in the range of large units required for modern farming.

In general, the farm-buildings of Scotland are not old. Few ante-date 1750, the oldest being mains- or home-farms attached to estates. The majority are younger than 1850. They came into being as part of the intensive and far-reaching agricultural improvements that changed the face of the country from the mid-eighteenth century onwards, built mainly by estates for their tenant-farmers. Estates are business organisations, and the farms they erected closely reflect the regional type of farming that was a basic source of income for the farmer and of rent for the laird.

In 1976, there were 32,507 'agricultural units' or farms in Scotland, full-time and part-time, representing eight types of farming, classified as hill sheep, upland, stock-rearing with arable, rearing with intensive livestock, arable rearing and feeding, cropping, dairy, and intensive units (pigs, poultry, horticultural). These are spread over the country in five regions, to which we have adhered in presenting our material:

1. Highlands: Argyll, Inverness, Ross and Cromarty, Sutherland, Shetland.
2. North-East: Aberdeen, Banff, Caithness, Kincardine, Moray, Nairn, Orkney.
3. East: Angus, Clackmannan, Fife, Kinross, Perth.
4. South-East: Berwick, East Lothian, Midlothian, Peebles, Roxburgh, Selkirk, West Lothian.
5. South-West: Ayr, Bute, Dumfries, Dunbarton, Kirkcudbright, Lanark, Renfrew, Stirling, Wigtown.

Regional analysis of full-time farm units shows that dairying leads in the South-West, stock-rearing, and stock-rearing and feeding in the North-East, cropping in the North-East and East, hill-sheep in the Highlands, South-West and Borders, a combination of hill-sheep and dairying in the South-West, and horticulture in the South-West and East.[1]

A study of Scottish farm-buildings must take the types of farming as an underlying criterion, and a major purpose of this book is to see how farm-buildings in these areas suit their functions. Since most farm-buildings in Scotland are relatively young, it is primarily the differences in function that account for differences in form. Nevertheless hints of older, traditional building forms come through occasionally, reflecting an older form of functionalism, especially in the North and West in the areas where the bulk of the part-time and spare-time farms are to be found. The long survival of the longhouse is one example. This is another kind of factor being considered in this study of Scotland's farm-buildings, though we are also very much concerned with them as examples of architecture in their own right, and with the many not necessarily functional features that mark estates and districts, and sometimes point to the work of an architect whose services were sought in more areas than one.

1

SCOTLAND : AGRICULTURAL DIVISIONS

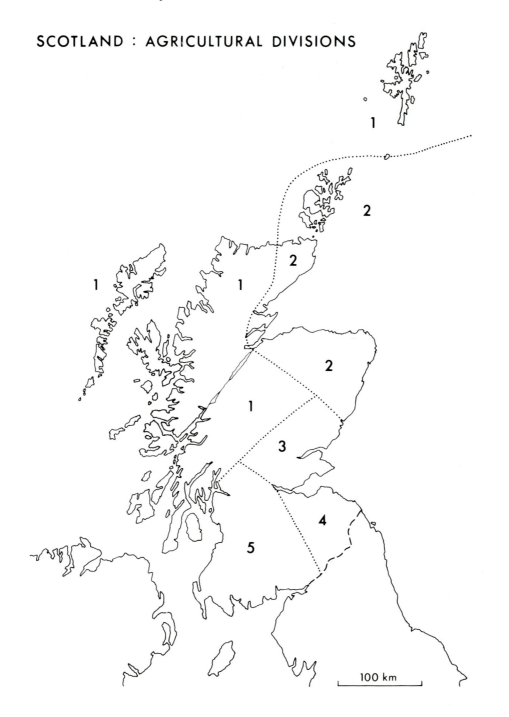

Fig. 1.   Scotland: Agricultural divisions. 1. Highlands. 2. North-east. 3. East. 4. South-east. 5. South-west.

Finally, this book is not concerned with recent building. Its purpose is to round up the historical background and to indicate regional variety. It is written in full awareness of the outstanding need for widespread, detailed surveying of farm complexes, with the specific intention of stimulating such activity. A new revolution is in progress. New farming needs are fundamentally altering, even eradicating, the farm buildings we know. Awareness of this is a strong source of motivation for the book. It is a record of what, in fifty years, may be gone.

It should be noted that dialect and technical terms are included—and explained—in the Index.

1

The Care of Buildings

THOUGH official attention has been paid to ancient monuments and historic houses in the past, farm buildings have been less regarded, since with some exceptions few have been considered old or elegant enough. Yet many are fine examples of architecture, and even though castles, tower-houses, palaces, country mansions, abbeys and churches, and burgh architecture have had more prominence in the writing and legislation, it is the farm-buildings that provide the most widespread and characteristic aspect of the country's architectural heritage.

There are various Government statutes with a bearing on buildings. The *Ancient Monuments Consolidation and Amendment Act, 1913* included buildings in the concept of 'monuments', with the proviso that any building coming under guardianship should not be occupied as a dwelling-house other than by someone employed as a caretaker. Effectively, this excluded most dwelling-houses, including farm-houses. A major step was taken in 1953 with the *Historic Buildings and Ancient Monuments Act*, which provided for 'the preservation and acquisition of buildings of outstanding historic or architectural interest and their contents and related property'. This Act also set up the Historic Buildings Council for Scotland to advise the Secretary of State, when required, on the exercise of his functions under sections 27, 28, 38 and 96 of the *Town and Country Planning (Scotland) Act, 1947*. These sections relate to buildings of special architectural or historic interest, and to preservation orders. The Act also made it possible for grants to be made to bodies like the National Trust for Scotland by way of endowment for such places, or to permit their acquisition.

The Town and Country Planning (Scotland) Act, 1947 was followed by others in 1954, 1959, 1969, and 1972, with some amendments to the 1972 Act in the *Town and Country Amenities Act, 1974*. The Act of 1969 made important changes in the law on historic buildings, incorporated in the 1972 Act which provides the current planning legislation. According to these Acts, the Secretary of State for Scotland is required to compile lists of buildings of special architectural or historic interest, or approve such lists made by others. Not only is the building itself taken into account, but also 'any respect in which its exterior contributes to the architectural or historic interest of any group of buildings of which it forms part; and the desirability of preserving, on the ground of architectural or historic interest, any feature of the building consisting of a man-made object or structure fixed to the building or forming part of the land and comprised within the curtilage of the building'. Allowance is made for consultation with specialists, if necessary, before listing a building. The lists, when finally agreed, are circulated and become the basis for the administration of both local and national conservation policies relating to buildings.

The work of listing is undertaken through the Scottish Development Department's Historic Buildings Investigators, and buildings in the resulting statutory lists are assigned to one of three categories:

A — buildings of national or more than local importance, either architectural or historic or fine little-altered examples of some particular period or style.

B — buildings of primarily local importance or major examples of some period or style which may have been somewhat altered.

C — good buildings which may be considered altered, other buildings which are fair examples of their period, or in some cases buildings of no great individual merit which group well with others in categories A or B.

In recent times category C has been upgraded from non-statutory to statutory. This is a major step as far as farm-buildings as well as other examples of rural and urban architecture are concerned, for the category is now taken to include small 'vernacular' cottages of seventeenth to early nineteenth century date, previously thought too modest to merit statutory listing; smaller laird's houses and old farm houses of the seventeenth and eighteenth centuries which have been refaced or altered but which show some traces of their origin in individual features; buildings in informal groups of 'mixed' quality; buildings in a planned estate or group which have remained substantially intact but are of modest individual quality; plain or very modest eighteenth or early nineteenth buildings with few special features; the last products of the Georgian tradition, viz. very late buildings of 1834-40, and secondary examples of Victorian and Edwardian architecture; nineteenth century buildings which have been aesthetically damaged by later alterations; and lesser industrial buildings (eg. grain mills) which have lost their machinery.

In practice, for all categories, all buildings before 1700 which survive in anything like their original condition are listed. For the 1700-1840 period most are listed, though selection is thought to be necessary. Between 1840-1914 buildings have to be of definite quality and character, except where they form part of a group, and the selection is designed to include, for example, the principal works of the better-known architects. Some listing of buildings between 1914 and 1945 is now being undertaken, and also works by living architects if the buildings are over 30 years old. It appears, therefore, that the remit is now wide enough to take into account the bulk of what is most characteristic of the country's architecture.

If a building is listed, in whatever category, it cannot be demolished, altered or extended without following the 'listed building consent' procedure. Such consent is got from the local planning authority or in certain cases the Secretary of State, in the same way as for planning permission. The penalty for failing to seek consent is a fine of up to £250, and in determining the amount, the court shall take into account any financial gain arising as a result of contravention. If consent is given for demolition, the Royal Commission on the Ancient and Historical Monuments of Scotland must be notified, so that they may have an opportunity to record the building before it disappears.

Owners of listed buildings are responsible for normal repair and maintenance in the same way as owners of any other buildings. Grants or loans may be available in certain circumstances from central government funds or from local authorities for the repair or maintenance of a listed building. Exchequer grants may be given for buildings of outstanding architectural or historic interest, through the Secretary of State as advised by the Historic Buildings Council for Scotland. Relatively few listed buildings, however, come into the 'outstanding' bracket.

B

Local authority grants may also be available, and are not restricted to buildings of outstanding interest or even to listed buildings. In practice, however, the local authorities have problems over the criteria for grant aid, which may mean that either very few buildings could hope to qualify, or too many buildings appear to qualify. Housing improvement grants are available for listed buildings, as for others, but where the cost of improvement or conversion is materially increased by measures taken to preserve the architectural or historic interest, the local authority may, with Secretary of State approval, give a grant above the normal maximum.

All this boils down to the fact that, though legislation exists, it operates chiefly on a basis of selection related to quality or special interest. Though housing improvement grants can be got, there is a risk that these in themselves are speeding up the process of erosion of features of traditional buildings, including the layout of rooms. Other kinds of legislation are also having an effect: for example, the requirement that tractors should have safety hoods means that the old-style cart-sheds are too low to serve as tractor-garages, so they have either to be heightened, or swept away in favour of a large, multi-purpose building in modern materials. It is not our purpose to seek to stop such changes. It is in the nature of farming to require changes from time to time in the farm-buildings. Our plea is not for fossilisation, but for surveying and recording as a basis for the reasoned selection, in appropriate areas and on appropriate sites, of buildings and their features that are worth preserving as part of Scotland's architectural and historical record. In these days of Government encouraged and subsidised amalgamation of farms, it should not be an impossible aim, nor need it interfere with the proper progress of farming.

For *walls*, elements contributing to character are all door and window openings with their margins, including shopfronts where these have architectural character; columns, pilasters, parapets, balconies, balustrades and all decorative work associated with them; the surface texture or decorative treatment of stonework such as rustication, pointing, harling, tile hanging and colour (even soot in some cases); and old lamps, fire insurance marks or any other fixtures. It is pointed out that stone cleaning can be particularly damaging to architectural character if done by unsuitable methods, though some latitude might be allowed in the case of modern finishes. Reinstatement of the original wet dash harl in place of modern dry dash, subject to a satisfactory specification and proper regard for other original detail, does not require the full planning consent procedure, but planning authority approval should be got and the SDD should be notified. The subject of harling, for example, creates a certain amount of heart searching. Proposed alterations to modern additions including shopfronts with no special architectural or historical interest do not necessarily require building consent, especially if the modern additions are at the rear and not generally visible, but the aim should be to bring unsatisfactory additions more into harmony with the original wherever possible.

For *external joinery, glazing and metalwork*, 'character' is associated with elements such as window divides, coloured, stained or traditional glasswork, door and fanlight joinery,

---

The Scottish Development Department (SDD), in a Memorandum on Listed Buildings and Conservation Areas, usefully identifies what is understood by the term 'character' in relation to listed buildings.

porches, conservatories, original rainwater heads, and other similar details. Alterations which may affect character include any traditional architectural detailing, ventilators, fanlights, external piping, most forms of advertising, and the introduction of patterned glass.

The 'character' of the *roof* usually lies in its pitch, the existence of dormers, roofing materials, skews and skew-putts, ridges, decorative treatment at the eaves, etc. Any new dormers or the enlargement of existing ones or any other new structure added to, or inserted into, the original planes of the roof require listed building consent.

Original *chimney* heads and detailing, modern chimney heads in original positions, shafts and ornamented fireclay cans all contribute to 'character' in a building.

Interiors are difficult to define for 'character'. Much depends on the category of listing required, but the elements to be looked at are chimney pieces, doorcases, doors and their fittings, window furniture such as shutters, pelmet boxes or curtain rods, panelling; ornamented plaster, wood and paintwork; original wall coverings; reliefs and statuary; fixed tapestries, tilework and mosaics; niches and pediments; floors where ancient or decoratively treated in wood, marble, mosaic, etc; balusters, newell posts, and tread ends; and any fixed furniture, such as bank or bar counters, or other fixtures of good quality down to about 1930. Any sub-divisions of rooms, particularly in the principal apartments and staircases, may be regarded as affecting the character.

For industrial buildings listed wholly or partly for the interest of their working, elements likely to contribute 'character' include all fixed machinery more than about 40 years old. In the case of cottages and smaller houses without designed finishes, and buildings largely listed for group value, 'character' need not be regarded as being affected by minor internal alterations unless the building retains interesting features such as box beds etc. in a good state of preservation. Alterations to plumbing do not require consent unless the fitments are of unique interest. Very particular consideration should be given to those houses of the mid-eighteenth century and earlier which have retained their original work throughout, or any building which has particularly rich and consistent interior work.

The curtilages are also relevant. They include the actual ground, particularly if this is covered by any traditional or original form of paving; basement areas, steps and railings, gates and walls; any items within the curtilage such as sculpture, sundials, urns, fountains and other ornaments; and conservatories, greenhouses, garden houses, mews and ancillary buildings such as stables, coach-houses, laundries and brewhouses. Old garden walls may also contain features of unusual interest such as bee-boles and charter boles (a recess on the proprietor's side to show that ownership of the wall is not mutual). Old outbuildings may contain dovecots and possess other interesting fittings.

2

Survey Bodies and Archives

The Royal Commission on the Ancient and Historical Monuments of Scotland (RCAHMS)

THE Royal Commission on the Ancient and Historical Monuments of Scotland was originally empowered to record monuments dating 'from the earliest times to the year 1707'. A Royal Warrant of 1948 gave power to include 'such further Monuments and Constructions of a date subsequent to that year as may seem in our discretion worthy of mention'. Subsequently the year 1850 has been in practice adopted as an approximate terminal date, and post-1707 structures are included only on a selective basis. Though small rural buildings may be considered for inclusion in the published *Inventories*, or may be the subjects of emergency surveys carried out prior to demolition or alteration in accordance with the *Town and Country Planning (Scotland) Act, 1972*, nevertheless it has no mandate for any general survey of buildings of this class. However, vernacular buildings have been examined, for example in Argyll, as part of the survey being carried out there. The *Inventory of Kintyre* includes a plan of the township of Balmavicar near the Mull of Kintyre, deserted in or before the last quarter of the eighteenth century, with details of two groups of shieling huts and of the large water-mill at Tangy, where the machinery was intact. In other parts of Argyll, the surveying has included pre-Improvement types of longhouses with cruck-framed, hipped roofs, some of them incorporating end-crucks. Details of thatching techniques have also been noted and in general, though the degree of involvement with such buildings is small, the amount of information gleaned is considerable.[2]

Forming part of the RCAHMS is the National Monuments Record of Scotland (NMRS), which began as the Scottish National Buildings Record, set up as a private body in 1941 to make and preserve records of historically important buildings in case they should be destroyed by enemy action. In 1954 it was taken over by the then Ministry of Works. It was transferred to the Royal Commission in 1966, and extended in scope to cover structures of all periods. The objects of the National Monuments Record are 'to make surveys of buildings of special architectural or historic interest which are threatened with destruction, and which are not yet published in the Commission's Inventories, and to establish a central archive of material relating to ancient monuments and historic buildings throughout Scotland'.[3] Examples of smaller-scale rural buildings recorded by the NMRS in its first *Report* are Blackpots Brick and Tile Works, Whitehills, Banffshire (now demolished); 84 farms and cottages in Caithness, surveyed in May 1971 following a proposal by the Caithness County Council to demolish ruinous or derelict small farms and cottages, mainly of late eighteenth to early nineteenth century date, on either side of the A9 road between Berriedale and Wick;[4] a clay-walled, cruck-framed barn and byre at Prior Linn, Canonbie, and the cruck-framed cottage with a canopied chimney-hood of clay and lath at Torthorwald, both in Dumfriesshire;[5]

A

B

Fig. 2 (a, b, c).   Turf House, Carse of Stirling, Stirlingshire: 1792. These contemporary drawings of 1792, by the artist Joseph Farrington, show an unusual type of turf house where the house was scooped from a solid block of peat left as the peat bog was cut away. These houses were replaced by brick ones after the reclamation of the moss was completed. a. exterior. b. in course of construction. c. interior. (British Museum Print Room: Farrington Albums).

C

the three-storeyed windmill-tower, High Mill, Carluke, Lanarkshire, erected about 1797, with mill-stones and machinery of later date; and several houses and farms on the Mainland of Orkney.[6] The second *Report* includes East Cluden Mill, Dumfriesshire, a late eighteenth century water-powered corn mill, now restored, though the kiln has been demolished; Achculin, Abriachan, Inverness-shire, an early nineteenth century township with cruck-framed buildings, stave-and-wattle partitions, and canopied chimney-hoods; a large cruck-framed, hip-roofed building at Corrimony Grange[7] and a single-storey thatched, cruck-framed cottage (now destroyed) at Tomatin, both in Inverness-shire; and a cruck-framed longhouse, probably of late eighteenth century origin, with a bed-outshot, two canopied chimney-hoods and the sill-beam of a former wattle partition, at Camsernay, Perthshire.[8] Such buildings, however, form a relatively small proportion of the NMRS Archive as a whole.

The Scottish Country Life Archive

The Scottish Country Life Archive in the National Museum of Antiquities of Scotland includes a substantial section on buildings in the countryside, organised to provide data on the background history of the buildings as well as on their regional variations. It is as much concerned with social and economic history as with architectural history. Its aim is to contextualise the buildings, to place them within their environment, and to see to

Fig. 3.   Davie Dean's Cottage. Houses of this type with large external chimney stack appear in a great many early prints of Scotland and continue into the early nineteenth century. No information is available which directly describes their construction (from a Vignette by Lizars, published in the first edition of Robert Chambers' *Traditions of Edinburgh* 1825)

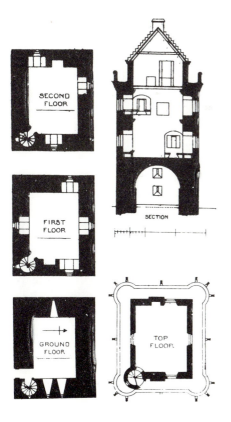

Fig. 4.   Minto Tower, Minto, Roxburghshire. A typical rectangular plan type tower house from the Borders area. The accommodation comprises a vaulted ground floor with an upper loft in the vault, and three stories above, the floors of which are of timber supported on stone corbels, the whole being served with a narrow wheel stair in the south east corner. The building measures 9.75 by 8.03 metres over the walls. The three upper floors each contain a fireplace. (Macgibbon & Ross: *The Castellated and Domestic Architecture of Scotland* III. 420-421)

Fig. 5.   Dunrobin, Golspie, Sutherland. A cap and dome type icehouse with entrance passageway. These structures were introduced into Scotland circa 1650. The ice was stored in the cap below the level of the entrance passageway, and the dome provided a cold room in which the foodstuffs were placed on a straw floor over the ice pack. Icehouses are often difficult to locate as they are normally semi-subterranean, and have a mound formed over the dome. The mound is often covered with vegetation to provide shade. (NMAS: 42. 20. 19)

what extent, in relation to available building and roofing materials and underlying types of farming, they are themselves the products of their environment. The information, sorted by county and by parish, derives from printed, manuscript and oral sources, and includes older photographs as well as recent ones taken in the course of field research. An important element is the material deposited by individuals, such as the record of 40 farm buildings on the Airlie Estate in Glen Clova, Angus, carried out by Ingval Maxwell, now of the Scottish Development Department, his later work on *Functional Architecture, Hopetoun Estate, West Lothian*, produced in two typescript volumes in 1974, and the photographs resulting from a survey of Midlothian farm-buildings carried out by him on behalf of the Midlothian District Council. The Archive holds the photographic collection of Alasdair Alpin MacGregor. A further major contribution comes from one of the present authors, Bruce Walker, whose surveying activities have been especially widespread in the East and North-East areas. The results are reflected in this book.[9]

The School of Scottish Studies
The Archive of the School of Scottish Studies of Edinburgh University complements

that of the Scottish Country Life Archive. It houses photographs of buildings from Lowland, Highland and Island Scotland, and its Central Index contains information extracted from, or to be found in, printed and manuscript sources, relating to dwelling houses and farm buildings, with more emphasis on rural than on urban material. Features such as roofing, windows, chimneys, fireplaces and box-beds are also touched on. The Photographic Archive includes copies of illustrations from printed sources, but consists mainly of photographs, especially of exteriors, taken by members of staff during field research. There are some plans of farm and village layouts. The Werner Kissling collection of photographs is kept here.[10]

A National Survey

Consistent efforts to achieve a national survey, particularly of rural buildings that did not appear to be fully covered by existing legislation, began in 1967 when, following a joint approach to the Scottish Development Department by the National Museum of Antiquities of Scotland and the Royal Commission on Ancient and Historical Monuments, a Scottish Vernacular Buildings Survey Working Party was set up under SDD chairmanship. Besides these three bodies, it came to include representatives of the Ancient Monuments Inspectorate, the Department of Architecture and the School of Scottish Studies, both of Edinburgh University, the School of Architecture of the

Fig. 6.   Cromarty, Cromarty, Ross-shire. A medium sized commercial icehouse built to supply ice to the salmon fisheries to allow the fish to be exported fresh to the London market. (NMAS: 42. 19. 29)

Bruce Walker 1980

A

B

BruceWalker 1980.

Fig. 8. Bonhard, Scone, Perthshire. A lectern type doocot typical of many built in the eighteenth century. This example has a double chamber and entry through ports provided in the vertical face of a step in the roof. Other examples might have dormer entries or ports in the wall above the rat course. The doorways are hidden behind the bushes in front of the building. (BW: viii. 76)

Edinburgh College of Art, and the National Trust for Scotland. The Working Party's remit was to consider existing facilities, including printed sources and archives, and to see how the neglect (at the time) of small rural buildings could be remedied. It was agreed that the SDD Lists, though constituting the only form of national coverage, were too limited in scope and were mainly concerned with external building features (though this situation has now improved). Following consultations with Dr R. Brunskill, of the School of Architecture of Manchester University, who directly and through his students had much experience in the field recording of rural buildings,[11] it was agreed that the likeliest solution was to aim at a survey of buildings to be undertaken over a period of about five years for the whole of Scotland. A four-week trial survey was carried out on the Glamis Estate, Angus, subsidised by a grant made by the National Trust for Scotland, and in order to publicise the Working Party's activities, a one-day conference was organised in Edinburgh University in 1968. The subjects covered were:

D. M. Walker. Estate Architecture and its Effect on the Vernacular Tradition.

A. Fenton. Traditional Building and Thatching Materials.

Dr A. Gailey. Building in Stone in the Scottish Highlands.

Professor P. Nuttgens, The Vernacular Tradition as Architecture.

The Conference was opened by the late Earl of Crawford and Balcarres.

Fig. 7 (a, b). Prestonpans, Prestonpans, East Lothian. A beehive corbelled stone doocot typical of many built in the sixteenth century or earlier. The birds enter through the open top and nest on simple stone ledges lining the interior. The projecting string course, commonly termed a "rat course", was to prevent vermin climbing the walls and destroying or eating the eggs. a. Exterior. b. Interior. (BW: vi. 75)

Fig. 9. Megginch, Errol, Perthshire. Castle offices and doocot forming a decorative cobbled courtyard close to the castle. The range of buildings to the right of the photograph was built of brick in 1707 and altered in the early nineteenth century when the other wing and the doocot were built. The doocot is a decorative Gothic structure with the pigeon house at first floor level over an open arched ground floor. The weathervane which surmounts the structure is in the form of a sailing ship. (BW: viii. 76)

Commentaries on the different lectures were given by J. G. Dunbar of the RCAHMS, Dr R. Brunskill of the School of Architecture of Manchester University, Dr H. Fairhurst of the Department of Archaeology of Glasgow University, Dr F. R. Stevenson of the Department of Architecture of Edinburgh University. The proceedings were summed up by Dr K. Steer, Secretary of the RCAHMS, and closed by J. Stormonth Darling, Director of the National Trust for Scotland. The lecturers and commentators together aimed at exploring a variety of basic topics—building in stone and in traditional materials other than stone, the importance of estate building from the late eighteenth century onwards—and sought to assess the value of such studies in the universities and for practical application by planning authorities and others faced with the problem of selecting buildings for preservation in situ or in open-air museums. The conference attracted 130 people representing university, museum, government and private interests, and the concept of a national survey sprang in part from the evident widespread enthusiasm.

The Working Party considered that a survey of the kind under consideration would fill one of the biggest gaps in our knowledge of the Scottish countryside, and allow the selection for preservation of a sufficient number of buildings showing regional types and social gradations to allow both visitors and residents to get a firmer historical feel of their area than will shortly be possible due to the great speed of present change. No man-made artefact can show the change and development in the various parts of Scotland over the last 250 years better than her buildings. As a form of three-dimensional history, they are irreplaceable. In addition, the survey material, adequately housed and sorted for public use, would provide a data bank for academic research as well as for planners, architects and all those with a concern for the built environment. A brief was prepared, but because of the difficulty of financing the survey project, the Working Party was not then able to go further.

The need remained no less strong, however, and in order not to lose what had been gained, some members of the Working Party decided to set up a Scottish Vernacular Buildings Working Group (SVBWG). Meetings on rural buildings were held in Edinburgh in 1972 and on village and urban architecture in Dundee in 1973, by which

Fig. 10. Carmyllie Manse, Carmyllie, Angus. The beeboles in the garden of the manse at Carmyllie form an interesting and decorative feature. The bee skeps were placed in the wall recesses, the iron bar placed in front of them and padlocked into position. Patrick Bell, the designer of the reaping machine, was the minister here. (NMAS: 43. 4. 10)

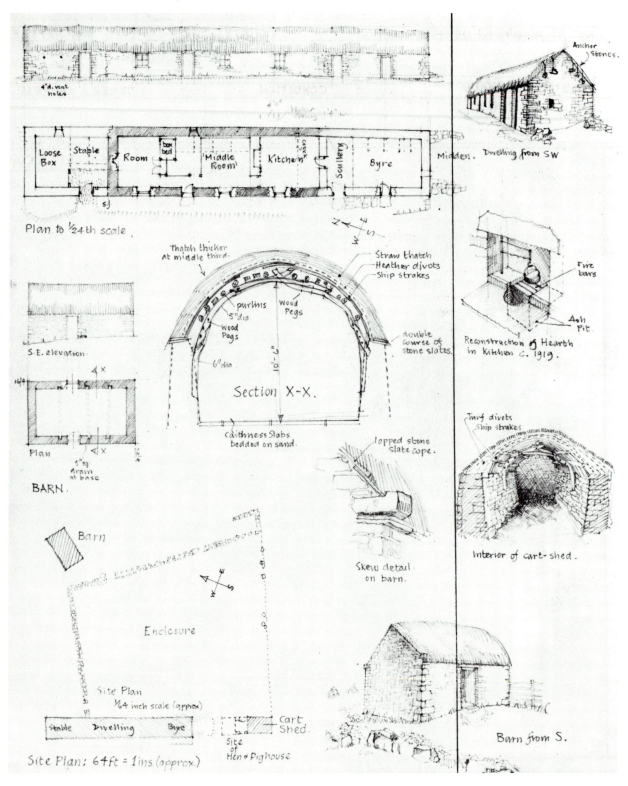

4"d. vent holes

Loose Box | Stable | Room | box bed | Middle Room | Kitchen | Scullery | Byre | Midden. | Dwelling from S.W.

Plan to ½24th scale.

S.E. elevation.

Plan

5" sq. drain at base

BARN.

thatch thicker at middle third.

Straw thatch
Heather divots
Ship strakes

purlins 5"dia
Wood Pegs
Wood Pegs

6"dia

Section X-X.

double course of stone slates

10'-0"

Caithness Slabs bedded on sand.

Reconstruction of Hearth in Kitchen c. 1919.

Fire bars

Ash Pit.

Anchor Stones.

lapped stone slate cope.

Skew detail on barn.

Turf divots
Ship strakes

Interior of cart-shed.

Barn

Enclosure

Site Plan ⅟64 inch scale (approx)

Stable | Dwelling | Byre

Cart Shed.

Site of Hen & Pighouse

Site Plan: 64ft = 1ins (approx.)

Barn from S.

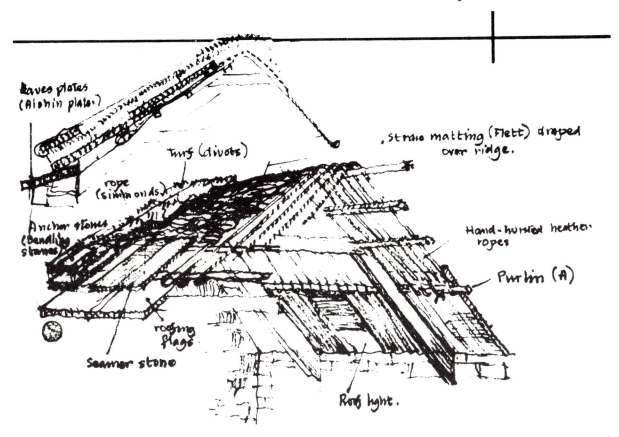

Fig. 12. Estabin, Firth, Orkney. A Survey sheet showing the structural analysis of a barn roof of unusual construction. The roof comprises a turf roof covering, roped and weighted with stones and supported on straw matting over heather ropes and purlins, the whole being supported by simple A-frame trusses. (RCAHMS: ORD. 5. 1)

time the Group had become big enough to justify establishment on a more formal basis, with the intention of uniting lay and professional interests in the common aims of:

    a. providing a meeting point for individuals and institutions concerned in some way with the architectural, historical and social aspects of vernacular buildings

    b. meeting at regular intervals in different parts of the country to discuss specific topics within the field of the subject

    c. diffusing knowledge of the subject through discussion and through publication of information

    d. stimulating more systematic activity in the surveying and recording of vernacular buildings in their regional and social settings

    e. encouraging the study and teaching of the subject in the curricula of universities and colleges of architecture.

Fig. 11. Laidhay, Dunbeath, Caithness. A Royal Commission on the Ancient and Historic Monuments of Scotland survey sheet showing the wealth of information that may be collected on a single sheet. (RCAHMS: CAD. 29. 1)

Fig. 13.   Auchindrain, Kilmichael Glassary, Argyll. Plan of an eighteenth century "ferm toun" which has survived comparatively unaltered into this century and is now an open air museum. (From J. G. Dunbar, *The Historic Architecture of Scotland,* London 1966, 248-49)

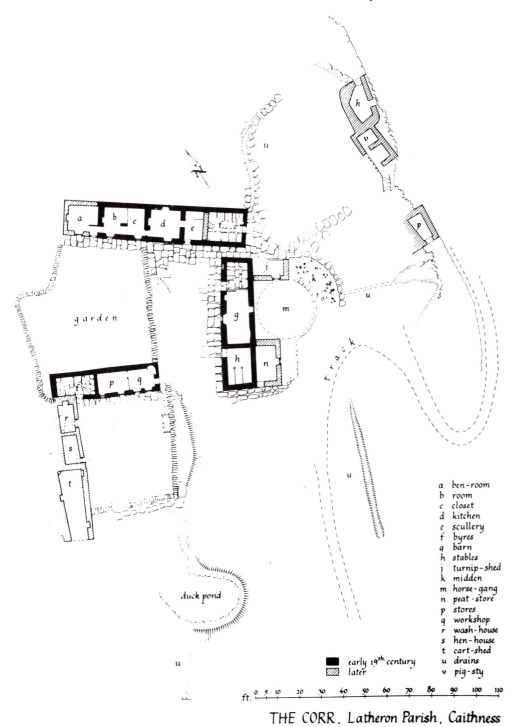

a ben-room
b room
c closet
d kitchen
e scullery
f byres
g barn
h stables
j turnip-shed
k midden
m horse-gang
n peat-store
p stores
q workshop
r wash-house
s hen-house
t cart-shed
u drains
v pig-sty

■ early 19th century
▨ later

ft. 0 5 10 20 30 40 50 60 70 80 90 100 110

THE CORR. Latheron Parish. Caithness

Fig. 14.   The Corr, Latheron, Caithness. Plan of an early nineteenth century farm steading with later additions. (RCAHMS: CAD. 33. 2)

C

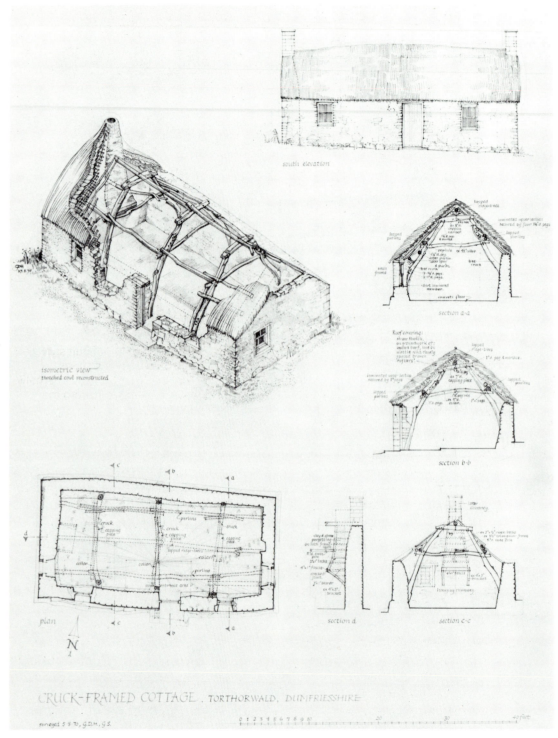

Fig. 15.   Torthorwald, Dumfriesshire. Survey drawing of a small cruck-framed cottage with "hingin lum" at one end. (RCAHMS: DED. 108. 1)

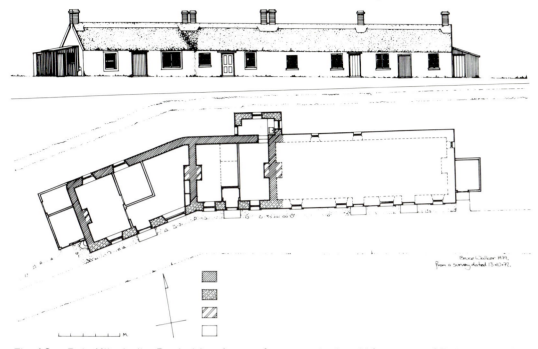

Fig. 16.   Rait, Kilspindie, Perthshire. A row of cottages in the old fermtoun of Rait surveyed by architectural students from Duncan of Jordanstone College of Art, before recent alterations. The house on the right was occupied and therefore was not surveyed internally. Copies of the original drawings by Espen Skordal and Pal Strom are deposited with the Country Life Archive, National Museum of Antiquities of Scotland.

The existence of the Scottish Vernacular Buildings Working Group, therefore, is due to the fact that there is little formal study of vernacular buildings in the universities and architectural colleges, and that insufficient attention is being paid to farms, cottar houses, craft workshops, tradesmen's houses, and other such buildings of a lowly kind. Yet their value can be greater than their individual merits for architectural, social, and economic history, reflecting in their form, structure and groupings the history and resources of a district, and establishing better than any other human artefact the regional character and identity of their district. They demand study not only by architects, but by historians as well if their full significance is to be extracted.

Because few extensive studies of Scottish vernacular buildings at this level exist in print, there is as yet no informed body of knowledge that can convincingly demonstrate that it can be in the national interest to draw attention to the importance of buildings that are often labelled as being of no more than local interest. National history is an amalgam of the history of the regions, and regional identity is itself part of the national picture. As with historical studies in general, it should never be forgotten that the fact of regionality is basic to the history of the nation.

The creation of the Scottish Vernacular Buildings Working Group marks a step in the attempt to remedy the neglect of an important subject, by fostering an interdisciplinary approach, and by encouraging a greater measure of protection and care for such buildings. The group now publishes an annual Newsletter, and has embarked on a programme of publications to provide source material and make the subject more widely known.

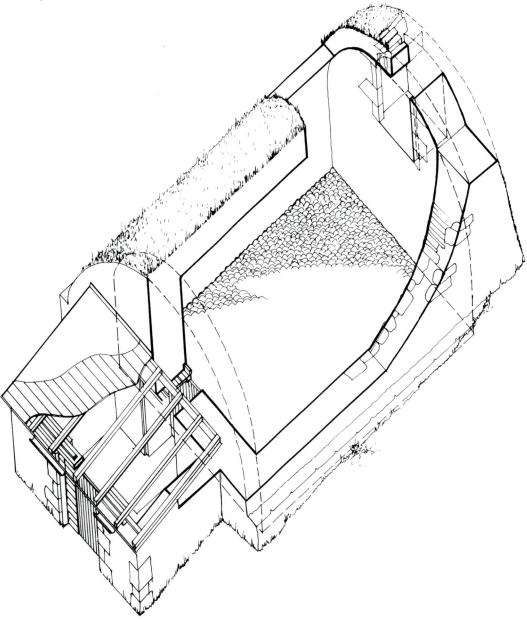

Fig. 17.   Seggieden Cottage, Kinfauns, Perthshire. A small commercial icehouse in the garden of the above cottage surveyed by architectural students from Duncan of Jordanstone College of Art—John Bradley, whose drawing is shown here, Nenad Lorencin and Stewart Mackay. This was the main distribution point for the Kinfauns salmon fishings and was possibly supplied with ice from less permanent structures at regular periods over the fishing season.

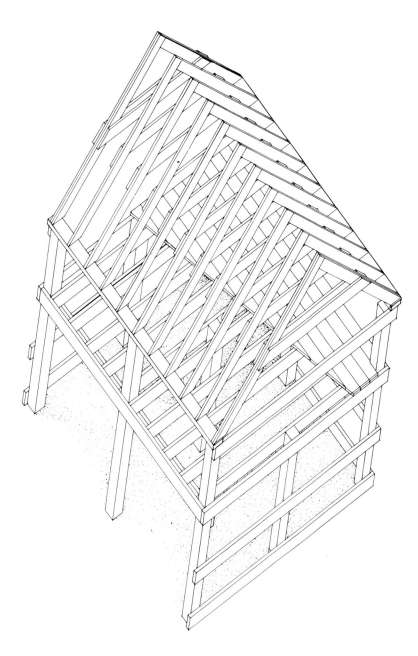

Fig. 18.   Millhill Cottages, Longforgan, Perthshire. A two-storey woodshed forming part of the offices of the above cottages. The survey was carried out by Nevin McMurray, Duncan of Jordanstone College of Art, whose drawing is shown here.

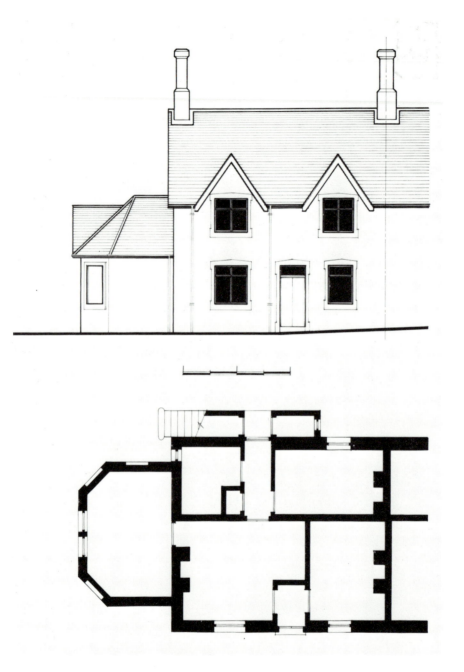

Fig. 19.   Knapp, Longforgan, Perthshire. Concrete cottage with chapel at first-floor level and forming part of a two-storey terrace in the village. Surveyed by Ian Stout, architect, Dundee, in preparation for alterations. Drawings of this kind prepared by architectural firms for their own use can provide a valuable source of survey material.

3

Printed Sources

A pioneering book on *Norse Building Customs in the Scottish Isles* was published by the Dane, Aage Roussell, in 1934. This dealt chiefly with buildings in Shetland, Orkney and the Outer Hebrides. Colin Sinclair's book on *The Thatched Houses of the Old Highlands*, 1953, looked at the Outer and Inner Hebrides and the West Mainland. Sinclair made a broad division of Highland houses into three types: the Hebridean, with a hipped roof and a double-skin wall with a broad roof-ledge on which a man could walk; the Skye type, hipped, with a single wall which the thatch overhung; and the Dalriadic, with gable ends and overhanging thatch. Though his divisions were over-simplified, this marked the beginnings of attempts to analyse such buildings in a systematic way. The book inspired Dr Isabel Grant to carry out further research, partly as a background to her work for the Highland Folk Museum, of which she was the founder. In the 1960s, when the Department of Geography of Glasgow University was surveying crofts in the Western Isles, Sinclair's three-fold division was still being used.

The chapter on Small Rural Houses, Farms and Villages in John Dunbar's *Historic Architecture of Scotland*, 1966, was one of the first of the more general surveys, looking at improved farms and cottages as well as at buildings of traditional character in the North and West and in the Central Highlands, at townships and villages, and, briefly, at kilns and mills. Robert Scott Morton's *Traditional Farm Architecture in Scotland*, 1976, concentrates on farm-buildings in Lowland Scotland, excluding Shetland, Orkney and the Highlands and Western Isles. The book, essentially a photographic record, gives a visual impression of the great variety to be found in Scottish farm-buildings. Orkney and Shetland buildings are examined in Chapters 13 to 23 of A. Fenton, *The Northern Isles, Orkney and Shetland*, 1978.

Several articles on specific topics have now appeared in print. The SVBWG's first publication, for example, dealt with the organisation of the building industry in Scotland during the seventeenth century (J. G. Dunbar), building with stone and slate, with special reference to quarrying (I. Fisher), timber construction (G. D. Hay), thatch and thatching techniques (A. Fenton), regional variations in building techniques in Angus, Fife and Perth (B. Walker), and the evidence for building materials and methods of construction revealed by the archaeological excavations at Broad Street, Aberdeen (J. S. Dent).[12] Clay as a building material in North-East Scotland was examined in the Group's second publication,[13] which took further an earlier study of clay building and clay thatch in Scotland.[14] A method of building using alternate courses of stone and turf, thought in 1968 to be obsolete,[15] has now turned out to survive in gables noted in Angus, Aberdeenshire, Perthshire and Inverness. An example of building in turf at its most extreme, the houses themselves being cut from the living peat, is linked to the late eighteenth century reclamation of Kincardine Moss in southern Perthshire.[16] Seventeenth century evidence for roofing and walling techniques

A

B

Fig. 20 (a, b). a.Farmyard, Dunfermline, Fife: 1694 (Slezer: *Theatrum Scotiae* plate 46).
b. Westown, Errol, Perthshire. Note the similarity in form between the rear building in the
Dunfermline farm group and the Westown steading. Both are built to running levels, are about
the same size and were both thatched. Westown lost its thatched roof in the 1920s when a tree
fell on the rear gable, demolishing both gable and roof. The steading walls are constructed of
shuttered tempered clay, in places faced with stone rubble.

Sheelins in JURA and a distant View of the Paps.

A Cottage in ILSAY.

Fig. 21. Buildings on Jura & Islay, Argyllshire. Eighteenth century illustrations such as these, although interesting, show a structural naivete. From Pennant 1769.

and house types in Lowland Scotland has been extracted from estate papers as part of a study of agrarian change.[17]

A subject that has provoked much study in England and some in Scotland is that of cruck construction. Perthshire examples were published in the 1950s and 1960s,[18] and more recently, others from Wester Ross,[19] Inverness[20] and Dumfriesshire.[21] The farming township of Auchindrain in Argyll includes hipped buildings with gable-end crucks as well as side crucks.[22] End crucks, though known elsewhere in mid-Argyll, appear to be rare in other parts of the country. Though some analysis of recorded cruck forms has

Fig. 22.   *A View of St Andrews (Fife) from the West with the sea combat of the Dolphin & Solboy with the Bellile, French Frigate, 1758.* Views such as this show forms of vernacular buildings in the foreground. The windmill to the left of the scene is approximately on the site of the Royal and Ancient Golf Club House. According to some members of "The Friends of the Byre", large timbers were found on or near the site of the club house during excavations for the building. (In the possession of Bruce Walker)

Fig. 23.   Cottage interior, Inverness-shire, showing a group standing round a central hearth on which an oatcake is being dried. Certain artistic licence appears to have been taken with the structure of the building as the large cross tree, from which the crook and links hang, does not appear to rest on either the cruck or the purlins, but simply disappears into the sarking. (NMAS—C.65 from d'Hardivillier, *Souvenir des Highlands* Paris, 1835)

Fig. 24. Falkland, Fife. A view of Falkland published in 1850. Note the sharpness of detail on the Palace and the small pantiled building in contrast to the more "vernacular" structures to the right of the scene. (NMAS: C4089; from *Scotland illustrated* 1850. Plate XXX).

Fig. 25. "Upper-Quais", Mainland, Orkney. Sketch of a typical Orkney group surveyed in 1900. (NMAS: C.5811; from Dietrichson and Meyer, *Monumenta Orcadica* 1906).

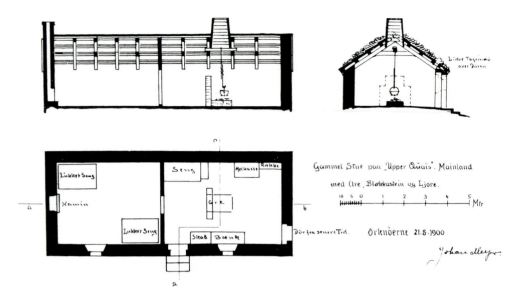

Fig. 26. "Upper-Quais", Mainland, Orkney. Plan and section of house showing the layout of furniture as surveyed by Johan Meyer in 1900. (NMAS: C5810; from Dietrichson and Meyer, *Monumenta Orcadica* 1906).

been made, neither the full range of types nor their distribution is yet clearly known. Probably they were used in most of the counties of Scotland, though there is little or no evidence from Shetland, Orkney and the Outer Hebrides. Surprises are sometimes found too, as in the crucks in fishermen's cottages at Ardersier in Inverness-shire, where a crown-post rises from a tie beam between a pair of crucks whose blades have not been carried to any great height. The crown-posts are forked to contain the ridge-tree, some with a pillow in the fork to level up the bed.

The single-skin longhouse and its double-skin form as the blackhouse (localised in the North-West) has been an object of interest since the mid-nineteenth century, having been seen by antiquarians as an example of the past surviving into the present.[23] In parallel with this approach was the view of the blackhouse and the areas in which it stood as examples of retarded culture. Such houses were also seen as fit subjects for the attention of health authorities concerned with domestic sanitation.[24] Scandinavians studying the spread of Viking settlement examined these houses in order to establish relationships with those in West Norway, the Faroe Islands and Iceland. The 1930s saw a good deal of systematic activity on this line of thinking,[25] which provided a basis for later studies.[26] Shieling huts have been included in a number of the publications referred to, because they reflect earlier building techniques with turf and stone.[27]

Several articles have appeared on functional features of farm-buildings and associated structures such as kilns and mills. Small four-sided corn-drying kilns have survived in Shetland,[28] especially in the northern islands, but the circular kiln is more widespread in the southern islands, in Orkney, and in Caithness. Its tower-like form at the end of the barn gives a characteristic mark to the farm buildings.[29] In other parts of Scotland, small kiln-barns were to be found, for example in Lewis, but the majority of the small kilns

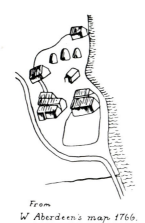

From
W. Aberdeen's map 1766.

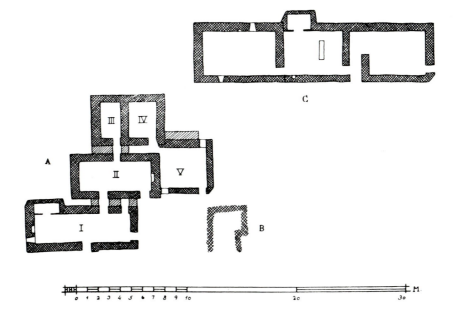

Fig. 27.   Thickbigging, Firth, Orkney. Plan of house and steading as surveyed in 1934 compared with W. Aberdeen's map of 1766. (From Roussell 1934. 89)

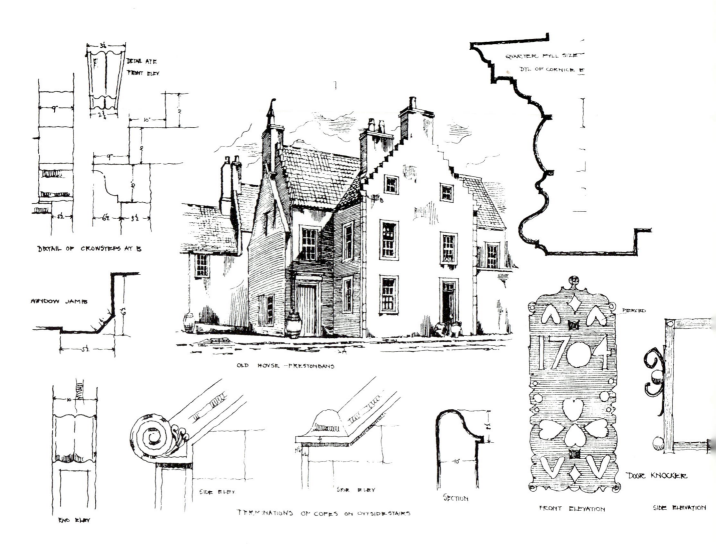

Fig. 28. (Old House), Prestonpans, East Lothian. Sketch of house with related details as published by the Edinburgh Architectural Association in 1896. Information of this kind can be particularly useful as many of these buildings have since been altered or demolished. (James Gillespie: 1922: *Details of Scottish Domestic Architecture* plate 34)

were away from the houses, and often built into the side of a slope. The stone-lined bowl, shaped like half an egg, is the distinguishing feature.[30]

Horizontal mills, in which the water wheel turns horizontally below the mill and drives the upper millstone directly, without the benefit of gearing, have attracted a good deal of attention. Their area of survival in Britain, in some cases till the present day, is in a crescent stretching from Shetland through Orkney and Caithness, the Hebrides and the West Mainland of Scotland, to Galloway, Ireland and the Isle of Man.[31] Mills with vertically turning wheels and intermediate gearing, usually with a large kiln attached as part of the same building, have had less thorough treatment, apart from some local studies in Orkney,[32] in the North-East,[33] in Fife, where a pattern of approach has been set by the fine survey of water-mills on the River Eden by the Dane, Anders Jespersen,[34] in East Lothian,[35] in Galloway,[36] and in Fife.[37] Windmills have also been investigated.[38]

Buildings and structures of other kinds have been examined too. Horse walks attached to barns for driving the threshing mill are being studied on both sides of the Border, and a recent survey by Bruce Walker has pinpointed the astonishing numbers that still survive in parts of Scotland.[39] Doocots have attracted attention,[40] as well as ice-houses,[41] lime-kilns[42] and toll-houses.[43]

Bibliographical data assembled for Scottish buildings by the Vernacular Architecture Group, appeared first in typescript lists, and then as part of a consolidated *Bibliography on Vernacular Architecture*.[44] A glossary of Scottish building terms also appeared recently.[45]

Fig. 29. Ackergill, Wick, Caithness. Many excellent photographs, such as the farm steading at Ackergill, by George Washington Wilson, are found in collections of glass plate negatives, or in old postcards. This is an exceptionally large and well-built farm steading for this area, having a steam-powered threshing mill with a brick factory-type chimney on a stone plinth. Note the large cartshed with a granary over, the large gabled roofs without raised skews and the decorative fence in the foreground. (GWW: C.4895)

4

Surveys and Survey Methods

SEVERAL limited surveys have now been undertaken, partly to establish the basic criteria for surveying, and partly to assess the rate at which work could proceed. In 1968, a four-week survey was made of vernacular buildings on the Glamis Estate in Angus by a student of art history, Hugh Dixon, on behalf of the Buildings Survey Working Party. Photographic records and brief descriptions of fifty buildings were made, as well as scale sketch plans of thirteen of the more interesting examples. Four more weeks were spent in collating the material and preparing a report and drawings.

This short probe brought to light even within the restricted area of the Glamis Estate several methods of building construction. Various types of local building materials were shown to have been in use during the eighteenth and nineteenth centuries, for example thatch, stone slates, and slates for roofing. Of the fifty buildings examined, only about six were included in the Scottish Development Department's Lists. The method of rapid superficial visiting, followed by a detailed survey of selected buildings, appeared to be satisfactory, and it was considered that a standardised record sheet based on that

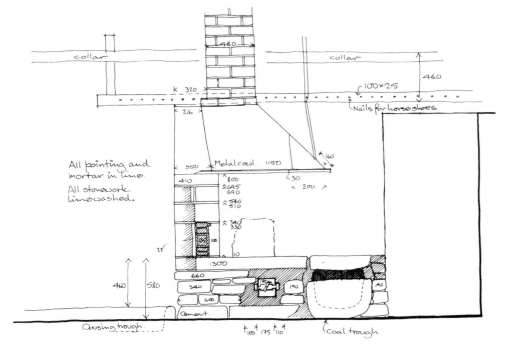

A

Fig. 30 (a, b). Eassie Smiddy, Eassie & Nevay, Angus. Two of a number of survey drawings of the forge made in preparation for it being moved to the Angus Folk Museum, Glamis. (Bruce Walker)

used by the National Monuments Record was likely to prove more satisfactory than the more elaborately classified system devised to suit English conditions by the Manchester School of Architecture.[46] However, not enough ground plans were made and the steadings were mostly ignored, so that functional relationships and the suitability of the buildings to their function in architectural terms could not be readily extracted.

In 1969, a survey of forty farms on the Airlie Estate, Angus, was completed by Ingval Maxwell, as a thesis subject for the Duncan of Jordanstone College of Art in Dundee. The method followed was again that of a rapid survey with sketch plans of layout and notes on features and materials, supplemented by photographs, and followed by more detailed surveys of selected examples. Considerable use was made in advance of large-scale Ordnance Survey maps, which show the layout of buildings on a farm for the period of their publication, providing a base against which later changes can be assessed.

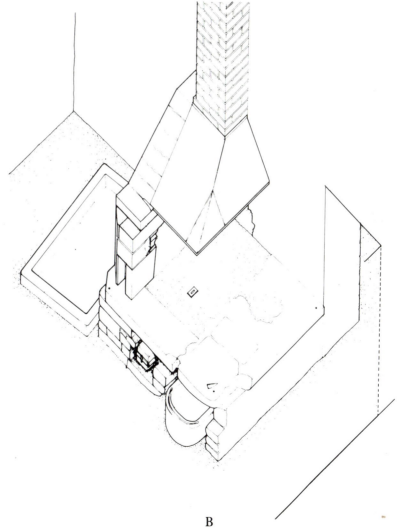

B

D

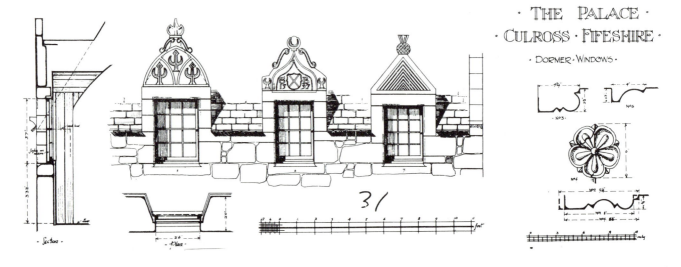

· THE PALACE ·
· CULROSS · FIFESHIRE ·
· DORMER · WINDOWS ·

Fig. 31.   The Palace, Culross, Fife. Dormer window details from the sixteenth and seventeenth centuries. Books of measured drawings showing details of domestic buildings can provide an excellent source of material.

Ingval Maxwell related his survey to farm size and type, using two sheets for recording data. One gave the farm name and map reference, with entries relating to the arable, cropping and rough grazing acreages, the numbers of cows, sheep, and pigs, the nature of any steading developments and the accommodation provided in it for stock, manpower, machines and equipment. This contextualised the farm. The second sheet went into more detail on the architectural-historical background, farming changes, mill and power, work horses, obsolete equipment, construction and materials, roofing, walling and flooring.

The forty farms chosen gave a good cross-section of the types in the area, from the small pendicle upwards. The acreage in relation to the former numbers of horses and other stock (reflected in the size and number of byres and stables, and the number of cart-sheds—as a rule a pair of horse can be reckoned for every cart-shed entrance), and the nature of the threshing machinery and the means (water, horse, engine) by which it

Burnshot steading
pre. 1826

A   Mill course shed which will repair with little cost

B   Barn the walls of this house to be raised and a loft put in for holding unthrashed grain - 52´x 18´

C   This stable is in bad order and should be converted into a straw house - 32´x 16´

D   This shed is in ruin

E   Present feeding byre in pretty good order

F   A loose house in very bad order

G   Scullery might repair

Plan of Burnshot steading as it stood before the alterations and additions proposed in 1826

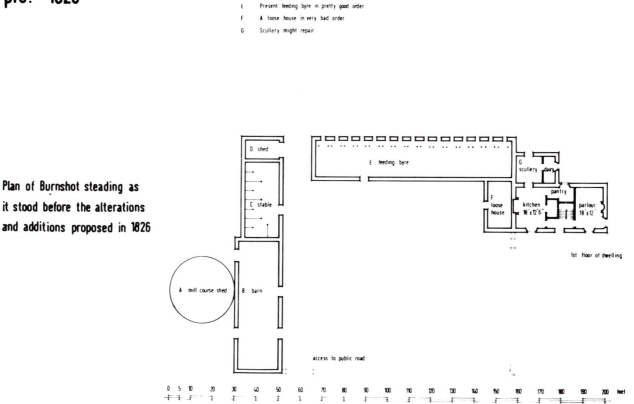

Fig. 32.   Burnshot, Carriden, West Lothian pre-1826. Plan of steading as existing before the alterations and additions proposed in 1826, as drawn by Ingval Maxwell from the original plans in the Hopetoun Muniments. (NMAS: C.2408)

was driven proved to be the basic essentials affecting the structure and layout of farm buildings.

The historical background was also investigated, using published material, and the extent of change assessed following the late eighteenth and early nineteenth century improvements, including a common change in steading layout from L- to U-shaped.

This survey gained for Ingval Maxwell a Royal Institute of British Architects' award, which was used to carry out a detailed survey of twenty-six farm buildings on the Hopetoun Estate in West Lothian.[47] Data sheets were used as for the Airlie Survey, and sketch plans made for each farm unit examined. The field study technique involved sketching the plan of the steading to establish functional relationships. On the assumption that structural supports are required wherever eaves, gutters or valleys exist in a roof plan, the ground plan of a building group could be readily prepared if the roof plan was plotted first. Once blocked out, the sketch interior detail could be infilled, and

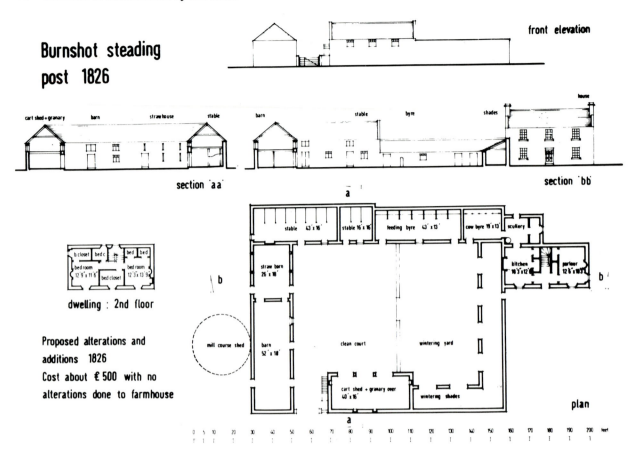

Fig. 33.　Burnshot, Carriden, West Lothian post-1826. Plan of steading showing proposed alterations and additions of 1826, as drawn by Ingval Maxwell from the original plans. (NMAS: C.2406)

windows, doors, floors, columns, beams, roof trusses, fittings and other details plotted within the blocked-out areas. Subsequent discussion with the farmer usually helped to establish the sequence of changes that could be observed. The modern layouts worked out in this way were related to a sequence of maps, in particular Roy *circa* 1752, Armstrong 1773, Forrest 1818, and the one-inch Ordnance Survey maps of 1857, 1898 and 1963. Thus a visual impression of change over a period of two centuries was obtained, and the existence of dated steading plans in the Hopetoun Muniments was an added bonus. Air photographs were also used, and it is apparent that by intelligent use of such sources, a great deal of purposeful preparatory work can be done in the library or archive before going out to study buildings on the ground.[48]

The elements examined on the Hopetoun Estate ranged over background topics such as enclosure, the amalgamation of farms, geological influences, and specific architectural features and units such as masonry work and techniques, the farm house (and its relationship to the steading), cot-houses and bothies for housing the farm-workers, the barn with its sheaf loft, threshing floor, threshing mill and granary, sources of power (horse, steam, water, oil), the cart and implement sheds, stable, byre,

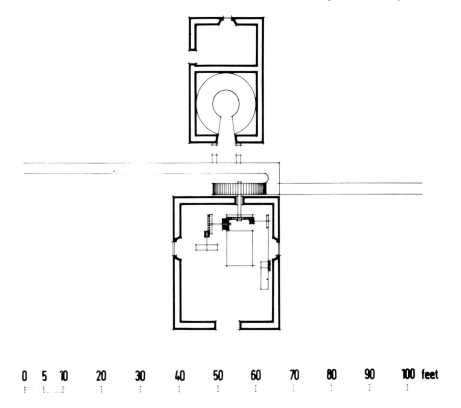

0 5 10 20 30 40 50 60 70 80 90 100 feet

Fig. 34. Philpston Mill, Abercorn, West Lothian: 1784. Plan of a corn mill on the Hopetoun estate in 1784, as drawn by Ingval, Maxwell from the original plans. (NMAS: C.2405)

wintering court, turnip shed, hen-house, boiling house, smithy, and the surrounding walls, gates and pillars. Fourteen tables bring out a variety of factors often related to acreage: the size of the farm house, the number of cot-houses or bothies in relation to manpower, the siting of the barn with the nature of the power source for threshing and grain processing machinery, the number of cart shed bays in relation to work horses and stabling, details of byres, with wintering courts and turnip sheds, and supplementary units such as hen-houses, boiling houses and smithies.[49]

A further survey is being undertaken by Ingval Maxwell in South-West Scotland, an area where milk production affects farm types. A study of about 150 farms, steadings and cottages in Midlothian has also been carried out by him at the request of the Midlothian District Council. In each case, the techniques worked out for the Hopetoun survey are being applied.

The Mackintosh School of Architecture in the University of Glasgow began to take an interest in vernacular architecture in 1973, concentrating on buildings in western Scotland. This led to detailed measurement and drawing of Kempleton Mill, Kirkcudbright, and of a group of blackhouses in the village of Garenin, Lewis.[50]

The School of Architecture, Duncan of Jordanstone College of Art, of the University of Dundee, is the most active centre at the present time. Ingval Maxwell is a product of the School, and a pupil of Bruce Walker. Besides the widespread survey work undertaken personally by Bruce Walker, several students have produced or are working on relevant dissertations:

J. Brewster, *Seven Fife Farms (Kerse Estate)* 1977;

K. Davie, *Power Sources for Threshing Mills in North Fife* 1979;

T. Drysdale, *The Historical Development of the Harbours of the East Neuk of Fife* 1977;

A. Duncan, *Cast Iron Structures (Dundee)* 1976;

A. R. Edwards, *Some Aspects of Peasant Housing in Scotland: influences on roof construction* 1977;

C. Gratton, *Clay Housing in Errol* 1973;

G. Grzywa, *Eighteenth and Nineteenth Century Building Materials and Constructional Techniques in the Carse of Gowrie, Perthshire* 1978;

C. Hughes, *Colour and Decoration in Scottish Vernacular Buildings* 1981;

E. Kelly, *Development of Auchmithie, Angus* 1977;

J. A. Leask, *Scottish Water Mills* 1969;

I. Maxwell, *Functional Estate Architecture—an historical study and appraisal of traditional farm building* (4 vols) 1969 (thesis subject);

D. Miller, *Railway Architecture—Aberdeen to Dundee* 1979;

D. Murray, *Aspects of Environmental Control* 1977;

J. Reid, *Water Power on the Rossie (Priory) Estate, Perthshire* 1976;

G. F. Simpson, *Railway Architecture of Fife* 1971;

C. A. Smith, *Organisational Procedures for Farm Building Projects* 1976;

T. Somerville, *The Lime Kilns of Angus* 1977;

A. Tragham, *Bothies—Angus and Perthshire* 1979;

G. White, *The Influence of the Low Countries on the Architecture of Fife and the Forth* 1977;

In 1977-78, a survey of buildings in Grampian Region, sponsored by the Countryside Commission for Scotland in conjunction with the Regional Authority, was carried out by Bruce Walker. This involved a review of published sources, field recording, and investigation of farm plans kept in architects' offices. The main features of buildings erected during the first and second phases of agrarian improvement were pinpointed from the documentary evidence, and checked against a form of field sampling, which consisted of following a series of lines drawn over the map, the length being based on the possible distance that might be covered in a day, allowing for visits to a number of farms on either side of the route. Since a main purpose of the exercise was to seek criteria for establishing regional identity, substantially altered structures were ignored, and the survey concentrated on reasonably intact survivals. Where farm houses and steadings of similar type occurred, only one was examined in detail and notes made on any obvious external differences in materials or constructional techniques on the others. Every effort was made to visit large, medium and small units, and to include crofts. Details of the analysis are given in Chapter 10 below.

One of the most potentially interesting present developments is a survey started in 1978 which, in effect, takes up the idea that the Vernacular Buildings Working Party originated. Through the firm of Sir Frank Mears & Partners, and financed by the Countryside Commission for Scotland, this survey aims to cover the whole of Scotland, though on a selective basis because of the time and cost factors. This should, for the first time, allow a reasonably firm assessment, at least in broad outline, of the regional variety of rural buildings in Scotland, and provide planning authorities with a body of computerised comparative data, suitable as a basis for selecting buildings for preservation. The knowledge gained of existing forms could permit architects to design modern buildings in keeping with the spirit of the past, even if adapted to suit modern materials and the modern idiom.

5

Roofing Materials

THROUGHOUT the country, as in other European lands, farms were grouped in clusters, *ferm-touns*, that stood with their arable, meadow and rough-grazing patches within a dyke that kept the bulk of the stock out on the hill or moorland grazing during the summer.

In Berwickshire, for example, there were four such villages in Mertoun in 1740. One contained six farmers, their cottages, and two or three tradesmen. Another contained 50 houses. By the 1790s, only a tenth part of a third remained.[51] The farm of West Laws in Whitsom and Hilton, with its dwelling house and offices, and its cottages for hinds and dependents, formed a little village by itself, as also at Legerwood.[52] In Fogo, several former villages were demolished as new, improved farms were made,[53] the best of which had three small low-roofed rooms, one of them a kitchen, with clay floors, bare, whitewashed walls, no ceilings, and rarely lofts.[54] In Fife too, about 1750, the mining communities had their farms grouped in one 'closs'.[55] In Angus the unimproved farms were often in clusters, with intermediate houses for cattle, forming a village without any plan.[56] The same was true throughout Scotland. In the improving lowland areas such villages vanished mainly in the period 1750-1800, but in the north and west they lasted longer and are still identifiable, for example at Fladdabister near Lerwick and at Aith in Fetlar, Shetland. The township of Auchindrain, six miles west of Inveraray in Argyll, is a former joint-farming community now preserved as an open-air museum.

Roofing Timbers : Lairds' and Tenants' Roles

In all such farming villages, and also in the smaller tenant farms of a later date, roofing timbers were the most valuable parts of the buildings. In many areas, from Caithness to Galloway, it was the laird who provided timbers capable of being shaped into cruck trusses, whilst the tenant saw to the walling which, as a consequence, tended to be built of ephemeral material like turf in no very workmanlike manner (though turf, if cut from well-established grass and properly built, could be a first-class material). This timber was the *master wood*,[57] *master's timbers*[58] or often *great timber*.[59] The tenant got the wood on inventory, and as a rule he was bound to leave wood of an equal appreciated value at the end of his lease, or to make an appropriate payment to the incoming tenant, the date of entry always being Whitsunday.[60]

The system prevailed in the seventeenth century as much as in the eighteenth. Accounts and leases relating to estates in Lowland Scotland show that pans and purlins, and cabers or rafters might be supplied as well as the 'great timber'. Where timber was scarce, the lairds had to use material imported from Norway, and it is no great wonder that they tended to be parsimonious about repairing or replacing timbers.[61] In the 1750s in Annandale in the South-West, tenants who were rebuilding their houses could get help from the estate factor, which was a matter of some importance for the local woods had become exhausted, and money was scarce for buying foreign timber.[62] However, it

Fig. 35.   Cruck-Framed Structure, Ross-shire. An interior photograph showing typical highland crucks with joints at the elbow and formed of timber with the bark left more or less intact. It is however more common to find the lower portion of the cruck built into the wall and standing on a large stone in the base of the wall to form some protection from rot. (NMAS: viii. 25. 24A)

was noted in Clackmannan in the 1760s that home-grown fir of 35 to 40 years old, at half the price of foreign wood, was dearer in the end for it lasted only up to 20 years as opposed to a century for imported material.[63] Local planted fir was the timber supplied by the laird in the parish of Dallas in Moray.[64] Oak and ash were preferred to fir, but hardwood was certainly too expensive for use in roofing the buildings at least in small tenants' holdings. Inevitably, crucks had to be repaired and as a result many must have had a re-used, patched-up appearance. Old rafters were used for new cottages. In

Fig. 36 (a, b).   Achmore, Lochalsh, Ross-shire. a. exterior
b. interior.
A small barn on a croft in Wester Ross with very sophisticated cruck blades, still with elbow joints but of dressed timber, and more akin to modern laminated timber in appearance than to the more normal highland cruck. From R. O'Malley, *One Horse Farm* 1948. Facing 51.

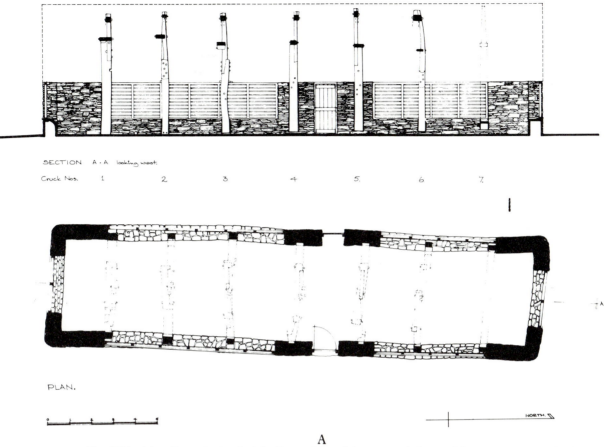

SECTION A·A looking west.

Cruck Nos.   1   2   3   4   5.   6   7.

PLAN.

NORTH

A

Fig. 37 (a, b).   Fernaig, Lochalsh, Ross-shire. A large cruck-framed barn, constructed using second-hand timbers of unusual section, as the largest dimension in section runs parallel to the walls and not at right angles as would be more structurally logical. This construction may be related to boat-building techniques as there the longer dimension is turned parallel to the planking to provide greater space in the hull of the boat.

Sutherland, roofing couples were of birch, and if taken from the laird's natural woods, remained his property. Lengths of moss fir from the bogs, however, were by custom the property of the tenants. They were laid across the couples to support the turf. If the tenants moved, they took their moss fir with them. They could also carry off their doors.[65] Here, therefore, there was sharing of a customary nature, and the situation was much the same in Atholl, Perthshire, where the Duke's forester allowed the tenants to get their small timbers or cabers free, though they had to pay for the main timbers.[66] On the estates of Skibo and Pulrossie in the 1790s, wood was supplied by the proprietors for the turf-built houses.[67]

The sharing of roles in this way between laird and tenant did nothing to improve the quality of the housing. Some lairds were evidently concerned about this, for already by 1701 on the Barony of Urie in Kincardineshire, removing tenants were being forbidden to pull down any more of the house walls than was necessary to let them take their timbers with them. Here the timbers seem to belong to the tenants. It was further

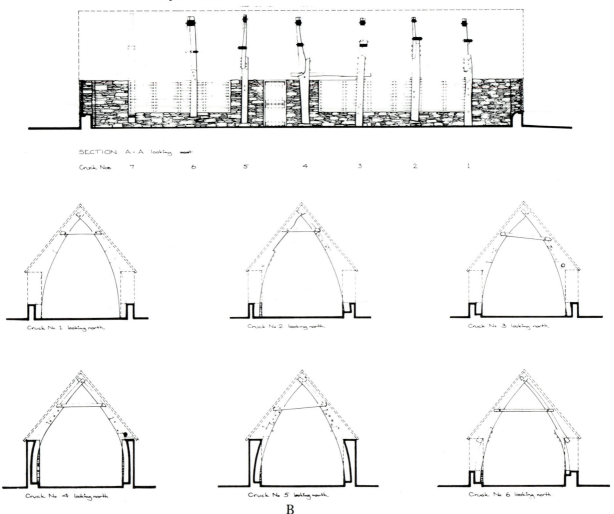

SECTION A·A looking east
Cruck Nos.   7   6   5   4   3   2   1

Cruck No 1 looking north.   Cruck No 2 looking north.   Cruck No 3 looking north.

Cruck No 4 looking north   Cruck No 5 looking north.   Cruck No 6 looking north

B

decreed in 1712 that timber should not be removed from office-houses without first offering it to the incoming tenant.[68] By the 1760s in Inverness-shire, some lairds were beginning to doubt the propriety of allowing tenants roofing timber because it led to sub-standard walling. Mr Grant on the Seafield Estate ceased to let his tenants in Urquhart have timber for the side walls, so forcing them to built in stone.[69]

In the Hebrides, interaction between laird and tenant was of a different kind. Presumably because of the island situation, where timber was not readily available except in the form of driftwood, the situation was that the tenants had to get their own roofing-timber, and the walls belonged to the laird.[70] In Kilmuir, Skye, lotters and small tenants bought their timbers from the Mainland, in the form of six to eight 'rude cupples' of unsquared timber, with a few purlins.[71]

Either way, since the responsibility for the buildings was shared between laird and tenant, this allowed plenty of scope for traditional building forms and features to survive, without the benefit of architect's advice. Building by tenants was almost general. In Stirlingshire they were left to provide a house and offices, each according to

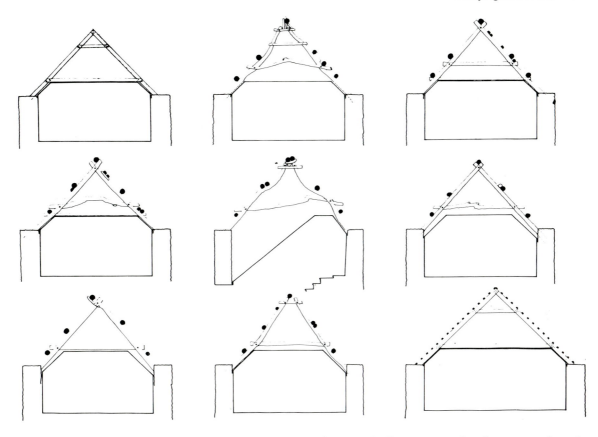

Fig. 38.   4 Gladgate, Auchtermuchty, Fife. A number of different types of roof truss were found in the roof of this house. The oldest type was spaced at approximately 3 metre centres, constructed from natural branches partially checked together to form an A-frame with a yoke collar at the ridge (2, 5 & 8). The joints are formed with tapered square pegs driven through round holes, and the trusses support purlins at ridge, mid span and eaves which in turn support close spaced branches running from eaves to ridge. The second type was constructed from quartered logs, pegged together in the same way to form an A-frame with crossed blades at the ridge (3, 4, 6 & 7). These trusses had been inserted between the older type to reduce the purlin span to approximately 1 metre. These trusses had been constructed with green timber which had warped considerably after installation. The third type was a simple A-frame constructed from scientific section timber, half checked at the joints and secured with blacksmith-made nails driven through the joints and turned over at the back. One of these (1) forms a truss, the others (9) formed couples spaced at approximately 60 cm centres to support thatching battens. All three types of truss were built into the wallhead. (NMAS: C.3889).
(Top line: 1—3, 2nd line: 4—6; bottom line: 7—9; all left to right).

his inclination and ability, which led to the retention of the two-roomed house with byre and stable usually under the same roof.[72] In Arran farmers built their own houses with crucks,[73] in Stirling till the early 1800s the lairds let the tenants provide their own houses and offices,[74] and similarly in most places. In Galloway it was noted that when houses were tenant-built, they were poorer than those built by the estate.[75] In Fife, as elsewhere, the question of whether a tenant or landlord should build depended on the

Fig.39.   Barvas, Lewis, Ross-shire: 1936. A shieling hut situated on the west side of Barvas on the Stornoway road. Note the rubble base to the turf walls and the large flat divots used to form the roof covering. (O.G.S. Crawford 227.2)

Fig. 40.   Stenness, Shetland. A group of rubble-walled fishermen's huts with gable entrances and turf-covered piend roofs. The turf on these roofs appears to be uniformly sharp, suggesting a recent cut and that all the huts had been re-roofed at the same time. This was an annual occurrence in this area. (NMAS: iii/44/34)

Fig. 41. Killiecrankie, Moulin, Perthshire. Broom-thatched cottages with turf ridge and skew. These two, single-roomed cottages have false stone chimney heads at either end and on the mutual gable. The actual chimney heads are constructed of timber on the inside face of the false stone chimney. This is a fairly common detail in Highland Perthshire. (GWW: F 1445)

length of the lease.[76] But tenant building was not absolutely general, for before 1740 in the Barony of Chirnside, Berwickshire, the houses of the village were erected at the lairds' expense and provided free to tenants.[77] This is scarcely characteristic, however. In Shetland for a time in the late eighteenth and nineteenth centuries, lairds often erected dwelling-houses and left the tenants to deal with their own outbuildings,[78] in which case the steading usually remained in an older style. All such factors helped to retain traditional features in buildings. For this kind of reason, it is sometimes possible to get glimpses back beyond the improvements, in farms that still stand at the present day.

Roofing Timbers : the Cruck Truss

The use of cruck-trusses was common throughout Scotland, except in Orkney and Shetland and the Outer Hebrides. The lower ends rested on a stone on the ground, or on top of a base course of stone. In spite of the way in which old crucks must have been

Fig. 42.   Hill of Hatton, Auchterless, Aberdeenshire. Photograph of a croft house where the corrugated iron roof covering had been blown away during a gale exposing an undercloak of turf used for insulation. Had this turf been intended to be the outer covering larger divots would have been used and laid with laps as in a slate or tile roof. It should be borne in mind that corrugated iron was available as building material before most of the Aberdeenshire crofts had substantial stone houses of this kind and therefore the corrugated iron could be the original roof covering. (NMAS: iv.29.8)

cobbled up as parts rotted away and had to be removed, a range of regional varieties can be distinguished. The characteristic half-barrel shape of the Caithness cruck, for example, is a result of composite construction from relatively short lengths of wood

Fig. 43. Overbrae of Fisherie, King Edward, Aberdeenshire. A stone-built hen house with rush-thatched roof held by chicken wire pegged at the eaves and skew with timber pegs. At the time the photograph was taken the thatch was in a poor state of repair and due for renewal, a process which was carried out by the female owner of the croft. (NMAS: S449)

pegged together. Where wood was more plentiful, bigger and sometimes elegant crucks with substantial side pieces were built, as in the Corrimony barn. Only a few cruck-framed rural buildings were two storeys high, as at Pitcastle, Perthshire.[79]

In Peebles in the South-East, where timber was scarce in places, some buildings had the unusual feature of 'stone couples' instead of roofing timbers. These were rough arches of stone, 18 in (46 cm) thick by 20 in (51 cm) deep, springing from the walls, meeting at a point, and set at 6 or 7 ft (1.8-2.1 m) intervals between the gables.[80]

In Ayrshire in the South-West, the crucks in farms up till the 1740s were set at 8 to 10 ft (2.4-3 m) intervals. Here, as in Roxburgh and Renfrew, crucks were known as *siles*. The cross-beams were the *ribs* or *pans*, the ridge-pole the *roof-tree*, and the arm-thick branches that made a bed for the thatch, the *cabers*. Smaller spars set on top of the wall to fill in the space were *upstarts*. The whole wooden interior of the roof got the general name of *bougars*, a term largely confined to South and East Central Scotland. The walls stood 5 ft (1.5 m) high and the houses were 12 to 13 ft (3.7-4 m) wide.[81]

E

Fig. 44.   Callanish, Lewis, Ross-shire. A crofter's cottage with heavily roped thatched roof anchored with stones resting on the wide wallhead. Note how the ropes are carried round the piend end by the use of a 'crow' stick at the end of the ridge but springing from the gable. (GWW: C2616)

In Perthshire in the East, the cruck legs rested on large stones 2 or 3 ft (0.6-0.9 m) above floor level. The *pantrees* or purlins were overlaid with *cabers*, branches stripped of their leaves and smaller twigs, as a bed for the thatch. At one time, the cabers were interwoven with other rods to form a kind of wattle.[82] In Angus it was much the same.[83]

A detailed description of crucks comes from the North-East. The old buildings, rarely over 12 ft (3.7 m) wide internally—though ranging in length from 30 to 60 ft (9.1-18.2 m)—had cruck couples with a perpendicular leg on each side, 4½ ft (1.4 m) long. They were set in position when the walls had been built up to a height of 18 in (0.5 m), with the foot of the couple resting on the inner part of the wall. They were set at intervals of 6 to 10 ft (1.8-3 m), so that a house 40 ft (12.2 m) long needed three or four trusses. They were made of whole trees squared a little with the adze or axe, or sometimes with 'half-trees', which were whole ones cleft down the middle. The units were joined by wooden pegs. The rafters did not join at the top, where a space was left for the roof tree, which lay along the crowns of the couples. The upper, short cross beams were close under the roof tree, whilst the longer, lower ones were about two-thirds of the way down. Two or three rows of purlins or run-joists lay across the couples

Fig. 45.   Brakins, Foula, Shetland: 1902. Closely roped thatch on croft buildings on Foula. Note the rounded form of the roof and the raised skews in rubble stonework. (NMAS: C6030; H. B. Curwen)

and gable tops, at equal distances apart. Over them at right angles went the smaller spars of fir, *watling*, as a base for the thatch. Their lower ends rested on the wall heads.[84] Further details from Banffshire add to this Aberdeenshire report. The couple arms that spanned the house were called *hoos*. The upper cross-piece was the *croon piece*, the lower was the *bauk*. There were three or four purlins or *pans* at each side, covered with *cabers*, and the *reef tree* lay at the ridge.[85]

In Caithness, crucks got the name of 'Highland couples', and it was already noted in 1795 that they had a semi-circular form. In the 1760s, there were two straths in Berriedale that produced trees big enough to use for roofing, but these were being converted to agricultural purposes by 1812. In the mosses lying towards Sutherland, bog fir was found, and used for roofing houses.[86]

In Argyll, in the Highlands, the poorer tenants, who were in the majority, had long, low, cruck-framed houses in the 1790s. The crucks were set about 6 ft (1.8 m) apart. The upright could be of one piece with a natural bend, or of two pieces pegged together at eaves' level.[87] In Inverness-shire, as in Perthshire, there were examples in the early 1800s of cruck couples overlain by interwoven wicker as a base for the thatch.[88] In Ross-shire, lotters' houses, much poorer than those of the farmers, still had crucks of unsquared alder, to which crossbars were fixed with tree nails, in the 1840s.[89] The

Bruce Walker 1980

Fig. 46.   Whigginton, Lochlee, Angus. A late nineteenth-century single-storey farmhouse with cross-roped thatched roof swept up to encase the timber chimney heads. Note the lathe just above the eaves to provide a secure anchor to the base of the thatch. (NMAS: C5413 per Glenesk Folk Museum)

smaller tenantry in Sutherland also lived in houses with cruck-frames, the side timbers of which were of birch or fir 7 ft to 10 ft (2.1-3 m) long by 4 to 6 in (10-15 cm) in diameter, fixed in the ground at one end and attached by wooden pins at the other. Lengths of moss fir from the bogs, used as cabers, were about 3 ft (0.9 m) long by 1-2 in (2.5-5 cm) in diameter.[90]

In every one of the five main regions, therefore, except for the Northern Isles, cruck-frames were the commonplace of pre-improvement buildings; only with the improvements did the use of crucks, and usually with them the longhouse where men and animals were under one roof, become confined to the smaller farming units and lower social levels.

Roofing Timbers : the Improvement Period

One of the consequences of building improvement was that much greater expense went into the house. A-frame couples, with their ends resting on the stone wall-heads, became the norm. The increasing use of slates led to an increased use of foreign timber, for they required a level bed which native timber could not so readily provide.

A factor of importance here already in the seventeenth century was the growing use of lime mortar, especially on the east coast around the Forth and Tay estuaries, but also in

Fig. 47.   Lochaber, Argyllshire. A highland cottage and outhouses with thatched roofs secured by laths. Note the swept corners to the stone walls of the house and outbuilding and the difference in the character of the stonework between these two buildings resulting from the house walls being pointed and lime washed. (GWW: F4247)

the North-East, Roxburgh, Lanark and Galloway. At first used on the houses of the gentry, it gradually spread to the bigger tenants' houses, for example on the Aberdour Estate in Fife in 1625. Most of the estate-paper references, however, lie between 1660-1700. Lime mortar permitted the construction of fully load-bearing walls associated with close coupled rafters, and buildings two or even three storeys high. It should be noted, however, that other materials could also permit the construction of fully load-bearing walls—for example, clay mortar, tempered clay, clay and bool, and timber frame. A survey of the Barony of Lasswade near Edinburgh in 1694 showed that the houses of the larger tenants, farming 65 to 130 acres arable, were of two and in one case three storeys, with lime-mortared walls. Some of the out-buildings were grouped into separate wings forming L-shaped steadings, or, in one instance, a Z-shaped plan. The best of them were built about 1693.[91]

It can, therefore, be assumed that where farm-houses or buildings of more than one storey appeared, A-framed couples were normally in use.

Fig. 48.   Skye, Inverness-shire. Cottage with thatch held by wire weighted with stones. Note the swept corners to the stonework and the changes of ground level on either side of the doorway. (NMAS: C5042)

Fig. 49.   Balbirnie Bridge, Markinch, Fife. A row of cottages with reed-thatched roofs and turf ridges. (NMAS: C2827)

Fig. 50.   Aberdeenshire, probably New Pitsligo area. Clay-thatched roof with large closely roped timber chimney head. The dormer top of the ground floor window is a reasonably common feature in Aberdeenshire and Banffshire. (Original in NMAS)

Thatch

Roofing thatch could be of various materials. Straw was common in the seventeenth century in the arable farming areas, that of wheat and rye being preferred where possible to that of bere and oats, as in the Lothians. Turf could underlie the straw, or could serve as thatch in its own right, especially but not exclusively for outhouses. Heather was common in Galloway, Ayrshire and the North-East, to judge by estate records, but was a relatively expensive form of roof-covering that tended to go with better-quality buildings, or on the dwelling house rather than the outhouses. It was also harder work to thatch with heather, and was sore on the hands.[92]

Wide use was made of broom and whin as thatch, or as a bed for turf, straw or heather.[93] In 1759, for example, the houses of tenants on Deeside were said to be built of

Fig. 51.   Inverness, Inverness-shire. Cottages with dormer windows set into the thatch of the roof. (NMAS: C5613 Inverness Museum. Photographer A. Cooper & Co., Inverness)

loose stones and covered with turf, heath, broom or fir branches, 'like so many mole hills'.[94] Bracken roots, rushes, bent grass, indeed any kind of material could be used, provided it could be spread so as to run the water.

That there were many different forms of thatching in the country is evident from information in the scattered sources, and it is also clear that the improvement situation had its effect on types of thatch. In the South-East, new Berwickshire farms were sometimes using by the 1790s a 'lately approved covering of corded thatch', presumably a particular form of sewn thatch.[95] At that period in Selkirk, most farms were of one storey, and thatched. In the higher-lying areas a fresh covering of rushes or *sprats* was put on each year.[96] In Peeblesshire, about 1800, bere straw was either sewn to the rafters with tarred twine, or else there was an underlay of divots into which the straw was thrust in small handfuls, twisted together at the top, into holes made obliquely upwards by an iron-shod, dovetail-pointed tool called a *sting*. Heather was applied by neither of these means, except for the first course at the eaves, which was sewn to the rafters. It was then laid in courses from gable to gable, each course being beaten close with mallets, and the top was secured by a ridging of sods.[97]

In the South-West, heather was a common Ayrshire thatch which continued into the improvement period. Though around 1800 it cost £2 10/- (£2.50) per rood to collect and

Fig. 52.   South Cairnton, Fordoun, Kincardineshire. A large steading with blue slated piend roofs to byres, stables, and covered courts. Note the use of metal flashings on the roof hips. (NMAS: 39. 29. 21)

Fig. 53.   Ancum, North Ronaldsay, Orkney. Stone-slate roof comprising large irregular flags laid with laps and pointed with mortar. (NMAS: A. Fenton 1964)

Fig. 54. Swordale, Thurso, Caithness. Very large stone slates on the roof of a field shelter. The walls are constructed of the same material in smaller pieces but split to thicker sections. (NMAS: vi. 24. 30A)

put on, it could last for 70 to 80 years and so was a long-term economy.[98] In Bute straw was used, but more often heather, tied down with a network of heather ropes and retained by stones dangling at the eaves.[99] Straw thatch was normal in Renfrew,[100] and in Dunbarton, though some parts used thatch of heather or bracken, both of which were very durable if properly applied. The heather, cut before harvest, was laid on the house stems downward. Bracken was pulled with the root at the beginning of October, care being taken that the fronds were not brittle. They were used with the leaves, which would fall off if the fronds were withered when pulled. They were laid in rows on the roof, roots downward, in rows about 3 or 4 in (8-10 cm) apart, so that almost nothing but the root was exposed to the weather. Bracken thatch could last about six or seven years on the side of the roof exposed to the sun, or upwards of thirty on the north side.[101] In Dunbarton too, in the early 1800s, thatch of wheat-straw, sewn with twine on to light spars of wood, was coming into use.[102] In Lanark, thatch was the commonest roofing medium, especially in the parishes of Wandell and Stonehouse, till the 1840s.[103] In Dumfries, fern, pulled by the roots, was said to last about 20 years, five times longer than straw. The roots were laid downward as for bracken, and exposed to view, the tops being covered. Strong heather was said to last even longer.[104] In Galloway, as generally in the South-West, the areas of longest survival of roofs thatched with straw, fern, or sometimes heath, were the moorlands.[105]

In the East, old farmhouses surviving in Kinross in the early 1800s were roofed with straw, turf or rushes.[106] Most of the farmhouses and offices in Atholl, Perthshire, were thatched with broom in the 1760s.[107] In the Central Highlands generally, the older buildings in the 1790s had thatch of straw, rushes, heather or fern, the latter plucked by the roots or cut very close to the ground in October. The gables and ridges were finished off with a layer or *seal* of thick sods.[108] Straw was the most common thatch, and fern or broom were used if it was scarce. Heather was common in the higher-lying areas, and though it gave a dark, gloomy appearance, it was more durable than other organic materials.[109] Here as elsewhere, where small tenants did their own building, straw thatch on top of turf was the usual roofing medium. As part of the improving movement, however, reeds were being cultivated for thatch on the Rivers Tay and Forth, starting with Henry Crawford of Monorgan in 1776.[110] Reed-beds at Powgavie, Seaside and Errol were planted in 1836.[111] The reeds were cut, made into bundles about 3 ft (91 cm) in circumference, and sold by the hundred bundles.[112] Errol was said to be producing over 40,000 bundles a year in the 1840s.

A bracken thatch roof was recorded at Broar, Perthshire in 1978, under a tin roof. In Angus roofs of turf and straw thatch, roped down with straw ropes, were normal, even on improved farms, many examples surviving until the age of photography and relatively recent times.

In the North-East, old farms were still to be found in Kincardineshire in the early 1800s, with thatch of straw or rush, roped with the same materials and renewed annually.[113] In Aberdeenshire, sewn thatch and heather thatch were counted as improvements in the 1790s. Heather was especially common in the higher parts of the country. The heather was first pulled by the roots, and made into bundles. It was said to last for over 60 years if carefully put on, though it was a high fire risk. In the lower areas, 'thatch and divot' was the main form of roofing, the thatch being retained by a criss-crossing network of straw ropes.[114] The getting of material for thatch required a considerable effort. On the improving estate of Monymusk, for example, 107 thraves of heather were pulled, at a rate of 7 thraves a day, in 1748, making a total of over 15 days' pulling. Broom was also used on some of the houses.[115] In Cluny, the straw or broom thatch was renewed every two or three years.[116] The thatch was drawn round the angles of the ridge and skews and tied with straw or heather ropes. The gablets forming the upper triangle of the gable, and the course of turf that usually topped the stone walls, may well have survived longer because they made an easy bed for the thatching pegs that held the securing ropes.[117]

From about 1785, a small number of the houses in Keithhall and Kinkell had been *stob-thatched*, or else covered with a deep coat of straw.[118] Stob-thatching became a widespread technique in the North-East in the nineteenth century.

In Moray and Nairn, the later eighteenth century roofing in the higher areas was of sods and straw under a netting of straw rope, and bracken was used if straw was scarce. On the lower ground, the offices on the farms were usually thatched, the straw being applied in overlapping layers as for slate, the upper half of each course being securely

Fig. 55.   Jericho, Glamis, Angus. Regular stone-slate roof (known locally as grey slate) on eighteenth century weavers' houses. Note the absence of flashings on the hip of the roof. (NMAS: 35. 12. 17)

bedded in clay.[119] By the mid-nineteenth century, the one-storey buildings of smaller tenants were still invariably, and the two-storey buildings of bigger farmers occasionally, thatched.

In Caithness, in the 1760s, there was a neat way of thatching the better-class houses. Flags were laid on the lower part for about 4 ft (1.2 m), then on the upper part straw ropes were laid close together and drawn tight. Lesser buildings were covered with sods and straw, laid regularly, or else piled on loose and well tied with straw ropes, in which case the roof had to be renewed every year.[120] About 1790, the technique of thatching with straw and clay was introduced. For this, the straw was threshed whole in the sheaf, without the band being untied. Four sheaves were then made into one bundle, and as many bundles made as necessary. The thatcher put his ladder within 3 ft (0.9 m) of the right-hand gable, and spread one of the bundles on the lower part of the roof, between the ladder and the gable. If there was turf underneath, he had to twist the upper part of the straw into a knot, and then with a special stick force the knot under or through the divots. The work proceeded from the bottom to the top. The course was then clayed all over, the ladder was moved, and the next course begun. Wheat, rye, barley or oat straw was used, in that order of preference. It was applied not less than 6 in (15 cm) thick, but 8 in (20 cm) was better. Divots, formerly considered the best foundation, were found to rot the straw, so straw alone, stitched with rope yarn, was preferred. The thatcher was

Fig. 56. Tyninghame, Tyninghame, East Lothian. Single-storey pantiled cottage. Pantiles were used as a utilitarian roofing material in much the same way as corrugated asbestos is today, and houses with pantiled roofs were rare prior to the 1850s unless as an inexpensive substitute for thatch. The use of pantiles for houses is a late nineteenth-century feature and their introduction to this class of building caused considerable controversy. (NMAS: C1649)

paid 6/- a rood, the straw being supplied, and he paid his assistant out of this. A roof of straw alone could last for 20 years, but had to be 2 in (5 cm) thicker than when clay was used. A roof of divots, straw and clay could last 17 to 20 years, and could be mended easily. If the available clay was stiff, a cart load of sand could be mixed with every two loads of clay.[121]

By 1812, Caithness had a number of slate-roofed farm houses with five to nine 'fire-rooms' in each, and squares of office houses which were generally slated or sometimes thatched with divots of thin turf. A thousand divots would thatch 1½ roods. They were tied with heather or straw ropes. If straw was put over the divots, the roof would last only 3 or 4 years before it was ready to be repaired or put on the dunghill.[122] Turf continued to have much importance in Caithness, and in the 1840s tenant services in Wick parish still included the annual casting of 400 *feal* or sods for building houses, and 300 divots for thatching them.[123]

In the Highland area, thatch was of various kinds. Argyll conformed to neighbouring districts to the east, with roofs of divots covered with straw, sprots, rushes, or less often ferns or heather. The thatch was laid loosely and tied with ropes of the same material, or of heather. The main area of innovation was Kintyre, where straw thatch was fastened by being driven into the roof in bunches with a thatching stob, as in lowland Scotland. Here too, A-frame couples, the feet of which rested on the wall-heads, had begun to come in in the 1790s. At the same period, heather was recommended as preferable for farm houses. It was said to last up to a century, if the timbers would last as long. Heather, however, was not especially common. It was heavier than straw, and ideally needed a steeper pitch and couples set rather more closely together. Fern was capable of lasting ten to fifteen years, if well put on.[124]

In the mid-nineteenth century, in Inveraray the houses and barns of the poorer tenants were thatched with rushes, lasting 2 years, or ferns, lasting 7 years.[125] In Glenurchy and Iniskail, the better tenants had slated houses of stone and lime, though the roofs of the steadings were of straw, fern or rush thatch.[126]

In the county of Inverness, houses in St. Kilda were described in the 1690s as being roofed with thin turves covered with straw which was secured on each side by double ropes of straw or heather, held in place by numerous stones.[127] Turf roofing was evidently common on the mainland in the mid-eighteenth century. Divots were fixed on the roofs with ropes of twisted heather, taken backwards and forwards from one end to the other, and fixed at the bottom of each side with big stones in the loops of the ropes, to prevent the wind from stripping the roofs. Because of the winter gales the houses had to be freshly covered each year.[128] Where straw was applied, it was laid loosely and not very thickly. The heather ropes, as appears from a comment in 1768, were placed about a foot (30 cm) apart.[129]

In the double-skin blackhouses of the North-West, in the 1790s, the timbers were erected on top of the eaves. The beams and spars were bound by ropes of heather or bent, and placed standing on the eaves. Purlins were then bound on very firmly, and rows of ropes 'wrought very close' to keep the stubble thatch from falling through. The beams and roof-tree, with the side timbers available, would not have been able to take the weight of a solid roof of divots, hence the need to plait the ropes more thickly over them. Finally heather ropes, anchored with dangling stones, were laid across the roof to hold the thatch.[130] Skye houses had straw, ferns or heather overlying turf-covered rafters.[131] Ross and Cromarty had a similar range of straw, fern roots or heather.[132] In the early 1800s, smaller tenants in the Loch Carron and Applecross area, who had put up new buildings of stone and lime, were nevertheless thatching with fern and heather.[133] In Glenshiel, rushes were also mentioned in the 1840s,[134] and in Stornoway in Lewis there could be on the blackhouses a thatch of stubble or potato stalks, tied with heather or straw ropes fixed to anchor stones. The soot-saturated thatch was stripped every summer and strewn as fertiliser on the potato or barley field,[135] as also happened at Golspie in Sutherland.[136] In Eddrachillis in Sutherland, most of the houses had thatch of straw, long grass, rushes, ferns or heather, bound with ropes of heather or straw, or of the twisted roots of trees. A fresh cover was put on each year to keep them watertight.[137] The two-storey manse at Kildonan had offices roofed with turf and finished off with straw and clay thatch, but the actual church and manse at both Ach-na-h'uaidh and Achness were roofed with straw thatch and heather ropes.[138] In Shetland, as in Orkney, the standard thatch was of well-roped straw, overlying turf.[139]

Clay and Heather Thatch

It is evident that up till the end of the eighteenth century, a variety of relatively ephemeral and annually (or nearly so) renewed types of thatch were in use, not the least important element being the turf that was often used alone, or as a bed to which the outer covering was pinned. From the 1790s on, more attention was being paid to thatch. From the Borders to Caithness, new buildings were appearing with thatch, partly of wheat straw, sewn directly to the rafters. Old forms of thatching might then be relegated to the outhouses only, or else the dwelling houses were slated and tiled, and the outhouses thatched. In many areas thatch whether of an improved or older type remained in use on smaller farming units right down to the twentieth century. However, every rule may be broken, and in Angus a number of survivals, as at Moss-side of Balinshoe, Kirriemuir, at Tealing, and elsewhere, show that the dwelling-house could sometimes be thatched when the offices were grey-slated.

The effect of improvements on thatching techniques may be seen in the appearance of clay thatching, involving a roof of straw so heavily impregnated with a moist clay mixture that no roping was necessary. Documentary records and recent survivals show that it was to be found mainly on the east side of Scotland, in Caithness, Sutherland, Ross, Inverness, Moray, Aberdeen, Banff, Kincardine, Angus, Perth, Fife and Ayr. The kernel area seems to lie between Moray and Fife. The Caithness and Sutherland occurrences mark a spread, and here the Kildonan example is significant, for manses were likely to be affected by innovations more quickly than the houses of the ordinary people. The Ayrshire outlier is also innovatory. About 1770, a method of thatching with straw and mortar was introduced to the Kilmarnock area by Mr Macdowal of Garthland. Well prepared 'mortar', which probably means clay mixed with cut straw, was thinly spread over the thatch with a large trowel. The thatch was expected then to last up to forty or fifty years.[140] The clay dressing for clay thatch could be improved by using blue clay from the bottom of the peat bog and mixing it with cow dung before applying the mixture to the roof. The result was a shiny waterproof covering, according to Mr Henry, Overbrae of Fisherie, Aberdeenshire, who was speaking of thatching in the 1930s.

Clay was applied to bent grass, straw, rushes, heather, reeds and even broom and clay thatch was easy to repair by means of small bunches of the thatching material, big enough to pass through the closed thumb and forefinger. These were doubled over straight, or given a twist at the bend, and then thrust into the roof by a tool with a forked iron or flat wooden head. Other tools were a hand rake and a trimming knife. Sandy Mackenzie, a thatcher from the Muir of Urquhart in Moray, described how he thatched in courses 12-18 in (30-46 cm) wide, over divots. If the old thatch was being re-covered, the old surface was first combed down with the side of a trowel. Clay was then laid on, and after that bunches of straw were thrust in (according to another thatcher, Mr Brockie of Cranloch, the bunches could be of unequal size and so arranged that in their overlapping a level surface would be achieved), and well clayed, especially at the top. Each now came half way down the one below. When the course was finished, the straw was worked smooth and straight by hand, then raked down. To finish off, clay of a pea-soup consistency was poured on and percolated into all the cracks. The rain was said to wash it in, not off. In some cases the strip along the eaves, below the straw thatch, was packed with heather as a deterrent to birds, because they could make holes that gave access to the wind. Usually nothing was used to tie down a clay thatched roof, apart from a strip of wood laid just above the eaves to strengthen the weakest point against the power of the wind. Rye-straw was sometimes used in the Moray and Nairn area.

In Aberdeenshire and Banffshire, the thrusting tool was the *stob*, corresponding to the Peeblesshire *sting*, and the bunches of straw were *tippets* or *grips*. The *stob*, however, is not confined to clay-thatching: it is essentially a means of thrusting straw into underlying turf. Some thatchers did this with their hands alone. At least eight tippets were required for each row in a course 2 to 3 ft (61-91 cm) wide. 'Tippeting' was referred to in a farm diary from Lewes, Fyvie, in the 1820s. A thatching needle might also be used to sew the thatch on to the rafters underneath, but again this was not primarily a clay-thatching tool. It was also used, for example, for stitching reeds, as by Mr Lawrence, thatcher in Rait, in the 1970s. The depth of clay thatch was about 9 in (23 cm). Oat-straw would last about fourteen years, wheat or barley straw about eighteen.[141]

Clay could also be used in conjunction with heather thatch, which appears to have been becoming more common in Aberdeenshire in the 1830s than in previous years. John Collier, a thatcher from near Turriff, pointed out that the pitch of the roof had to be considered in relation to the type of thatch. The pitch varied in proportion to width, and usually buildings being thatched with heather had an internal width of 12 to 16 ft (3.7-4.9 m). If the heather was sewn on to the rafters instead of being laid over turf, the pitch should be raised about 4 in (11 cm). If three or four rows of slates or of pantiles were laid along the eaves, the heather could be laid thinner there, and the pitch lessened. Examples of thatch laid over pantiles and slate have been noted in the New Pitsligo area and around within the last decade.

According to Collier, the best heather thatching came from close-growing beds with slender stems 18 to 24 in (46-61 cm) long, which were too weak to support their own weight without leaning. It should be pulled by the root rather than cut, then bound in sheaves and laid in straight regular rows on the roof. Rope yarn could be used to compact the heather and sew it tight on the roof, but as it was apt to be bitten through by vermin, good clay was considered a better binding medium. The heather was not laid, like straw, in vertical courses from eaves to ridge, but in horizontal courses from gable to gable, as in Peeblesshire, from the bottom of the roof to the top. The upper rows did not need to be clayed as thoroughly as the lower courses. They should be angled at 25° to 30°, to match the slope of the roof. To run the rain better, the roof was made to swell slightly towards the middle by using the longest strands of heather at this point, or by packing more heather in. The ridge was topped with clay mixed with cut straw. Such a roof could last 20 to 30 years. For each rood of length (5.3 m) 576 sheaves of heather and two cart-loads of clay were required.[142]

Slate, Tile and Flagstone, c. 1770-1850
When Lord Belhaven discussed his ideal for farm buildings in 1699, he saw them as being roofed with thatch, and not slates or tiles. It was nearly a century later before these

began to be common, at first only on the bigger buildings that were being erected.

In the last decade of the eighteenth century in the South-East all new buildings of two storeys or more were slated with blue or, as sometimes in West Lothian, grey slates. The steading roofs occasionally matched those of the houses, but more often were tiled or thatched where the houses were slated.[143] In East Lothian, roofing tiles could be bought in the 1780s from the Musselburgh Tilework Company. Both dwellings and steadings were most likely to be slated in areas where slates were plentiful as in Tweeddale. There were, for example, two seams in Stobo parish, of a dark blue colour,[144] and a slate quarry in Traquair.[145]

The South-West area retained the single-storey farm in general, with some exceptions, and slating on any scale belongs mainly to the first half of the nineteenth century there. Because foreign timber was preferred for slates, its greater cost meant that for a time other roofing materials were preferred. In Ayrshire, slating was on the increase by 1810. By 1845 slates had largely replaced thatch in Colmonell, Dalry, Dundonald, Mauchline and Straiton, but in Riccarton, Ochiltree and Symington only the newer and larger farm houses were slated, and in Craigie only about half.[146]

In Cumbrae in Bute, the houses were of stone, slated, and cast with Irish lime. In the parish of Kilbride, a few slated houses had begun to replace the old ones.[147] Slate was available in several places, such as near Kames Castle, at Inchmarnock and Ardmalash.[148] In Renfrew, in Houston and Killallan, thirty-five new houses were erected between 1781 and 1791, of which six were of two-storeys, and two slated.[149] By the 1840s, slating was general in every parish.[150] In Dunbarton and Stirling tiles were used, but only to a small extent for they were nearly as expensive as slate, and far less durable. Slate was itself slow to come in.[151] The parish of Calder in Lanark had eighteen slated houses—about half of them recently built—in 1793,[152] and by the 1840s slated roofs were common in the county except on the farms of the small tenants known as *planners*.[153]

Dumfries, with its sea access, could import slate, and 200 tons were taken to Gretna from Lancashire and Wales in 1793. Slating, therefore, proceeded more quickly here, as also in Kirkcudbright and Wigtown. The spread of slate roofs, however, was not helped by the Act that imposed a 33⅓ per cent duty on slates and freestone for roofing borne by water beyond the limits of a custom-house district. They cost about 9/- per square yard, including the cost of timber.[154] Another form of roofing in the area was thin red freestone flags, as in some of the buildings in Wamphray,[155] but they made a heavy roof that drew water through the pores unless the stone was well chosen and laid steeply enough. Builders preferred slated roofs done on laths. The weight of the flags was against them, and an occasional compromise was to have two or three rows laid at the eaves, and the rest of the roof finished with slates.[156]

The East had a mixed character. In Clackmannan, by the 1790s, thatch and divot had been largely replaced by pantiled roofs, though these often suffered from gales, and had poor qualities of insulation. However, they cost less that slate. One man, experimenting on a Yorkshire analogy, tried to combine thatch and tile. He nailed tile-lath on the undersides of the couples, filled the spaces between the couples with wheat-straw, and

F

tiled over this in the normal way. To reduce the fire risk, he later nailed thin quarter-inch (0.6 cm) lath boards under the couples.[157] Pantiles were also found in Fife,[158] in Perth, often on outhouses,[159] and in Angus. Tiles or thatch were used if the house happened to be far from a slate quarry.[160] Two-storey farms were almost invariably roofed with blue or grey slate from the 1770s onwards, and were fairly numerous in parts of the area from an early date, the slates being got locally, or from Easdale. A characteristic Angus roof was formed by sandstone flags. These came from the Sidlaw Hills, and were made into 'slates' 14 to 16 in (36-41 cm) broad by 18 to 20 in (46-50 cm) long by ½ to 1 in (1.3-2.5 cm) thick, for roofing. Many were larger. They were coated with mica scales, or talc, for easy separation, and turned grey or brownish in colour after exposure. They needed strong rafters, and had to be laid in plaster lime or fog, *Sphagnum palustre*. The principal quarries were centred around Carmyllie, and a branch line of the Arbroath-Dundee railway was installed primarily to assist in the export of this stone. The common name for the big slates in Angus was 'Carmyllie flags'. They were also produced in quantity on the Hill of Balnashader, in the moor south of Forfar, the north side of the Hill of Turin at Aberlemno, the south side of the same hill at Rescobie, and the south side of the Sidlaws at Carmyllie. They served not only for roofing, but were also exported from Arbroath to Leith, London and elsewhere, for footpaths and for paving the ground floors of houses. Cologne Cathedral is reputed to be paved with 'Arbroath stone', as it was called on the Continent. Their use avoided the payment of duty on water-borne slate. In general, most farms of 100 to 200 acres in size were built with stone and lime, of two storeys, with flagstone or slate roofs, and lathed and plastered inside.[161] Recent surveying, however, has shown that stone and clay mortar was much more common. Lime appears more on the periphery of Angus, in Glenesk and Glen Isla, at either end of the Grampians and on the coast in Craig parish, south of Montrose.

In the North-East, the better Kincardine farms, of two storeys, were coming to be roofed with blue slate by the 1790s, whilst smaller-scale improved farms were content with the less expensive grey slate.[162] Slated farmhouses were found only in the better-favoured Aberdeenshire parishes, such as Forgue and Monquhitter,[163] but thatch kept a firm grip and slating was becoming more general only towards the middle of the nineteenth century, as in Banffshire. Some tile roofs were also to be found. In Banffshire, Lord Findlater was already erecting two-storey, slated houses by 1759, between Cullen and Banff.[164] Good roofing slates were got near Letterfourie and Boat of Bridge. Tiles were made at Blackpotts on the edge of Whitehills, and at Marnoch.[165] The offices were sometimes slated as well as the houses in Moray and Nairn by the 1790s, but thatch was more common, because less costly. Ballachulish or Easdale were sources of slate, as well as the Earl of Moray's quarry in Rafford parish, and Enzie in Banffshire.[166] Still by the 1840s, however, even two-storey farms were to be found with thatched roofs, and smaller houses were almost invariably thatched.

Slating came slowly to Caithness, though flagstones were used for roofing, especially of outhouses. Orkney, however, is the main area for flagstone roofing. Both flagstone and a thinner kind of course grey slate were used for roofing. The latter were better for the climate than Easdale slates, but did not look so well. The flags were laid loose, covered with a little thatch, and the whole kept tight by heather ropes.[167] The technique of covering the lower part of the roof with flags and the upper part with a thick packing of ropes has survived till the present day.[168]

The Highland area varies enormously from east to west. In Argyll, because of the availability of slate, even some of the crofters' houses had slated roofs, for example in Strachur and Stralachlan,[169] and many of the village houses were slated. In Bowmore in 1794, 50 houses had blue slate roofs, 20 tiles, and 40 thatch.[170] Ardnamurchan had 11 slated houses before 1780, and 17 by 1798.[171] Slate was also appearing in the islands. Between 1789 and 1793 in Gigha and Cara, two new two-storey slated public houses were built, and there were also five slated houses. The two-storey tacksman's house was also slated.[172] The slate used on these buildings came from Easdale or Bute and was, therefore, available in most parts of Argyll. The limiting factor was the high price of fir, which restricted the use of slates to the proprietors. Tile roofs were not much favoured in the 1790s. By the 1840s there were also two newly built slated farms in Gigha and Cara, and several slated farm offices.[173]

The Easdale slates came from three quarries on the Earl of Breadalbane's property, and in the early 1800s the slate works were carried on by him and John Campbell, WS, Edinburgh, as the Easdale Company. In 1808 there were 257 quarriers in the village. The slates were made in two sizes, a larger one, 9-18 in (23-46 cm) long by 6-14 in (15-36 cm) broad, at 35/- per 1000 (which weighed about 1½ tons), and a smaller one, 6-12 in (15-30 cm) long by 4-6 in (10-15 cm) broad at 12/6 per 1000. Shipment was made in thirteen sloops and two brigs, and the numbers produced between 1802-1807 were as follows:

	Large	Small
1802	4,048,100	812,100
1803	3,376,700	915,200
1804	4,076,700	670,300
1805	4,626,300	740,500
1806	4,237,600	1,262,600
1807	4,530,300	1,821,800

At another quarry on the inlet of Belnahuagh, Mr E. Stevenson of Oban employed 26 to 42 men.[174] In Inverness-shire, houses of the best class in the 1790s were of one storey and slated,[175] and in North Uist the only slated houses were the church, a mill, a house at Lochmaddie intended for a public house, and a ruined one in the island of Vallay.[176] Tacksmen's houses in the Hebrides were normally slated. Towards the eastern mainland, good farm houses were mostly of two storeys, and roofed with blue or grey slate.[177] In Ross and Cromarty, Stornoway in Lewis had 67 slated houses, and on the coast opposite, Ullapool had 35 slated houses out of a total of 72.[178] New Black Isle farms were either thatched or slated.[179] In the early 1800s, a good slated farm house for a farm rented at £200, cost £400, with outhouses at £300.[180] Slate was appearing on the roofs of croft houses by the 1840s. Lochs in Lewis, for instance, had three such roofs by that period.[181] In Kildonan in Sutherland, the two-storey manse was the only house in the parish roofed with blue slate in 1800.[182] In the east of Sutherland, between 1809 and 1820, twenty-seven sets of new farm offices had been built. The farm at Cyderhall, for example, was erected in 1818. It was of stone and lime, and was roofed with Easdale slate. Significantly the occupant was a Mr Rule from Roxburghshire. Other examples were the farm erected for Earl Gower at Skelbo in 1811; Morvich farm, 1812; Culmaily farm, which in 1810 had been 'covered with black huts'; Dunrobin farm, 1810; Inverbrora, 1820; Kintradwell, 1819; and Lothbeg, 1813.[183] Between 1862 and 1883, the Duke of Sutherland was allowing annual grants for improvements in crofters' dwelling houses. These included the purchase of slates where superior dwelling houses were erected. Within the period 60 such had been built, and over 20 more had been improved.[184] In Shetland, by the 1840s, some farm houses in Bressay, Burra and Quarff were roofed with slates or flags shipped from Bressay.[185] By the 1870s there were two-storey slated houses at Vatsie, the Haa of Swarister and Gossabrough House in Mid and South Yell, and one-storey slated houses at Newfield, Springfield and Newhouse. The croft of Barkland in Fair Isle had a flagstone roof, due to the fact that it was built in 1880 by an Orcadian from Westray, to whom this was a normal building technique.[186]

Composition Roofing

Slate and tile were relatively expensive for roofing and for long the cheaper alternative to them was thatch. Composition roofing, which later in the form of tarred felt spread very widely, appears to have originated in Greenock in 1792. It was made of sheathing paper (so called because used in sheathing ships). This was dipped in tar heated to boiling point to make it penetrate the paper more deeply. Two days' drying soaked up the tar completely, after which the sheets were dipped again at a lower temperature. They were then nailed on to the roof, overlapping in the same way as slates. The whole roof was covered with a coat of tar boiled to the consistency of pitch, over which sieved smithy ashes were spread to reduce the fire risk and prevent the tar melting. With this early form of felt, the pitch of the roof could be made quite shallow, the average proportion of the elevation being one foot (30 cm) in twelve (3.7 m). The lightness of the sheathing paper meant that the roofing couples could be much slimmer, about 3 in (8 cm) broad by 1½ in (4 cm) thick. The cost was about half that of slates. It was first used on the roofs in a village of 50 houses associated with an alum manufactory in Campsie parish, and then by the agricultural improver, Mr Spiers of Culcruich. The earliest example of it, on a public store-house in Greenock, was put on in 1792 and was still good 20 years later. It was introduced to Stirlingshire in 1807.[187] Such composition roofs may have spread quite widely, for in later years they are said to have been common in Shetland.

6

Walling Materials

Stone and Turf

THE available evidence does not suggest that stone was prominent as a building material before the improvement period. This is demonstrated by the value of the roofing timbers and the numerous complaints or comments about the poor quality of the walls of turf, or of stone and turf, erected almost as an infill between the legs of the crucks. Because the stones used were often little more than field boulders, unshaped, a means had to be found of welding them together. One method was to make a kind of many-decker sandwich, consisting of alternating courses of stone and turf. The base course was normally of stone, to provide a reasonable foundation for the cruck ends.

Building in alternating stone and turf courses was first noticed in print in 1629; a thatched house at Langholm in Dumfriesshire may have been of this construction,[188] though the description could also indicate simply a single course of stone with another of turf above, as was common in a number of areas such as Aberdeenshire and Caithness.[189] However, the alternating technique was well known in the Borders at a later date, for example at Heriot in Midlothian in the 1740s.[190] About this period too, cottar houses in the Lothians were often clustered by themselves at a little distance from the farm houses. They were about 12 ft (3.7 m) square, with walls about 5 ft (1.5 m) high—which was a fairly standard height for the walls of unimproved houses—built of round land stones and turf, layer about. The turf, in effect, provided a bed that helped to keep the stones in position. A day was enough to build such a house, if the material was assembled beforehand.[191] Two rows of sods generally went between each row of stones. Shepherd's cottages in Roxburgh and Selkirk had walls of this form,[192] though it was obsolescent by the first decade of the nineteenth century. Examples survived in Wamphray in Dumfries till around 1800.[193]

In Angus not only cottages but also farm houses and steadings could have such walls, especially in the clustered township groups that lasted into the 1800s in the Grampian districts, and also the homes of weavers and other tradesmen, rapidly knocked up on allotments of waste land.[194] Comparative figures from Kincardine give the relative costs of building in different techniques around 1810: a house of stone and turf was cheapest at 50/- to £3, one of stone with clay mortar cost 15/- to 20/- more, one of stone and lime with a stob-thatched roof sewn on with rope yarn was £15 to £20, and if slated £20 to £25.[195]

In Banffshire, alternating stone and turf was mainly confined to crofters' houses,[196] as in the higher parts of Moray. Further north, examples of the sandwich technique were to be found in Cromarty,[197] and in Sutherland in the church itself at Ach-na-h'uaidh. Here the ground course was of stones, 2 ft (61 cm) deep, and thereafter turf and stone courses alternated.[198] In the West, small one-roomed farm houses in the island of Arran were being built in this way as recently as 1816.[199]

The technique, as noted in the sources, is concentrated in the Border hills and around

Fig. 57.   East Geirinish, South Uist, Inverness-shire. Turf-built hut of the simplest kind.
This type of hut was occupied by squatters in many parts of the Highlands and especially in
the outer isles prior to the clearances. These dwellings and the people occupying them did
not appear in the rental books of the period as the whole holding was less than £4 in value.
(NMAS: 7. 6. 1)

the Grampians, though this may do no more than indicate a contraction of what was
once more widespread. In South Scotland and parts of the North-East, alternating stone
and turf buildings were often of a relatively temporary nature, for use by shepherds,
day-labourers and artisans. In Angus and Arran, farm houses forming parts of township
groups come into the question, as does a church in Sutherland. A range of social strata
and conditions are represented, which in itself suggests that the technique is old. In fact,
it occurs in excavated houses of Viking date in North and West Scotland.[200] It survives
till the present day in one known example from Sutherland, three in Angus (Waggles,
Glenesk; Moss-side of Balinshoe, Kirriemuir; Murroes Cottages, Murroes) and one in
Perthshire (Rait Village, Kilspindie).

   Another combined form of turf and stone was vertical. In the thick-walled
blackhouses of North-West Scotland, it is evident from comments included in Name
Books by the officers of the Ordnance Survey, who were at work in and around Lewis in
1849-52, that most blackhouse walls had an inner face of stone and an outer face of turf.
This is the exact opposite of the Rules and Regulations of the Lewis Estate in 1879,
which said that walls should be of stone and lime, or of stone and clay pinned and harled
with lime, or with stone on the outer face, and turf or sod on the inside.[201] As they

Fig. 58.   Old U.P. Manse, Howford Bridge, Nairn. A turf-built cottage in the course of upgrading. The front has been rendered and limewashed and the left gable rebuilt. Cement or grey clay mortar is being used to seal the ridge and skews. Earlier photographs in the Elgin Public Library show the left gable propped and only half of the front rendered. (Miss I. Rae, Nairn, per R. Noble)

survive, blackhouses have both inner and outer skins of stone, with a core of peat mould or earth between the skins.

Buildings of turf alone were to be found, according to the literature, till the late 1700s in the Central Highlands,[202] and in the higher areas of Moray, where they were built and occupied by the poorer tenants. They could occur in lower districts too.[203] When Pennant was passing through Moray in 1769 he noted that the houses were entirely of turf, in contrast to those of Banffshire, and this remained true of areas such as the parish of Ardclach,[204] where some still remained in the 1840s. Turf building was still common in the early 1800s to the West of the Findhorn.[205] Caithness also had examples surviving to this period, though they had become rare. Tenants in Wick parish were still then required to cast a certain quantity of sods a year for building houses.[206] In the parish of Kiltearn in Ross, it was said in the 1790s that the houses were mostly of earth, razed to the ground once in five to seven years and added to the dunghill.[207] In Sutherland, many houses were built of large bricks of turf, said to have been cleared on to the dunghill every three years, and the buildings then put up afresh.[208]

Photographic evidence of the 1890s to early 1900s shows the existence of buildings with walls 5 to 6 ft (1.5-1.8 m) high, the lower half built in rough stones like a field dyke, with an upper course of turf. Pennant and other reporters described this technique in

Fig. 59.   Melvich, Reay, Sutherland. Alternating layers of stone and turf used to form the gablet of this small building. Once a very common building technique, it made use of the ease with which turf could be built whilst destroying less pasture and making use of stones removed from the fields. (A. Cameron, colour transparency, 1971)

the late eighteenth century. Turf gablets also appear in photographs, in towns like Kintore and Peterhead as well as elsewhere. They were also built on quarrymen's houses at Greystane, Carmyllie, Angus, as noted in 1974. The use of turf as beamfilling lasted into the nineteenth century, according to entries in the Glamis Estate Papers. Numerous examples survive in Angus and Perthshire.

Walls of solid turf also existed, as at Barry of Tentsmuir.[209]

Clay

Clay-walled houses survive in several parts of Scotland, some still occupied, some empty shells, some serving as implement sheds. They are or were distributed over parts of Ross, Moray and Nairn, Aberdeen, Banff, Kincardine, Angus, Perth, Stirling, Fife, East Lothian, Berwick, Roxburgh, Dumfries and Wigtown. In date they can be traced back to the sixteenth century, mud houses being mentioned as the homes of common people in Forres in 1586,[210] and some of the defensive peel towers in the Borders were also built of clay *(ex sola terra)* about the same period.[211] Socially, they range from the humble cottage, the farm house and steading, to manses, churches and peel towers, and in the town of Errol substantial clay houses of good urban appearance still remain.

The most northerly evidence is for Sutherland and Ross-shire. In Tain in 1789, two-storey townhouses of solid mud, 60 ft long by 20 ft broad (18.3×6.1 m), were being built by regular mud masons, with walls up to 16 ft (4.9 m) high. The only stone parts were 'the corners, door and window skimshions, Lintols and soles, chimneys and

Fig. 60.   Highland Steading, Kinlochewe, Ross-shire. A late eighteenth or early nineteenth-century steading using many pre-improvement building techniques. Note the drystone wall with turf-built upper section (above the shafts of the cart), and the cruck framed gable with timber boarding inside the cruck to form the gable wall. Note also the various types of thatching, the general clutter and the numbers of loose boulders lying about the farmyard. (GWW: F0748)

chimney heads, Sque and Wall tabeling, all of which is to be of the best quarry stones neatly hewed'.[212] In Moray and Nairn, clay buildings were also a town phenomenon, particularly characterising Garmouth, which in 1811 had several neat clay houses, some of two storeys, sometimes with foundation courses of stone.[213] As recently as 1974, five solid clay structures were located in the village.[214]

In the country around, and stretching into Banffshire, was a variant form of clay building to which the name 'Auchenhalrig work' or 'clay and bool' was given. Essentially this is a kind of wall in which the shrinkage cracks in the clay are controlled by a clay and straw mix laid in alternate layers with rounded stones ('bools'). As with walls of solid clay, only courses of two or three feet (61-91 cm) were built in a day, with three or four days allowed for drying off between courses. The outer face of the stones always touched the shuttering. Stones of equal size were used to give a very positive layered appearance, or sometimes they were set to form a herring-bone pattern. The impression could be heightened by cutting back the clay on the finished wall and pointing between the stones with lime. At first the stones were completely covered with clay, but the outside layer fell off after two or three years if left to itself, after which the

Fig. 61.   Barn, Balmacara, Ross-shire. Owing to the wet climate of Wester Ross, farm holdings there have larger hay barns than one would normally expect, to allow at least part of the haymaking to take place indoors. Traditionally these structures were ventilated through wattle screens, or as they are known in Scotland, "stake and rice" walls. Later, adjustable timber louvres replace the wattle. This photograph shows one such barn still retaining part of a wattle panel in the lower gable, a wattle gablet and adjustable timber louvres in the side wall panels. (NMAS: ix. 20. 26A)

wall could be pointed with lime and rough river or sea sand.[215] Three-storey houses could be built in this technique, which was recommended for threshing mills and horse gins because it was said to stand vibration better than ordinary work.[216] The terms 'ham and egg work', 'clay and dab' and 'clay and dash' were also given to it.

In Banff and Aberdeenshire, surviving clay buildings lie mainly in the triangle formed by the towns of Banff, New Aberdour and Turriff. Their builders were known as 'clay an' dubbers' (*dubs* = mud). The earlier distribution was somewhat wider. Mud work was used in Tarves Manse in 1684, and crofts, farms, churches and schools could all be built of the same material. A professional clay thatcher, James Strachan in New Pitsligo, who had some experience of clay building, related in 1965 that the first course was always made of big stones, and that each course was 27 in (69 cm) deep. In this area no shuttering was used, but each course was left for a couple of days to dry off. Hollows for chimneys were made as the walls rose, and hollows for presses etc. were put in with wooden uprights and cross members. Once the walls were up, they were never cut into.[217]

Fig. 62. Barn, Balmacara, Ross-shire. Detail of a "stake and rice" or wattle panel on the barn illustrated in Fig. 61. This type of panel often formed the base for a clay wall, tempered clay being applied to one or both sides. (NMAS: ix.20.28A)

In Kincardine and Angus, clay building was common in the eighteenth century and still in the nineteenth for cottages and small farms in areas where stones were scarce. The 'clay city' of Luthermuir was built by squatters who set up the first houses from the clay beneath their feet, scarcely troubling even to clear the foundations, towards the close of the eighteenth century. By 1840 this village, laid out afresh in 1828, was mainly occupied by handloom weavers. As they survived the clay houses in it had slated roofs, but the grey Angus slates were not so much used on clay buildings because of their weight, though such walls were fully load-bearing. Instead, thatch was normal, tied to the rafters with cords, and projecting to throw the water clear of the walls, as in Lord Gardenstone's planned village of Laurencekirk in the 1770s.[218]

Houses built of clay with an intermixture of chopped straw were described in 1813 as warm and impervious to wind and weather, looking well when whitened with lime plaster.[219] The Strathmore Muniments give details of the building of clay houses at Clippethills in Angus in 1771-76. Foundations were of stone, 15 in (38 cm) high, the chimneys were of brick, and the roofs were covered with thatch or slate. Here, such buildings were estate-inspired and of good quality.[220]

Fig. 63. West Bay, Portree, Skye, Inverness-shire. Timber was used throughout Scotland in the nineteenth and twentieth centuries for many types of utilitarian buildings, and in some cases for complete steadings. In this photograph we see a new timber shed (possibly in the last quarter of the nineteenth century) in proximity to more traditional forms of building. (GWW: B0635)

The Carse of Gowrie in Perthshire contains perhaps the most sophisticated of all clay buildings in Scotland, though earlier examples were of poorer quality. According to a letter of 1817 relating to the Scone Estate, clay was actually dearer to use as a building material than stone, so that an improved house in clay was by no means a sign of poverty.[221] The parish and village of Errol was a main centre of clay building, all old buildings except gentlemen's seats being of clay in the eighteenth century. The houses of the village are mostly two-storey, and many are terraced. The urban emphasis in the building technique is suggested by the way in which the buildings are normally split horizontally, as if one cottage were laid above another, with an outside stair leading to the upper dwelling. A feature of the terraced clay houses is the manner in which the gable flues are built in clusters rather than in line ahead in the more usual way. This allowed the flue to be built as a freestanding unit to which the clay walls were later butted.[222]

Outside the village, some substantial two-storey buildings can be found, such as

Fig. 64. Howe, Strathdon, Aberdeenshire. Detail of internal timber partition in a stone-built steading. The partition has a rubble base and is constructed from the offcuts from squaring logs, roughly flattened at either end to allow them to be nailed to a top and bottom rail. (NMAS: 34.10.14)

Horn Farmhouse, though one-storey clay cottages are more common, for example at Westown, a few miles north of Errol. At the farm of Flatfield, which has an excellent late eighteenth century brick dwelling house, the barn is of clay, with a structural feature that may be unique in Scotland. Every third joist of the first floor is carried through the solid clay wall and pegged against a timber plate on the outside of the wall. On the north side these joists are connected in pairs by short timber members stapled to the ends of the joists.[223]

In Stirlingshire, old buildings were said in the 1790s to have been mostly built of clay tempered with chopped straw, on a foundation course of rough stones, on which the ends of the crucks rested. The thatch had to be well maintained to keep the clay walls from spoiling.[224]

In the South-East, East Lothian had an old church at Aberlady, the walls of which were built partly of clay prior to 1773.[225] In Berwickshire the Coldingham Moor area retained remains of orange-coloured clay houses till recent times. The clay is not much mixed with chopped straw or heather, but with small stones up to the size of a fist, making a hard, durable mixture. The walls had stone footings, and the example surviving in 1970 had a red pantiled roof. In this area, clay was an element in building before 1740, but the date of the all-clay houses is probably not earlier than the

Fig. 65.   Feddan, Dyke & Moy, Moray. Timber internal partition in former stable comprising boards and cover straps in the upper portion and heavy horizontal boarding to form the trevis and lower section. The timber in this interior has been limewashed. (NMAS: 32.18.11)

nineteenth century.[226] In Roxburghshire, clay-walled, thatched houses were still to be seen in the 1790s.[227]

In the South-West, mud or clay houses were known in the Moss of Cree area in Wigtownshire[228] but the bulk of the evidence lies in Dumfries. In Scotland they may well go back to the seventeenth century, as an extension of the clay-building tradition that existed in Cumberland,[229] but by the 1790s the technique had almost died out, though examples survived till the 1840s in places like Hutton and Corrie.[230] It is from the parish of Dornock that one of the liveliest accounts of clay-building comes in 1792:

'The farm-houses in general, and all the cottages, are built of mud or clay; yet these houses, when plastered and properly finished within—are exceedingly warm and comfortable. The manner of erecting them is singular. In the first place, they dig out the foundations of the house, and lay a row or two of stones, then they procure, from a pit contiguous, as much clay or brick earth as is sufficient to form the walls and having provided a quantity of straw, or other litter to mix with the clay, upon a day appointed, the whole neighbourhood, male and female, to the number of 20 or 30, assemble, each with a dung fork, a spade or some such instrument. Some fall to the working the clay or mud, by mixing it with straw; others carry the materials; and four or six of the most experienced hands, build and take care of the walls. In this manner, the walls of the house are finished in a few hours; after which, they retire to a good dinner and plenty of drink which is provided for them, where they have music and a dance, with which, and other marks of festivity, they conclude the evening. This is called a "daubing", and in this manner they make a frolic of what would otherwise be a very dirty and disagreeable job.'[231]

Fig. 66.　Flatfield, Errol, Perthshire. A 1½-storey barn with solid tempered clay walls on a rubble base. This example is unusual in that it incorporates a form of timber detailing not normally found in Scotland. Every third or fifth first-floor joist is carried through the wall to project from the face. Round the joist end is a timber board which forms a backing to a timber peg which penetrates the joist horizontally to prevent the wall from falling outwards.

Clay-building was also going on nearby in Canonbie in the 1770s.[232]

In the Dornock description, no indication is given of the use of shuttering. This is surprising, since several accounts from other areas refer to the risk of the wall swelling out and going off the perpendicular if built too fast. The Dornock walls may have been very low, however, no more than a bottom course of stones and one course of clay. It is also surprising, since elsewhere, especially in the North-East, the walls were built in courses of about 24 to 30 in (61-74 cm) deep, each of which was left to dry off for two or three days, covered in case of rain, before the next course was added. The top of each course was levelled off with trowels or spades to make a smooth bed for the next. In some cases framing or shuttering was certainly used, as on houses of up to three storeys in height in Garmouth in the 1820s.[233] At Westown a few miles west of Errol the marks of boards used as shuttering in building clay walls can be clearly seen on one house.[234] There is no doubt that shuttering was known and used, but it remains to be proved that it was not the exception. The more important difference in technique seems to lie between houses with wooden frames, either crucks or upright posts, in the walls, where the clay was essentially an infilling, as in parts of south-west Scotland, Stirlingshire and Angus, and walls of solid clay mixed with small stones, straw, heather, bent-grass or the like, that took several days to erect and were fully load-bearing. The first method is the more primitive; the second reflects improvement conditions.[235]

Fig. 67.   Bauds of Arnbog, Rathven, Banffshire. A clay and bool wall showing the main characteristics of the technique. The stones are set inside the shuttering, touching either face, and packed round with tempered clay. When used externally the clay was allowed to weather back from the face of the stones, then the spaces between were pointed with lime and the whole wall limewashed. (NMAS: 32.20.35A)

Combinations and Alternatives : Brick and Concrete

Clay walls, especially those serving as internal partitions, were often formed of a structural skeleton of timber, either of uprights with ladder-like cross-pieces, or a wattle frame, clayed and smoothed on each side. The ladder-like form is infilled with a mixture of stiff clay and long straw, which may be left flush with the upright standards, or may cover them. In Easter Ross another form with uprights is called *kebber and mott* or *caber and daub*.[236] The technique was widespread, and a sample from a house in Kelso, dating from the 1820s, is preserved in the National Museum. In an internal partition at Braikie Castle, a tower house dated 1658 and sited between Friockheim and Montrose, rope was used instead of horizontal wooden members.[237] However, the form with a wattle base is probably the oldest and most widespread of all, even if judged only by the range of local names applied to it: *stake and rice, stab and rice, claut and clay, cat and clay, stud and mud, clam staff and daub, daub and stower, rice and stower, riddle and daub, strae and rake, rod and daub, split and daub, clay and mott, wattle and daub, clay and wattle.* If straw or heather rope was used as an alternative to brushwood or wattle the term given could be *stake and tow* or *stab and tow*.[238]

The combination of clay with stone or brick was mainly for outer walls, the stone or brick skin being on the exterior, so giving protection to the softer clay in areas where

Fig. 68. Hill of Fearn, Fearn, Ross-shire. The gablet shown in the photograph is constructed in a technique known as "caber and mott". The wall comprises a number of straight poles placed vertically, almost touching, and held at top and bottom. Into this structure is pressed tempered clay, either on one or both sides. Externally these walls were finished with lime harl or both internally and externally with lime slurry which was then limewashed. The lower part of this gable is constructed of clay and bool and the chimney of poles, lathes and lime plaster. (NMAS: xxii.33.2)

impact from sharp objects or animals was likely. The skin was usually no more than 10 cm thick. Brick skins could be built independently, and samples of nineteenth century houses with an inner skin of clay and an outer skin of bricks survive, for example, at Cottown in the parish of St. Madoes. The remains of a former barn at Chapelhill nearby show an otherwise unrecorded form of walling consisting of two skins of brick with a solid clay core, the total thickness being equal to that of solid clay walls.

Clay was also widely used as mortar in stone buildings, as a cheaper alternative to lime, to such an extent that sources, whether written or oral, that refer to 'clay biggins' or 'clay walls' must be carefully checked. As often as not stone walls with clay mortar are in question, and not walls of solid clay. Source criticism is also necessary in relation to buildings said to be constructed 'of stone and lime', since this need not indicate lime mortar. Investigation in the Carse of Gowrie has shown that such a description might even be given to buildings of solid clay, whose walls were finished externally with lime slurry or lime harl.[239]

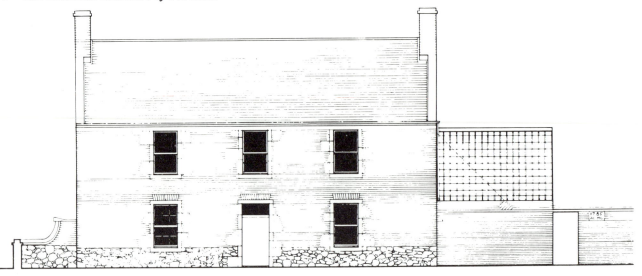

Fig. 69.   Flatfield, Errol, Perthshire. A two-storey farmhouse with brick walls dated 1785. The brickwork has been used as a direct substitute for clay, being built off a rubble base and having stone dressings at all the vulnerable points such as door and window jambs and lintels and at the wall head. Even the thickness of the walls is related to clay construction rather than to the capabilities of brickwork, being 60mm thick in solid brickwork. The house was originally thatched.

Fig. 70.   Fordoun, Fordoun, Kincardineshire. Concrete cottages by the side of the main road. Concrete was used as building material for both houses and farm steadings from the 1850s onwards.

Fig. 71 (A—J). Rubble Types. The varieties of rubble walls found in Scotland are infinite. A few examples are shown here, selected mainly to illustrate stonework not shown clearly in the other illustrations.

A. Bauds of Arnbog, Rathven, Banffshire. Rubble in a tempered clay mortar. (NMAS: 32.20.34A)

B. Craighead, Tomintoul, Banffshire. An irregular rubble wall built in courses approximately three stones deep. (NMAS: 32.23.7)

C. Mains of Panmure, Panbride, Angus. Dressed stone margins to wall ventilator in a late eighteenth-century steading. (NMAS: 41.20.31)

D. Upper Craighill, Arbuthnott, Kincardineshire. Split field boulders with the split face outwards, packed with sandstone slabs and pointed with lime. (NMAS: 39.13.15)

E. Mill of Morphie, St. Cyrus, Kincardineshire. Whin boulders packed with sandstone slabs with cherry calking on lines of principal joints. (NMAS: 40.28.5)

F. Nether Warburton, St Cyrus, Kincardineshire. Sandstone rubble with cherry calking. (NMAS: 41.3.25)

G.   Wester Leys, Drumblade, Aberdeenshire.
Roughly squared rubble with pinnings.
(NMAS: 32.12.27A)

H.   Kirkton of Fordoun, Fordoun,
Kincardineshire. Ashlar with pinnings.
(NMAS: 39.28.21)

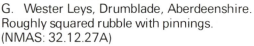

J.   Newton of Affleck, Monikie, Angus.
Aberdeen bond stonework in sandstone with
lime pointing. (NMAS: 41.30.29A)

Not surprisingly, in areas where the combination of clay and brick was found, there are a number of brick-built farm houses, such as Flatfield (1785), dating back to the late eighteenth century. Brick offices and garden walls were built at Megginch, Errol, around 1707. Early brick houses are found towards the north end of the village of Laurencekirk, marking the products of the late eighteenth century brickworks sited at the south end. In Kincardine, Perthshire, over three-quarters of the houses at the east end of the parish had been rebuilt in stone or brick by 1793.[240] In the 1780s a brick partition was built in the kitchen of the farm of Spittlerigg in East Lothian.[241] Garden walls were also done in brick, but not till the eighteenth century did whole steadings begin to be built in this man-made, clay-derived material. In dwellings of poorer class, brickwork was at first restricted to door and window jambs. Its use as a permanent shuttering, and in constructing fireplaces, flues and chimney heads goes mainly with nineteenth century techniques.

In the Carse of Gowrie, eighteenth century bricks have a soft, crumbly appearance, and the brick itself is somewhat shallower than later bricks, which normally have a hard, smooth appearance. The soft appearance, however, does not go with a poor performance in surviving even in exposed conditions. Large bricks of $30 \times 10 \times 5$ cm also appear in the eighteenth century, apparently as a means of beating a tax levied in 1784 on the number of bricks manufactured. At first bricks were made in temporary kilns set up on site, but later, mainly in the nineteenth century, brickworks were established.

Fig. 72. Achreaynie, Thurso, Caithness. Rubble-built steading showing slaty nature of Caithness stone. The bands of squarish stones appear to be bonding stones the full width of the wall, whereas the smaller stones appear to form two faces with a vertical joint up the centre-line of the wall. (NMAS: vi.20.29)

Fig. 73. Coulag, Castletown, Caithness. Another use of Caithness stone in large slabs to form an internal partition. Stones of this type may also be used to form fences, troughs, benches, and even clothes poles. (NMAS: vi.27.21)

Fig. 74.   Culdrain, Gartly, Aberdeenshire. Doorway in "cherry calked" rubble wall. Note the unusual double flat arch forming the opening. (NMAS: 32.9.6)

During the nineteenth century, the width of the brick wall was gradually reduced for single and two-storey buildings to approximately 22 cm, that is, to the width of a single brick, and occasionally, for single-storey buildings, to 11 cm, or a half-brick width. The cavity brick wall consisting of two half-brick skins with a 5 cm cavity between, does not appear to have been generally accepted until the late 1930s or 1940s.[242]

An extension of the clay walling technique is the use of mass concrete, and it is probably no accident that houses and sheds in concrete do occur in areas of clay construction, sometimes dating from the mid-nineteenth century. Garmouth, for example, has a number of outhouses built in mass concrete. In Errol parish, examples so far located all form part of the steading, and include cattle courts, stables, lofts and a henhouse. Two-storey concrete cottages on the Rossie Estate to the east and at Seggieden to the west appear to have been erected about 1880 to 1890.[243] Villages such as Fordoun, Kincardineshire, are built almost entirely of mass concrete, but these buildings date from the early part of this century.

Stone and Lime
The use of lime as a mortar or cement in building is attested by early medieval sources, though only in relation to buildings of the best quality, including manse and office houses such as those at Cramond which, according to the Kirk Session Records for 26 December 1689, were pointed with lime. In 1699 Lord Belhaven was recommending that the walls of farm buildings should be of stone and lime and not of the less durable clay and mortar,[244] but it was still to be some time before stone and lime for such

Fig. 75.   Glendevon, Kirkliston, West Lothian. Substantial rubble-walled steading
with stone forestair to granary from cobbled yard. (IM: 15.7)

buildings became in any way general. In the 1780s, lime for repairing the office-houses
at Spittlerigg in East Lothian came from Spilmersford.[245] In East Lothian barns, the old,
damp floors that led to spoiling of the grain that was threshed with flails, were being
replaced by the early 1800s by floors of sleepers and wooden boards, or else by
'a uniform stratum of round gravel, covering it with a coat of well-tempered clay, above
which a mixture of clay, brick-dust, forge ashes, and a small proportion of lime, will
make a hard uniform floor'. Natural drying was to be preferred, for some farmers had
cracked the surface by burning a thin layer of straw on it to dry it more quickly.[246]

By the 1790s, new farm houses generally had walls of stone and lime, and smaller ones
if built by the lairds, in the South-East area. In the more up-to-date areas, like
Midcalder in Midlothian, even the old farm houses and cottages were mostly of stone
and lime.[247]

In the South-West, new farm houses and offices erected by the Earl of Eglinton and
John Orr of Barrowfield had walls of freestone or whinstone cemented with lime.[248]

Fig. 76.   Three Mile Toun, Ecclesmachan, West Lothian. Steam engine house and stack base in dressed ashlar with rubble side walls to the engine house. (IM: 4.2)

Improved farms in Renfrewshire were of stone and lime, with hewn freestone corners, doors and windows.[249] In Ewes parish, Dumfries, lime was provided for improved buildings by the Duke of Queensberry,[250] and in that county, by 1812, most farm houses were of stone and lime, with corners, doors, windows and chimney tops of dressed sandstone, the rest of whinstone rubble.[251] The earliest evidence in the South-West area is for places like Annandale, where tenants with leases were already rebuilding their houses by 1759, using stone and mortar for the body of the building and stone and lime for the door cheeks. An allowance for building was sanctioned in 1769 for outgoing tenants. Estate regulations in 1772 decreed that tradesmen were to build houses in stone and lime or in stone and clay cast with lime, but no more houses of stone and turf were to be erected.[252] In Wigtownshire, on the estate of Basil William Lord Daer, where rebuilding began in 1786, nearly every tenant had a good house of two storeys with four, five or six rooms, and offices, all of stone and lime.[253]

In the East, old buildings in Clackmannan were being increasingly replaced by new ones in stone and lime from the 1760s. They were mostly of one-storey, and south-facing.[254] In Fife, the majority of farm houses were in stone and lime by the 1790s, as well

Fig.77.   Feddan, Dyke & Moy, Moray. Harl-pointed steading showing characteristic stone pattern where the large stones are coursed. (NMAS: 32.26.27-28)

as the steading.[255] In Perthshire, Redstone Farm in the Barony of Stobhill had a stone and lime dwelling house by 1773, and other examples were also to be found there.[256] When such houses appeared, the farmers often kept the old ones to house the servants.[257] Masons were employed in Monedie for new buildings, making walls of stone and mortar harled with lime, and thatching with straw and clay. Four such had been built by 1792.[258] Little Dunkeld had five two-storey, slated houses of stone and lime.[259]

In Angus, the practice of pointing with lime became common after road transport improved, a situation common to all districts where lime had to be brought in from outside.[260] In Dunnichen parish, it was found that marl burned in the kiln made very strong cement.[261] About 1813, pipe clay found north of Glamis was used by the people for whitewashing their houses. Clay called *cam-stone*, from the Sidlaw Hills, was used for whitening hearths.[262]

In the North-East, by 1813 in Kincardineshire, farm house walls were largely of stone bound with lime mortar. The larger two-storey farms were of the best masonwork.[263] In Aberdeenshire, change to walls cemented with lime came a little later than farther south. In areas like Keithhall and Kinkell a very few of the houses had been snecked or harled with lime from about 1785,[264] but there were no lime-built walls then in the country districts at least. But lime was available for town building and for prominent residences from a much earlier date, for in the seventeenth century there are several references in the Aberdeen Shore Work Accounts to lime boats and lime barks, and to bolls of lime forming parts of cargoes in the small boats that moved up and down the coast like mobile grocery shops at that period.[265] There were in Banffshire two-storey stone and lime houses about 1759 between Cullen and Banff, built by tenants of Lord Findlater; poorer tenants had houses of stone bound with clay, pointed or harled with lime.[266] In Moray, in richer areas like Cromdale, farmers had houses of stone and lime, some of two storeys, with glass windows, and also barns and kilns of stone and lime.[267] In this county, building stone came from quarries at Duffus, Lossiemouth, and the hill of

Fig. 78.   Lower Hempriggs, Alves, Moray. Harl-pointed house where the margins, quoins and occasional wall stones are left uncovered. The stone in this case is red sandstone and the harl pointing white. (NMAS: 32.25.29)

Quarrywood. Building lime was carried from Cairnie, Keith and Grange in Banffshire by crofters who traded in selling lime, at 2/- per cart load of three bushels.[268] In Orkney, lime mortar was being used for better-class stone-built houses in the sixteenth century, though it did not spread generally to farms for another three hundred years. Though it was said in 1789 that most of the 300 houses in Kirkwall were built of stone and lime, in fact this is an example of care being required in interpreting the term, for only a few years later it was noted that the houses were built with clay mortar, a little lime being used on the outside of the walls only.[269]

In the Highland area, geographical diversity led, as always, to considerable regional variety. There was also much social diversity, for the houses of the gentlemen and tacksmen were often of a quite different quality from those of the tenants. It was noted already in about 1734 that the houses of the chiefs were sometimes built of stone and lime in the Highlands, though not in the higher-lying areas. The story was told of a Highland laird who sent a number of men with horses to fetch lime from the Borders. It rained on the return journey, and the lime began to crackle and smoke, so the

Fig. 79. Aberdour House, Aberdour, Aberdeenshire.
Thin Scots harl applied to an eighteenth-century steading
entrance. The harl stops against irregular dressed
margins which have been limewashed to give a uniform
white colour to the wall surface. (NMAS: 32.21.20A)

Highlanders threw it in a rivulet to quench, as they thought, the fire.[270] In Argyll, tradesmen, labourers and even some of the crofters in Strachur and Stralachlan had slated houses of stone and lime by the 1790s,[271] as also in Tobermory in Kilninian.[272] Ardnamurchan had 27 cottages cast with lime.[273] In Inverness, Samuel Johnson saw Hebridean gentlemen's houses with walls cemented with mortar in 1775.[274] Better houses in Skye were also built of mortared stone.[275] Tacksmen's houses in the Hebrides were generally built of stone and lime, and were of two storeys.[276] In Ross and Cromarty, houses in the parishes of Cromarty and Ferintosh were more elegant, built of stone and clay and sometimes plastered with lime, usually with at least one chimney, one or two glass windows, and rooms. There were also new farms built on their own enclosed units of land, neatly built, and either thatched or slated. Improved farmers' houses were in

Fig. 80.   Muirhead, Alves, Moray. Harled farmhouse with brick lean-to extension on back wall. The limewash finish has begun to weather off the brickwork and is badly stained under the chimney heads which are constructed in ashlar. (NMAS: 32.25.24)

general built with stone and clay and primed with lime. Walls up to 7 ft (2.1 m) high cost 23/- per rood (5.3 m), from 7 to 10 ft (2.1-3 m), 26/-, from 10 to 16 ft (3-4.9 m), 30/-.[277] The two-storey manse of Kildonan in Sutherland was built of stone and lime in 1800, the interior partitions being of *cat-and-clay*, lime-plastered and whitewashed.[278] In the early 1800s, in parts of Sutherland, mason work cost 36/- to 56/- per rood of 36 square yards, according to the height of the wall. Quarrying the stone took 15/- to 21/- a rood, and carriage was extra. Freestone for doors and windows came to 9d to 1/- a square foot. Lime was imported from Sutherland at about 10d per barrel of 32 gallons slaked.[279] By the 1840s, houses in Golspie were built of stone and lime or stone and clay,[280] and in Tongue, later in that century, the laird was supplying lime and timber.[281] In late nineteenth century Shetland, the standard cottage was 28 to 30 ft (8.5-9.1 m) long by 8 to 10 ft (2.4-3 m) broad, with clay-mortared stones pointed inside and sometimes outside with a mortar of sand and lime.[282]

In considering the subject of lime pointing, it is to be noted that lime pointing is commonplace in all stone improved buildings, but the underlying mortar was often clay. Some lime workers' houses in Clunie Parish, Perthshire, for example, were built using clay mortar but pointed with lime. It was observed at Murroes in Angus that lime or cement pointing could give an alternating turf and stone wall the appearance of a rubble wall with wide joints.

Plastering, Snecking, Harling and Whitewashing
In pre-improvement days, drystone buildings were plastered with clay on the inside to reduce draughts, as in Cluny in Aberdeenshire in the eighteenth century.[283] The walls of

Fig. 81. Kintrochat House, Brechin, Angus. Large harled and limewashed farmhouse with dressed stone margins and string courses. (NMAS: 35.11.18A)

turf and drystone dwellings in Durness, Sutherland, were being similarly treated, even at a later date.[284] Cow dung was used as a plaster for the insides of cot-houses in Orkney in the 1880s,[285] and was a common ingredient in plasters, not only on walls, but also for coating the wattlework hoods of canopy chimneys. Its elasticity allowed it to withstand changes in temperature without cracking, and the technique must be old.

More sophisticated plasters of lime and hair were used on better-class buildings. The *Master of Works Accounts* for 1622[286] refer to the dressing of lime and hair for this purpose. A lime and hair mixture was used for plastering the kitchen at Spittlerigg in East Lothian in the 1780s,[287] at a lesser social level. Houses in Bute had plastered or whitewashed walls by the early 1800s,[288] as also in Renfrewshire.[289] Brick farmhouses in the Carse of Stirling were well plastered and finished inside even before this.[290] Two-storey Inverness and Ross and Cromarty farms had plastered walls,[291] though here, as elsewhere, the plastering can refer to an external priming with lime. Late nineteenth century Shetland houses were often plastered and whitewashed externally.[292] In parts of Orkney, the custom of applying an external wash goes back to the seventeenth century. In the island of Egilsay, sand was mixed with lime imported from the Firth of Forth, heaped up until the following year, and then the mixture was used to plaster the houses

Fig. 82.   New Galloway, Kirkcudbrightshire. Limewashed rubble walls to thatched cottage. (GWW: E1509)

on the outside. Lime was imported by people like David Traill—as in 1715—for limewashing houses, and the local folk who could not afford this burned cockleshells for the same purpose. This is recorded from Papa Westray, Walls and elsewhere, just as in the Hebrides.[293] Internal limewashing was also done, as in a Sanday kitchen (for servants) in 1766.[294]

Snecking is a term applied to closing a crevice in a rubble wall by filling the spaces between the larger stones with tightly packed smaller ones, or by pointing the interstices or joints between the stones with lime. The term was originally localised in Aberdeenshire and Kincardineshire, the earliest noted reference being to houses snecked or harled with lime about 1785.[295] The practice, but not the name, was recorded in late eighteenth century Angus, where there was a frequent custom of thrusting small chips of stones into the cracks between bigger stones.[296] Such small packing-stones were known in Aberdeenshire as the snecks. That the technique was even more widespread is shown by the fact that it also occurred in houses in the towns, for a traveller in the 1730s

Fig. 83. Hillockhead, Huntly, Aberdeenshire. Aberdeen bond stonework in light and dark granite on the principal facade with coursed pinned rubble on the gable. (NMAS: 32.6.27)

spoke of the rubble walls of town houses, composed of stones of various sizes, but many of them nearly round. As a result large gaps were left between, into which small, flat stones were driven. Finally, the walls were faced all over with mortar thrown against them with a trowel. This was known as harling.[297]

Harling, the practice of rough-casting with lime mixed with small gravel, has a history dating from at least the sixteenth century in relation to churches, tolbooths, and similar buildings, and also, in an Edinburgh source, to dykes.[298] The early references are to Aberdeen, Edinburgh and Haddington; later, as the practice spread more widely and sank through the social scale, the term and practice came to be found over the whole country. Office-houses were being harled in Berwickshire in 1760,[299] dykes in Cromarty in 1795,[300] and barn walls in East Lothian in the early 1800s.[301] The limestone in Lochlee was so full of sand that no addition was needed when it was used as mortar. It was stronger and stood the frost better than imported lime, and was good for exterior harling.[302]

In Kirkwall in 1824, masons earned 4/- per rood (5.3 m) for pinning and harling dykes, and 3/6 per rood for harling houses or walls built with mortar.[303]

It is clear that harling was regarded as a desirable finish for buildings of many kinds in town and country, and this has influenced restorers of eighteenth century buildings at the present day. The criticism levelled is that whereas the old harling was made with burnt slaked lime, sand and natural shingle, the modern versions consists of hydrated lime, cement, sand and often crushed stone chips. The old mix was used for pointing the joints and was then built up by dashing to form a thin coat over joints and stones alike. Now, after pointing, a coat of cement is plastered on, left to harden, then followed by another coat on to which harl is dashed. The result is a more glaring white than this country has ever known.[304]

Wickerwork

The use of wickerwork, generally in combination with clay or turf, is well documented from several parts of the country as a building material. At Langholm in Dumfriesshire, three English travellers stayed in 1629 in a house of stone and turf, with a door of wicker rods.[305] This method of closing the entrance was common in Ireland.[306] In Islay and Jura in 1772, some of the house doors were no more than faggots of birch twigs, presumably held together by wattling them. The wigwam-shaped shieling huts seen in Jura are clearly made of wattle covered with sods.[307]

In Ayrshire, farm houses up till the 1740s were often partly or wholly built of turf or of clayed wattle, the gablets being regularly of such materials, as well as the internal partitions.[308] Buildings in this material, known as creel-houses or basket-houses, were also to be found in Argyll. The builders marked out the required length and breadth, 'then drive stakes of wood at 9 in or a foot (23-30 cm) distance from each other, leaving 4 or 5 ft (1.2-1.5 m) of them above ground, then wattle them up with heath and small branches of wood upon the outside of which they pin on very thin turf, much in the same manner that Slates are laid. Along the top of these stakes runs a beam which supports the Couples and what they call Cabers, and this either covered with turf, heath, or Straw.'[309]

Evidence referring to the need for wattle to make good houses exists for the Glamis Estate in Angus in the early eighteenth century. The Strathmore Muniments include appraising tickets of the period, containing this information. The wattle appears to have been used in conjunction with clay.

In Inverness, Captain Burt stayed in a creel house in the 1730s. The walls were about 4 ft (1.2 m) high, 'lined with Sticks wattled like a Hurdle, built on the outside with Turf'.[310] Ruinous creel huts were seen at Derculich in the 1750s.[311] Samuel Johnson stayed in such a house at Anoch, Glenmoriston, in 1773. It had a chimney in one of its two rooms, and the other room, in which he slept, had a small glass window, and was lined with turf and wattled with twigs which kept the earth from falling—presumably from the divots on the roof. There was a garden of turnips and a field of potatoes nearby. The farmer kept 100 sheep, 100 goats, and 12 milk cows, and had 28 beef cattle ready for the drover. He was, therefore, a man of status, whose rent had been raised from £5 to £20 in the period between 1750 and 1773. Johnson also observed some creel houses of this kind in the Hebrides during his journey.[312] When Bishop Nicholson visited Strathglass, he observed that all the houses except those of lairds and people of consequence had walls of wattle turfed on the outside.[313] The technique survived into the nineteenth century, not only for barns, where it was common for the gablets to be filled with a wattle of broom or brushwood woven around upright spars, to allow access to the air for drying the produce stored within,[314] but also in the form of partitions in longhouses, separating the people from the animals. Such a partition, in Gaelic *tallan*, was noted in Kilmuir and Strath in Skye in the 1840s.[315]

Ross and Cromarty was another creel-house stronghold. Around Cromarty, barns and also houses could be 'basket-houses' in the 1760s, the barns differing from the houses only in having 'no turf fastened to their outer side from the ground up to the easing so that the wind blows through all parts of the barn . . . and dries their Corn.[316]

Evidently the houses had an outer cladding of turf attached to the wicker base, as in a late eighteenth century illustration of an inn in Ross-shire.[317] Creel barns were general in Ross-shire. They were built partly of stone, with large openings in the walls filled up with wickerwork, or sometimes built entirely of wickerwork, with the exception of the roof.[318] In the early 1800s, in the western districts, there were good creel barns of stone with large openings filled with wickerwork, and Mr Downie, the minister at Lochalsh, had erected several.[319] In some cases the creel barns at Lochcarron had wickerwork panels filling in the gaps between pillars of turf and stone.[320] Though creel barns were part of the improving habit of thought, the technique of building in wickerwork need not in itself have this character, for by Lochcarron, for example, in 1824, a hut of open wickerwork was seen 'pervious to all winds, and ill protected from the rain by an imperfect covering of turf'. The people in it, having been ejected from their farm, had been allowed by a neighbouring farmer to build the hut from his woods.[321]

In Sutherland, in the Highland straths towards Assynt, there were also barns in the 1800s with 6 ft (1.8 m) high walls and gables of drystone with some courses of turf, and gablets wattled with twigs of birch or willow.[322]

H

7

The Layout of Farm Buildings, with their Furniture and Fittings, c.1750-1850

IN 1649, West Gagie in Angus had the house and some of the offices on three sides of a square, whilst other outbuildings, including four byres, a stable, three barns and a henhouse, formed a second group, possibly around a second yard.[323] In 1699, Lord Belhaven outlined his ideas on the layout of farm buildings. Ideally, the dwelling house should lie east and west, with the barns running north and south at the west end. This let the house windows get the south sun, and the prevailing wind could pass through the barn doors to facilitate the winnowing of corn. For East Lothian farming conditions, three barns were recommended, one for wheat and barley, one for oats and one for pease, with the barnyard adjacent on the west side. The stable and byres should be across the close from the dwelling house, with the doors facing the house for easy access. The chaff-house should partly fill the remaining east side, with the entrance to the close alongside it. The dunghill was in the middle of the resulting square of buildings.[324] As yet, the separation of the dwelling house from the outbuildings was not even being considered. The factor for the Earl of Panmure at Belhelvie in Aberdeenshire had in 1705 a substantial dwelling house with one or more attached one-storey ranges of outbuildings, including three barns and four byres. How they were arranged is not known. His farm extended to a ploughgate of around 104 Scots acres. In Midlothian, the farm of Over Moss-houses on the Clerk of Penicuik estate had in 1717 a house flanked by two service wings, the fourth side being enclosed, possibly by a wall.[325]

There is no indication that these buildings were other than of one storey, and in spite of these examples and speculations, the real period of new building that marched hand-in-hand with general improvements in agriculture dates from about the 1760s, though as early as the 1740s in some parts. Surveys made in the 1760s and 1770s show how new farm houses and steadings were being built, often on former outfield areas, standing within their own blocked-out fields that no longer lay intermingled with those of their neighbours.[326] From numerous existing sources, it is possible to get a picture of the development and variety of farm buildings in the late eighteenth and early nineteenth centuries.

In the South-East, improvements began in Berwickshire in the 1740s. Before that date in Chirnside, there were no outfield farms, except those belonging to the three mills in the parish, and the existence of common property inhibited the extension of farms and steadings. The division of commons between proprietors facilitated such a spread on the one hand, and on the other it affected roofing materials, for example in Coldingham, where people who formerly used turf and divots from the moor had to change to slates or tiles after the commonty was divided about 1770. As new farms spread, as independent entities on their own units of land, the old farming villages disappeared.[327] By the 1790s, two- and even three-storey farms were to be found, with four to eight rooms including a back kitchen.[328]

102

Fig. 84.   Upper Sound, Lerwick, Shetland. A good example of a nucleated fermtoun photographed in the third quarter of the nineteenth century. (GWW: A0079)

By 1809, two-storey farm houses, with kitchens and offices paved with flat stones, were general, except where some of the old farm buildings remained on farms with unexpired leases. The dwelling house had moved from its central position in the row or square of buildings, facing the dunghill. First it was placed with the block of offices behind it, then it was placed a distance away. Internally, there was a living room and parlour on the ground floor, four bedrooms above, and a back wing with a kitchen and offices, and the nursery and women servants' room above. The milk-house, scullery, wash-house, pantry and coal-house were partly within the walls and partly built as lean-to sheds.

The outbuildings in their *stead*, *steadin* or *courtin* were on three sides of a square on big farms, with the barn, stables, byres and feeding sheds on the east, west and north sides. The dunghill in the middle was divided into three or four courts by cross-walls, for wintering cattle. The barn was also in three or four sections. One part, often on an upper floor beside the feeding board of the mill, held an unthreshed rick. One was for threshed grain, and could contain a pair of millstones driven by machinery to break corn and

Fig. 85. (Old) Scone, Scone, Perthshire—1693. A linear fermtoun settlement in close proximity to the mansion house. Note the rounded gables to most of the buildings and the openings high in the walls. The buildings are built to running levels.
(Slezer: *Theatrum Scotiae* Plate 35)

beans for horse fodder, and to grind cereals. There could also be a chaff cutter here. The third part, beyond the mill, was the straw barn, with a room for chaff, capable of holding the straw of two ricks, one for bedding and one for fodder.[329] Four-sided steadings also came into being, as in Westruther in the 1840s, with stable, byre, cattle shed, dairy, piggery and poultry house all set around the close.[330]

In East Lothian, data from the 1780s show a considerable degree of sophistication in building. At the farm of Spittlerigg, office-houses were being causeyed, and there was a bakehouse, for which a 6 ft (1.8 m) stone was got from Abbey Quarry as a vent. The kitchen was slated, with lead in the rigging, and flags from Tranent coalhill were laid on the floors of the washing house and henhouse.[331] As in Berwickshire, farm houses built from about this period were of two storeys, with parlour, nursery, kitchen, larder, milk house and laundry on the ground floor, and four rooms upstairs, besides closets and garrets. Many of the steadings formed a square within which lay a combined dunghill and cattleyard, or more rarely a cattleyard alone.

In the barns, threshing floors were being improved, and threshing machinery was spreading rapidly. Stables were of two types. The older ones consisted of an undivided range, longer or shorter according to the horse-power requirements, with a rack and manger running from one end to the other. The horses were not tied. Since the 1770s, however, stables had been increasingly divided into stalls each holding a pair of horses

Fig. 86.   Rait, Kilspindie, Perthshire. Part of the old Kirkton of Rait which takes the form of a linear fermtoun. When this particular group was partly demolished in preparation for renewal it was discovered that the building had been narrower—the large stones in the gable wall clearly marking the former corner—and that the buildings had formerly had rounded gables as in the 1693 print of Scone (Fig. 85). Note that these buildings are also built to a running level and bend in plan to follow natural features such as the burn which runs behind them. The present window openings are nineteenth or early twentieth century.

that normally worked together. Some stables were made wide enough for two rows of horses with a common channel down the middle to take off urine, but this type was not considered good, because of the danger of kicking across the passage. Evidently stalls were often made with open spars, though it was recognised that closely joined boards were to be preferred. Byres did not have partitions between pairs of cows, but upright wooden stakes to which the cows were individually fastened. East Lothian byres were normally wide enough for two rows of animals with a urine channel along the middle of the byre. In areas where turnips were regularly grown, the cattle being fattened on them were also tied to stakes in the common byre. Feeding byres generally had an opening with a flap board opposite each beast, so that they could be easily served with turnips. Included in the steading was a low building called a *cruive*, sometimes divided, and not very big, for keeping pigs, but otherwise not much attention was paid to them.[332]

In Roxburgh, another well-advanced area, the majority of the *onsteads* were two storeys high, with a garret floor. In general they were 36 to 40 ft (11-12 m) long with an internal width of 17 to 21 ft (5.2-6.4 m). On the ground floor of the house was the dining room and family bedroom, with a closet behind. Upstairs were four smaller and two larger bedrooms with closets, the beds being frequently sited in the closet so that the room could serve the purpose of a drawing room. Few houses were smaller than this,

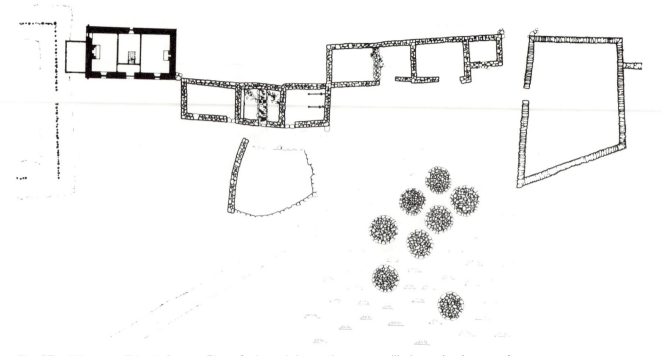

Fig. 87.   Waggles, Edzell, Angus. Plan of a late eighteenth, or more likely, early nineteenth-century farm which has been altered and extended several times during the nineteenth century. The farmhouse is late nineteenth century and replaced the former single room house at the west end of the steading block.

and many were larger, with a dining-room, drawing-room, four or five bedrooms, business rooms, a nursery and servants' quarters. Bigger places were built of hewn or rubble stone, and slated, whilst smaller ones, generally built by the proprietors, were built with clay or lime, and could be thatched or slated.

The buildings in the steading, which usually lay behind the dwelling house, had an average width of 15 ft (4.6 m), with walls 7 to 10 ft (2.1-3 m) high. When the house formed one side of the square, there were two, and sometimes three barns, 30 to 34 ft (9.1-10.4 m) long, on another side; stables for 10, 12 or more horses, and two byres for cows and young cattle on a third side; and feeding sheds for 20 to 50 bullocks on the fourth. If the house no longer closed the square, its place was taken by toolsheds, a henhouse, pigsty and so on. The dunghill generally lay in the middle. There was a hay loft above the stable or byre, in which the unmarried farm servants slept, and a granary overlay another shed, or an end of one of the barns.[333]

In Selkirk, some proprietors were active in building, like Mr Scot of Gala who in the twenty years following 1770 built six farm houses with complete sets of offices,[334] but in general farms and offices were not too good.

In Tweeddale in Peeblesshire, improved farm buildings were, by the 1790s, neat, roomy, well-sited and well-built, of two storeys with three or four rooms. On some of the smaller farms there were still houses placed in the lowest-lying parts, almost inaccessible because of wet in bad seasons. They were of one-storey, poorly built, covered with

Fig. 88.   Gogar Bank, Corstorphine, Midlothian. Illustration showing farmhouse and "mains" steading. Note that the farmhouse is shown as being slated whereas the steading behind is pantiled. (NMAS: C3923 from Robertson 1795. Facing 40)

thatch, and forming part of an irregularly placed set of offices, near the dunghill. These were, however, becoming few.[335]

By 1802, it could be said that the best farm houses were similar to the houses of the clergy, but they were smaller, with lower ceiling heights and a poorer quality of furnishing. Fifty two-storeyed dwellings replaced the former long, one-storey houses with walls 6 ft (1.8 m) high, measuring 46 by 15 or 16 ft (14 × 4.6 × 4.9 m) internally, entered from the front through a door near one end. They were divided into three units by means of box beds, with the kitchen in the middle, and the fire in the middle of the floor.[336]

Already by the 1780s in Midlothian, good farm houses with commodious offices had been built on the Buccleuch estate, and long leases were being given. Couden farm was one example. The proprietor was not always himself responsible for erecting new buildings, for Alexander Carfrae, on the Marquis of Lothian's estate, had built himself a large house, perhaps in anticipation of better times, for he was a bachelor. At Gilmerton and Dalhousie Mains the houses and steadings had been largely put up at the tenants' expense.[337] In the 1790s, the usual layout was still in the form of a square, sometimes open at the side opposite the house or bounded by a low wall or set of sheds. The houses were of two storeys, with five or six apartments in addition to the kitchen, dairy, larder and so on. The barns were usually 20 ft (6 m) wide with walls 8 or 10 ft (2.4-3 m) high. The actual length was in proportion to the size of the farm, and they could hold 50 to 100 bolls of corn in the straw at a time. As a rule they were in two parts so that different types of grain could be threshed at the same time. Occasionally a loft above the threshing floor served as a granary. The stables had stalls for pairs of horses, or more rarely for single horses. Sometimes milk-cows were also kept in separate stalls. On farms that kept *winterers*, the dunghill and court were in the middle of the close, but otherwise it was beginning to be put out of sight behind the stable. The scale of the buildings had a direct

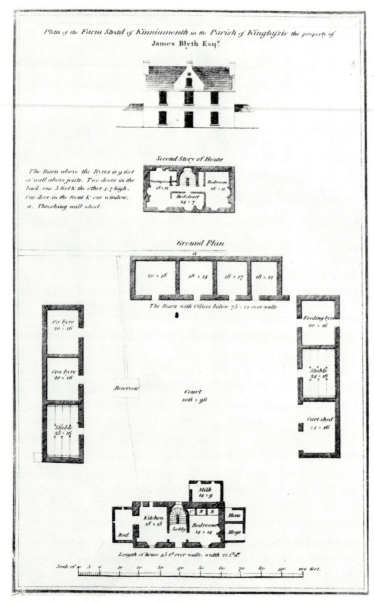

Fig. 89.   Kinninmonth, Kinglassie, Fife: 1800. Plan of a house and steading for a fairly large farm. Note the lack of trevises in the byres and the use of a first-floor barn, possibly to lift it clear of the damp caused by the water wheel on the north wall. This wheel would be used to drive the threshing machine. (NMAS: C3878)

relationship to the size of the farm in terms of space for stock and goods, and elegance and prestige for the dwelling house. A year's rent of the farm was normally allowed as the cost of building the houses, this amounting to £300-£400 in the low part of the country.[338] In this way, by collaboration between laird and tenant, fine new buildings, many of which survive, replaced the old low farm buildings arranged in a square. The master's house at one side had two or three rooms, earthen floors, low ceilings, and a few

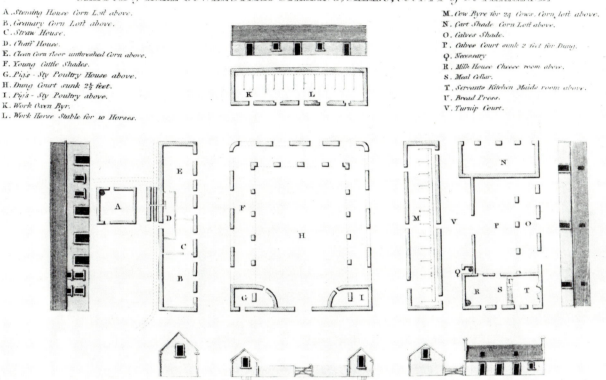

and Report

SKETCH of EARL GOWER'S FARM STEADING, SKELBO; COUNTY of SUTHERLAND.

A . Steaming House Corn Loft above.
B . Granary Corn Loft above.
C . Straw House.
D . Chaff House.
E . Clean Corn floor unthreshed Corn above.
F . Young Cattle Shades.
G . Pigs - Sty Poultry House above.
H . Dung Court sunk 2½ feet.
I . Pigs - Sty Poultry above.
K . Work Oxen Byr.
L . Work Horse Stable for 10 Horses.

M . Cow Byre for 24 Cows. Corn loft above.
N . Cart Shade Corn Loft above.
O . Calves Shade.
P . Calves Court sunk 2 feet for Dung.
Q . Necessary.
R . Milk House Cheese room above.
S . Meal Cellar.
T . Servants Kitchen Maids room above.
U . Bread Press.
V . Turnip Court.

Fig. 90.   Skelbo, Dornoch, Sutherland: 1812. A single-storey steading with 1½-storey barn wing to west. Note that the byres have trevises between every second animal as was common later and that there is a feeding passage at the animals' heads. This is a feature that normally only occurs on the most elaborate plans. (NMAS: C3981)

small window lights. The barn was cruck-framed, with walls up to 5 ft (1.5 m) high, and the stables undivided. The cattle were tied to upright stakes.[339]

In West Lothian, new houses were mostly of two storeys, with five or six rooms, measuring about 40 ft long by 20 ft (12 × 6 m) wide, with 7 to 9 ft (2.1-2.7 m) high ceilings.[340]

In the South-West area, in Ayrshire, a common plan was a dwelling house three units long, with garrets above, and offices at right angles at each end, forming a U-shaped court with the midden in the centre.[341] A good deal of rebuilding had been going on from about 1780, for example in Sorn. In Tarbolton, houses and offices were in a square, open at the front, and of one storey.[342] The bulk of rebuilding, however, did not start till after 1800, and the old form of longhouse survived for long, with the byre at one end and the cattle sharing the same door as the family. Doors were rarely over 5 ft (1.5 m) high, windows 18 in (46 cm) high by a foot (30 cm) wide, sometimes with boards instead of glass. The living area, the *in-seat*, was 12 to 14 ft (3.7-4.3 m) square, with a central or gable hearth but no real chimney. Larger farms had a second room, the *spence*, entered through the first one, and here were stores of various kinds, including the meal girnel,

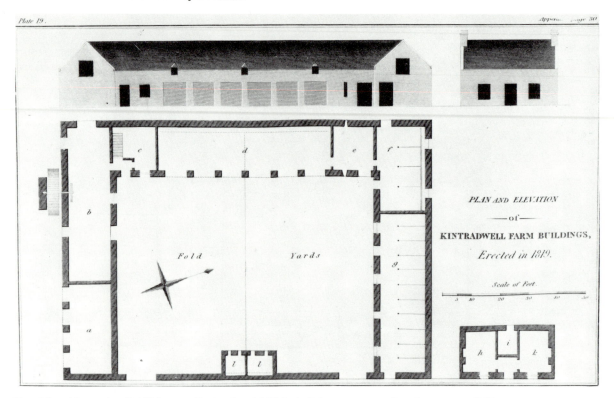

Fig. 91.   Kintradwell, Kildonan, Sutherland 1819. A 1½-storey steading forming a "U" plan round open fold yards and with the cattle shed incorporated into the main steading buildings. These sheds are often mistaken for cart bays especially if the fold has been removed. (NMAS: C7096)

sowen tub, a cask for urine to be used as lye in processing textiles, spinning wheels and reels, and a press. To the left of the entrance was the trance-door leading to the living quarters, to the right the *heck-door* leading to the byre or stable, the doors in each case being placed centrally in internal partitions. The entrance door or fore door was matched by another at the back, called the yard door. A 6 ft (1.8 m) wide causeway of large stones led up to the fore door, and the dunghill was sited 8 to 10 ft (2.4-3 m) away from it, with a pond called the *midden-dub*, no doubt a favourite spot for ducks to dabble.[343] In general there were few upper storeys on such buildings, and the floors were rarely even paved with flags.

In the island of Arran, Bute, farms were still arranged in irregular village clusters in 1804. The dwelling houses had two units. The living room was the larger with a screen or *hallan* of worked clay and straw on upright posts standing between the door and the hearth, which was of flat stones sunk in the floor near one end of the house, far enough out from the wall for people to walk round it. The smoke hole was a clay-lined opening in the roof, and a cross-beam supported the crook and the links. For supporting heavy boilers, there was also a swey. The inner room was sometimes separated by means of wooden beds, with a passage between them, and a door, or else by a clay screen which was whitewashed on the inside. Here there was a fireplace with stone jambs, on a flat

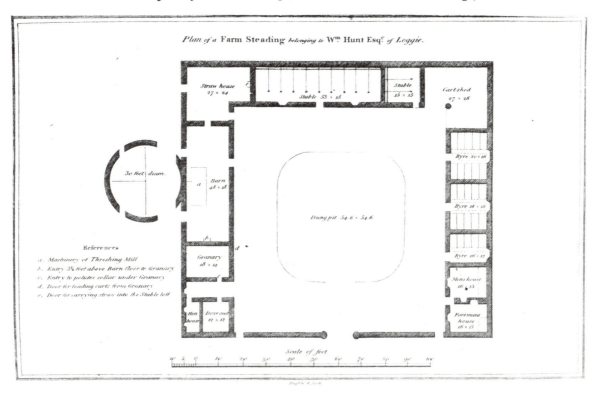

Plan of a Farm Steading belonging to W.ᵐ Hunt Esqᵗ of Loggie.

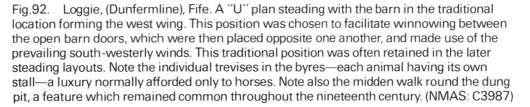

Fig.92. Loggie, (Dunfermline), Fife. A "U" plan steading with the barn in the traditional location forming the west wing. This position was chosen to facilitate winnowing between the open barn doors, which were then placed opposite one another, and made use of the prevailing south-westerly winds. This traditional position was often retained in the later steading layouts. Note the individual trevises in the byres—each animal having its own stall—a luxury normally afforded only to horses. Note also the midden walk round the dung pit, a feature which remained common throughout the nineteenth century. (NMAS: C3987)

base-stone, and a chimney in the gable. It could be paved with flagstones, but the luxury of a floor of wooden deals was coming in, with a deal floor above, forming a ceiling and with exposed joists, and plastered or whitewashed walls. The kitchen always had one window, generally of square boards in a frame, and rarely of glass panes. The inner room often had a glass window which could be larger than the one in the living room.

Though the byre was linked to the houses, and could be entered by a door from behind the hallan, the animals themselves had their own separate entrance. In addition there was a stable where the horses stood unbound, frequently up to their knees in mire; a small barn capable of holding a small stack of corn for threshing; a shed to hold carts, slide cars, and other implements; and sometimes a shed for peats.[344]

In Arran, the technique of building in alternating courses of stone and turf still prevailed in 1816. Doors in such walls were 4 to 5 ft (1.2-1.5 m) high, and the windows tended to be airholes only. One-roomed dwellings were common. Home-grown timber for roofing was becoming scarce, and new farms were usually still put up by the farmers

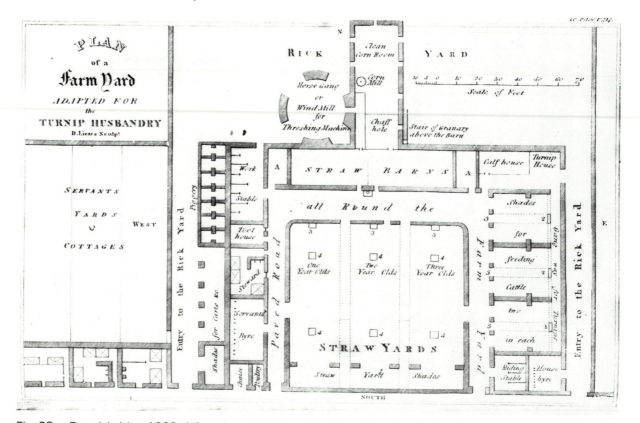

Fig. 93.   Berwickshire: 1809. A farm layout designed for "turnip husbandry" and showing various forms of byre and cattle sheds. Note that the house and servants' byres have a double pole arrangement to restrain the cattle—the poles being closed, and pegged in position, on either side of the beast's neck allowing vertical movement whilst restraining the beast; separate calf house; sheds for pairs of animals; and a central court, sub-divided to hold one, two and three year old cattle in separate enclosures. Note also the alternative power sources given for the threshing machine—viz horse engine or windmill. (NMAS: C3946; from Kerr 1809. Facing p.97)

themselves, or sometimes as a joint effort by the community for a newly married couple.[345]

Farm houses and offices in Dunbartonshire that in the 1790s had been recently built were good, well sited, and mostly in the form of a court, the dwelling house being flanked by the offices on the sides, and having the dunghill in front of it. Most were of one storey, with a large kitchen and a room or spence, and sometimes garrets that could be fitted up as sleeping places. The cost of the whole was about £160 stg. The majority of steadings were of the old type, however, small and poorly constructed, with house and offices in one row, under one roof, with a common entrance for house and byre. The old farms, therefore, were longhouses.[346]

The walls of farm buildings were in general 7 ft (2.1 m) high by 20 in (51 cm) to 2 ft (61 cm) thick, of drystone, or with a bonding of clay mortar or mud. There were two rooms, each about 12 to 14 ft (3.7-4.3 m) square, sometimes with a small closet between.

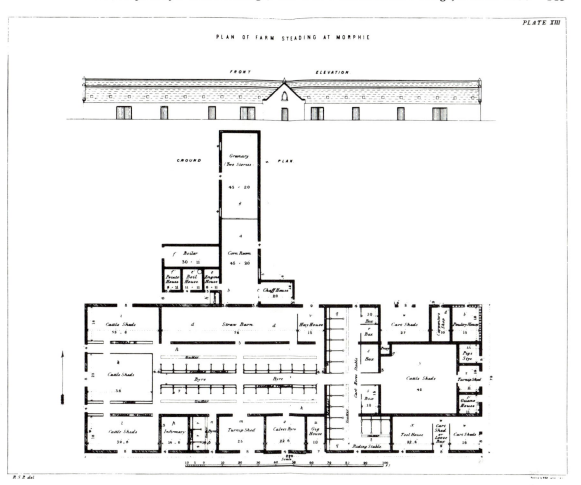

Fig. 94.   Morphie, St Cyrus, Kincardineshire. A large, complex but highly original and well organised farm steading which has been recently demolished and replaced by a large multi-purpose shed which utilises the original south wall and gables of the building shown here. Note the head to head arrangement in the byre with the feeding passage between the two rows of animals. The only inexplicable feature is the large cattle shed separated from the main cattle area by the stable to accommodate the twelve work horses. (NMAS: C7714)

The spence usually held two beds, and the kitchen one. The rooms were not ceiled, and the fires were at floor level. The windows were of four panes, of which only one or two might be glazed. An inner door linked the kitchen with the byre, in which the horses were also kept.

Many such farms were still surviving in 1811, though the newer ones were of stone and lime, with hewn freestone corners, doors and windows. The walls were increased in height to 9 ft (2.74 m). On the average they measured 40 by 20 ft (12.2 × 16.9 m), and the arrangement of two rooms and a closet, but with two garrets above, was retained. The walls were finished with plaster, the windows were sashed, and the floors paved or covered with boards.[347]

Some estates in Stirlingshire had two-storey houses. In the best-arranged farms, the

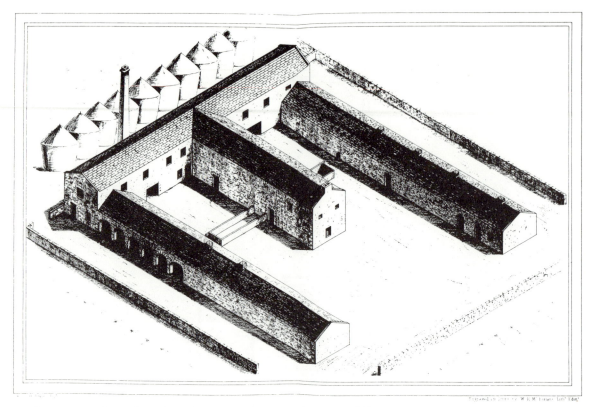

Fig. 95.   Carse Farm Steading—Isometric drawing. A double "U" plan steading comprising 1½-storey accommodation on the barn ranges in the centre and to the north, with single-storey accommodation elsewhere. Note the factory-type chimney for the steam engine to power the threshing machine and the large stackyard behind the main buildings. (NMAS: C7715; from Stephens and Burn 1861. Plate XXII)

buildings surrounded the yard where the cattle were foddered in winter, with a shed they could enter for shelter in bad weather. On the biggest farms, a white corn and a pease barn were found, but it often happened that little barn room was allowed, and the crop had to be stacked in the yard, 'a practice which generally prevails over all Scotland, and is attended with the best consequences'. Threshing floors were said to need improving, since they were of clay as a rule, and not of planks, which were said to be preferable.[348] In Gargunnock, the buildings were much better than in the 1770s, mostly with two rooms, each of which had a chimney and a reasonable window. The farms were still often longhouses, but the cattle were not allowed to enter at the same door as the family. In Campsie every 'decent' inhabitant had a house with a kitchen and one or more had two rooms, ceiled above and often laid with deal, with glass windows.[349] It was considered by 1812 that the most important aspect of the modern farms was the square, enclosed yard, paved with small stones and sloping towards the centre from every side. The entrance gate was on the south, and the other three sides had covered sheds for sheltering the cattle. On Sir Charles Edmonstone's estate of Kilsyth, every farm of £70 rent and upwards had such a straw yard.

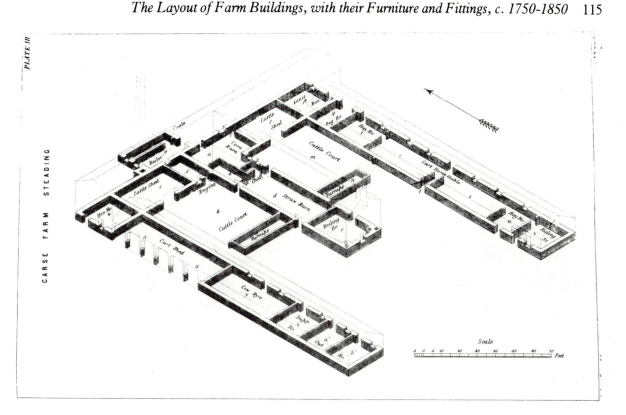

Fig. 96. Carse Farm Steading—Plan. Gives the detailed layout of accommodation for Fig. 95. (NMAS: C7712; from Stephens and Burn 1861. Plate III)

Since lairds allowed tenants to provide their own houses until the early 1800s, the result was that they were of no great quality. They were longhouses, with the byre and stable under one roof and separated from the kitchen by a partition of clay-plastered osiers on slender wooden posts. The master and mistress, children and servants, sat and ate together in the kitchen, whilst the spence, found only in the better quality houses, was where strangers might be received and where the heads of the family slept. Glass windows and chimneys were rare. Such buildings were still to be found in 1812, though in decreasing numbers. Their survival was in part due to the smallness of most carse farms, which seldom exceeded 20 acres, so making the erection of costly buildings economically impossible.[350]

In Lanarkshire, though there were some two-storey, slated examples, the majority were still of the old style. They were of one storey, with a kitchen at one end, a *far room*, and a small family room leading off the passage between. The garret was rarely floored or plastered. Beds were to be found in all three rooms. The biggest was the kitchen, with its central hearth set about 6 ft (1.8 m) out from the gable. In this space was a long wooden seat with arms, the *lang settle*, where the young lads sat during the winter evenings. The chimney or *brace* was a square-mouthed box 5 to 6 ft (1.5-1.8 m) wide suspended over the fire at a height of about 6 ft (1.8 m). It contracted to 2 ft (61 cm) square at the top and was carried straight up through the roof close to the gable, or else

A

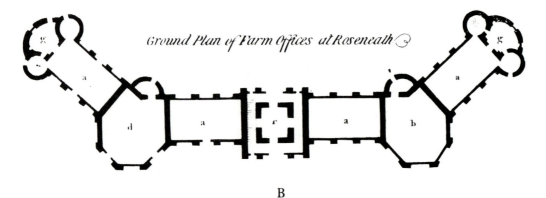

B

Fig. 97 (a, b).   Roseneath, Roseneath, Dunbartonshire: 1811. Formally planned farm offices in an elaborate gothic style showing the lengths some landowners would go to, to embellish the home farm buildings. (NMAS: C3939 & C3945; from Whyte & MacFarlane 1811—(a) following p.26, (b) facing p.27)

was led into a stone chimney in the upper part of the gable. The wooden projection stood 3 ft (91 cm) above the ridge, and was wound around with straw ropes, or sometimes slated if the rest of the roof was slated.[351]

In parts of Dumfriesshire, for example at Annan, a soft red freestone was plentiful, and was used for door and window frames for the thatched houses. Arched door frames were also made of it for the barns around 1760.[352] This must have given a good appearance to the buildings. By 1790, improvement was well advanced. In the first stage, the best farms were built on three sides of a square, with the house to the front, stable and byres on one side, and barn, cart-shed and granary on the third. Sometimes

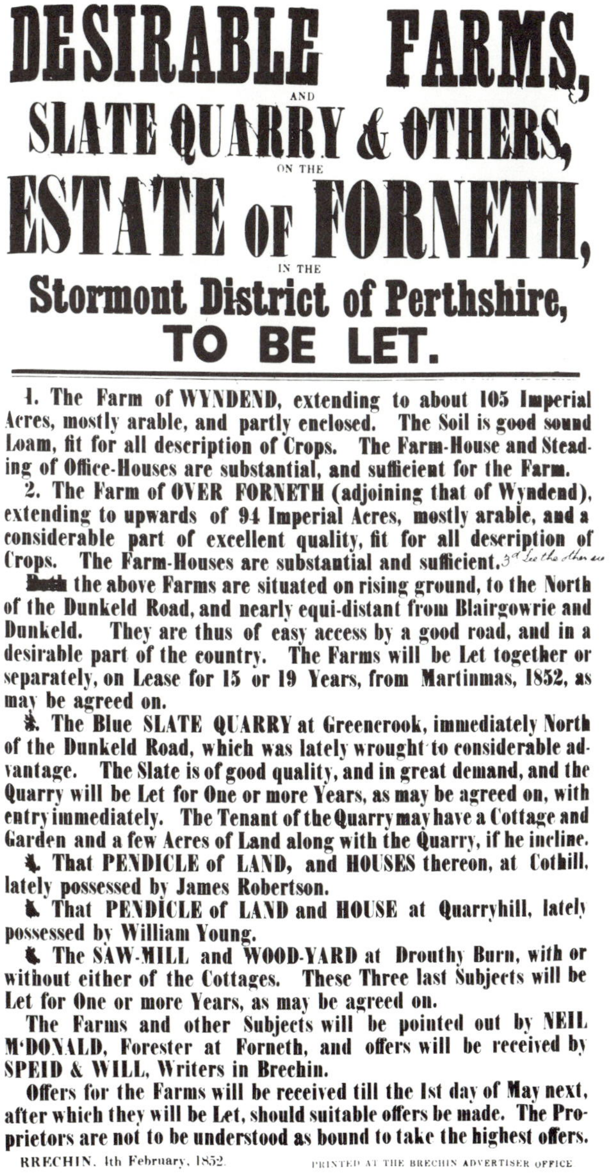

DESIRABLE FARMS,
AND
SLATE QUARRY & OTHERS,
ON THE
ESTATE of FORNETH,
IN THE
Stormont District of Perthshire,
TO BE LET.

1. The Farm of WYNDEND, extending to about 105 Imperial Acres, mostly arable, and partly enclosed. The Soil is good sound Loam, fit for all description of Crops. The Farm-House and Steading of Office-Houses are substantial, and sufficient for the Farm.

2. The Farm of OVER FORNETH (adjoining that of Wyndend), extending to upwards of 94 Imperial Acres, mostly arable, and a considerable part of excellent quality, fit for all description of Crops. The Farm-Houses are substantial and sufficient.

Both the above Farms are situated on rising ground, to the North of the Dunkeld Road, and nearly equi-distant from Blairgowrie and Dunkeld. They are thus of easy access by a good road, and in a desirable part of the country. The Farms will be Let together or separately, on Lease for 15 or 19 Years, from Martinmas, 1852, as may be agreed on.

3. The Blue SLATE QUARRY at Greencrook, immediately North of the Dunkeld Road, which was lately wrought to considerable advantage. The Slate is of good quality, and in great demand, and the Quarry will be Let for One or more Years, as may be agreed on, with entry immediately. The Tenant of the Quarry may have a Cottage and Garden and a few Acres of Land along with the Quarry, if he incline.

4. That PENDICLE of LAND, and HOUSES thereon, at Cothill, lately possessed by James Robertson.

5. That PENDICLE of LAND and HOUSE at Quarryhill, lately possessed by William Young.

6. The SAW-MILL and WOOD-YARD at Drouthy Burn, with or without either of the Cottages. These Three last Subjects will be Let for One or more Years, as may be agreed on.

The Farms and other Subjects will be pointed out by NEIL M'DONALD, Forester at Forneth, and offers will be received by SPEID & WILL, Writers in Brechin.

Offers for the Farms will be received till the 1st day of May next, after which they will be Let, should suitable offers be made. The Proprietors are not to be understood as bound to take the highest offers.

BRECHIN, 4th February, 1852.   PRINTED AT THE BRECHIN ADVERTISER OFFICE

Fig. 98.   Farm Advertisement: 1852. Note that even as late as 1852 this comparatively fertile area was only partly enclosed and that in many areas of more marginal land the enclosures were even later. (NMAS: C3931)

the fourth side was filled with sheds for young cattle, and houses for pigs and poultry. In the second stage, the style was to put several buildings in a long range with the dwelling house at the east end, so saving several gable walls.[353]

In Penpont and in Johnstone, the population increased by about 100 between 1776 and 1791, due to the division of some large farms.[354] The same happened in Kirkmichael because of the division and cultivation of a large common, but the increase was

Fig. 99.   Balmoral Home Farm, Crathie, Aberdeenshire. An Aberdeenshire farm typical of many erected in the last decade of the nineteenth century, though this may be earlier. The features which are particularly common in Aberdeenshire are the single-storey dormer windows to the house, the gabled ranges to the steadings, the "H" plan form of the main block with midden to the north (type 3.3), and the double cart bay in the gable of one range. Note the sawmill to the rear of the farm steading. (GWW: C1048).

restricted because of the practice of 'leading' farms, by which one large farmer owned another smaller one. The number of farms diminished by 20 between about 1730 and 1791. There were still in 1791 three farm villages, two of 70 to 75 and one of 100 inhabitants.[355] In Glencairn, there were 90 farms in 1792, many of them occupied by one tenant only. There was a two-way process at work in several parishes. In many, old runrig multiple ownership farms were being blocked into individual holdings, whilst in others, large farms were being divided into smaller possessions. The population of the parish could decrease or increase accordingly.[356] Evidence of rising living standards can be seen from the common use of clocks, mostly of wood, in Kirkpatrick Juxta, and from the fact that every house had at least one glass window, though there were only two houses with glass window panes about 1720.[357] Forty-three new houses were built in

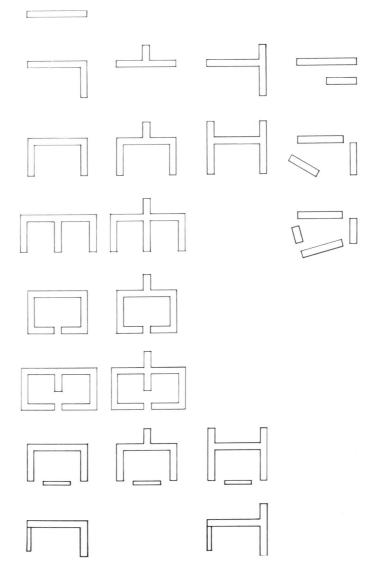

Fig. 100. Farm Plan Types. Typical steading plans in Grampian
Region (Walker 1979).

Johnstone between 1780 and 1791. In Closeburn, the principal farmers had good
houses, but the subtenants often built their own much poorer ones, alongside the main
road. This social difference was probably fairly widespread.

By 1812, most farm houses were of stone and lime, with corners, doors, windows and
chimney tops of dressed sandstone, the rest of whinstone rubble. The steadings were
built close on three sides, and the fourth was supported on sandstone pillars, with strong
lintels of red fir, couples, and a roof of slate. A new element was storage sheds for
potatoes, built either long and narrow, or wide with internal wooden partitions.[358]

Fig. 101. Little Powgavie, Inchture, Perthshire. A late nineteenth-century steading with circular horse engine house, and cart bays on the north elevation. Note the piend roofs and the jerkinhead dormers. The arches of the cart bays in these late nineteenth-century steadings tend to be false, the wall being supported on timber safe lintels. behind a thin stone skin which forms the arch. (NMAS: 41.19.6)

Fig. 102. Goukmuir, Fordoun, Kincardineshire. A nineteenth-century farm steading with cart bays in the west range facing the former stackyard. These openings are formed with timber lintels. (NMAS: 39.28.15)

Fig. 103.   Gateside, Linlithgow, West Lothian. Cart bay range with granary over, from the early nineteenth century. Arches at this date were true arches the full width of the wall. Note the slate roof over the granary for extra protection from damp, but pantiles elsewhere. (IM: 1.8)

Tenants in Galloway were building their own houses about 1790, having been given twenty-one year leases by the Earl of Galloway. They were of one storey.[359] Till shortly before 1810, longhouses survived, in which cattle and people were not even separated by a partition. There were no chimneys, and the small holes for windows were closed by wooden shutters.[360] As recently as 1896, some of the old farms with house, byre and stable in one long range still existed,[361] though these were probably originally of the improved type, and not longhouses. In Whithorn, Wigtownshire, farms were improving and often slated. Sheds and strawyards were becoming general, providing greater comfort for the animals, whilst the physical wellbeing of the inhabitants was improved by the acquisition of seven-day clocks, and glass windows. Around 1735 the windows were merely unglazed light-openings on each side of the house stuffed with straw on the windward side if necessary. Some sub-divisions of larger units took place,

Fig. 104.   Towmill, Premnay, Aberdeenshire. Home made trevises in a byre for feeding cattle. These trevises were constructed by the present farmer approximately forty years ago. (NMAS: 32.5.3A)

for example in Kirkinner, where one large farm was split into thirteen or fourteen small holdings around 1780, and several subtacks were also created on another farm that had been long under pasture.[362] The same was true in Mochrum, where Sir William Maxwell divided up several large farms.[363] In Kirkowen, on the other hand, the enlargement of farms since 1750 had led to a decrease in population. Multiple-tenancy farms in Wigtown, with two, four, or even twelve tenants, had all been replaced by single-tenant units.[364]

By 1810, considerable progress had been made. Nearly every barn had a water- or horse-driven threshing mill. Other estates followed this example, though not all improvements were appreciated by the tenants. Several of them took a long time to get used to the idea of sheds and strawyards, thinking they would lead to a waste of fodder and check the growth of young cattle.[365]

Fig. 105. Whinhill, Fordoun, Kincardineshire.
Home made trevis in croft byre. (NMAS: 39.28.32)

In the East, by the 1790s, in Clackmannanshire, few of the old steadings remained. Their walls were no more than 7 ft (2.1 m) high, and the window openings closed by two boards that opened in the middle, with a small pane of glass in each of the upper parts of the boards. From the 1760s, such buildings were being increasingly replaced by new ones built of stone and lime, with larger, glazed windows. New houses mostly faced south, and were of one storey, with a garret. The barns, about 16 ft (4.9 m) wide and 30 to 35 ft (9.1-10.6 m) long internally, were usually set on the west side so that they and the stackyards alongside were open to the prevailing wind direction. The cart-shed, at the end of the barn, had its end open to the south, which allowed larger items to go into it than if it had been open at the side. The walls of the buildings were seldom more than 7 or 8 ft (2.1-2.4 m) high. The stables and byres lay opposite the barns.

In this area, where farms were small, and each needed the basic units of barn, stable

Fig. 106.   Newton of Foulzie, King Edward, Aberdeenshire. Typical timber byre trevis from architect-designed farm steading. (NMAS: 33.3.16)

Fig. 107.   Upper Wanford, Alvah, Banffshire. Less typical timber byre trevis with hind post carried to a rail under the rafters. (NMAS: C33.1.3)

Fig. 108. Nether Warburton, St Cyrus, Kincardineshire. Typical stone byre trevises. These are sunk at least 600mm into the floor and restrained at the top against the byre wall. Concrete trevises often take the same form. (NMAS: 41.4.11)

and byre, landlords were hardly likely to put out much expense on them, though they normally took the responsibility of building them. The tenant's share was the carriage of material, maintenance, and leaving in good condition on expiry of the lease. The landlord might also give a tenant a sum of money for erecting buildings, say about £30 to £100 for small farms. Not very much could be done for this sum.[366]

In Kinross, the old one-storey buildings were entered from near one end. It was necessary to pass through every room to get to the end one. New houses were often of two storeys.[367]

In Fife in the 1750s, farm buildings were irregularly placed, often as multiple-tenancy runrig farm-villages. The houses were low and smoky, without separate apartments except for divisions made by the furniture. Steadings had low walls, and ponderous, leaky roofs. In a few cases they formed a square with house, barn, stable and byre facing onto the dunghill in the centre,[368] and as in the parish of Kettle, houses were of two storeys with garrets.[369] The steadings formed a square, sometimes at the back of the house and including it as part of the square, and sometimes set a little apart from the house. The buildings included byre, stable, barn, implement sheds, strawyards for feeding cattle, milk house and hog house. Naturally, there were several degrees between the best and the worst, and not all were suited to the size of the farm. Some had no granaries or lofts for holding threshed grain. Some had no sheds, or none large enough to store the implements. Some had no strawyards or feeding byres, and no proper milk house. Many only had threshing floors of damp clay.[370]

By 1773, in Perthshire, agricultural improvement was leading to the appearance of

Fig. 109.   Rathvenmill, Rathven, Banffshire. Stable trevis with typical upsweep at the horse's head to prevent biting over the top. Note the slatted pallet in each stall to keep the horses off the stone floor. (NMAS: 34.3.5A)

new farm buildings, in the midst of their own fields. In the Barony of Stobhall, Mr Gibb erected Redstone Farm, with a stone-and-lime dwelling house, slated; John Greig at New Mill had built a house, offices and corn mill; Alexander Robertson at Brunty a two-storey house 50 ft long, slated, with offices in proportion, a lint mill, and a corn mill.[371]

Such buildings replaced huts built in the Central Highlands of thick turf, and later of stone without cement. The walls were rarely over 5 ft (1.5 m) high, the doorways were low, and the windows often unglazed.[372] Longhouses still remained in the 1790s, with only a partition between men and animals, though the entrance doors were made separate,[373] but much progress had been made. In Inchture, nearly all the farms were rebuilt between 1776 and 1792.[374] In Monedie there were four new farms by 1792,[375] and in Logiealmond twenty, two of them of two storeys, with garrets.[376] Little Dunkeld had five two-storey houses.[377] In the east end of Kincardine, over three-quarters of the houses had been renewed.[378] Fowlis Wester had two new one-storey and four two-storey farms.[379] In Lecropt the farms had been recently enclosed and subdivided into fields in 1796, and neat steadings built.[380] Auchtergaven had 20 or 30 new farms of similar type.[381] Longforgan had two-storey farms for the most part, with two fire rooms, and a large, light closet on each floor.[382] In Bendochy, windows were formerly covered with wooden boards, but now all had some glass. Three-foot (91 cm) square chimneys were beginning to be built in some of the low, thatched houses, these presumably marking canopy chimneys. There were five two-storey farms.[383] By 1797 in the parish of Longforgan

Fig. 110. Quithell, Glenbervie, Kincardineshire. Covered cattle court in the centre of a formerly ''U'' plan steading. (NMAS: 32.22.18)

there were 50 to 60 new houses measuring 28 to 30 ft (8.5-9.1 m) long by 15 ft (4.6 m) wide internally, with floors of earth or clay, two good rooms and a smaller one in the middle, garrets above laid with deal, and a thatch of sewn wheat straw, or tiles or slates, with skylights.[384] South of the Teith, in Kilmadock, there were several two-storey houses, with tiled offices on each side, forming a square. This type was becoming general.[385]

In Angus, longhouses had died out about 1800. They had the fire in the middle of the floor, and a smoke hole let out the smoke. An improvement was the placing of a screen between the door and the fireplace, to direct the draughts. A window with a wooden shutter was first put in it, then a pane of glass. For more light, a window was put in the outer wall, with one to four panes of glass. A number of farms remained like this in the early 1800s, especially towards the Grampian mountains. Box beds formed a division between the fireplace and an inner room used for storing lumber, which, in the course of improvement, acquired a stone and clay chimney, and became the room for the farmer and his family, The servants then occupied the kitchen end.[386] New buildings, however, were generally arranged round a square court with a strawyard in the centre,[387] and many parishes had two-storey farms.

In the North-East area, Barclay of Urie in Kincardineshire was one of the leading improvers of his day. In the 1770s, he already had very substantial farm offices. They were about 200 ft (61 m) long on each side, and 160 ft (49 m) on each end overall. The internal width was 20 ft (6.1 m), and the walls were 12 ft (3.7 m) high. Two stables on the

Fig. 111.   Stone of Morphie, St Cyrus, Kincardineshire. Interior of covered cattle court showing manger or heck and troughs. Note the difference in level between the feeding passageway and the floor of the court. This is to accommodate the build up of dung over the winter months. (NMAS: 40.27.33)

south side held 8 and 14 horses respectively, and both had hay lofts. Behind them were houses for pigs, hens and calves, and a room for servants. There were three voids for wagons, each measuring 10 ft (3 m), and a tool house with a granary above it. On the north side was a barn 180 ft (55 m) long with doors big enough to take loaded vehicles. Below it were sheds with 8 ft (2.4 m) spaces between the pillars, and a granary above. On the east side was a covered gate 10 ft (3 m) high by 14 ft (4.3 m) wide, a byre, and seven voids for vehicles with a grain loft above and a hatch above each void for filling grain into carts. The west side, at that time not finished, was planned to match the east side. In addition, a mile or two to the south, there was a barn 68 ft (21 m) long by 20 ft (6 m) wide

Fig. 112.   West Hillhead, Monikie, Angus. Cattle feeding in covered court. (NMAS: 42.3.10)

with walls 14 ft (4.3 m) high, with a porch 12 ft (3.7 m) square, two lean-tos, a straw house, and a cattle yard surrounded with broom faggots standing 10 ft (3 m) high. A similar barn and yard was planned for a spot 1½ miles to the east. Nearer the sea there was a mill that ground the estate's wheat and barley, and another for oats, pease and malt. The flour was sold and delivered in Aberdeen in sacks, after the London method and at London prices.[388]

For any part of Scotland this was advanced for the time. The average reality was different. Improvements began in general about 1760 to 1770, though the earliest efforts were still of a fairly humble nature. At first the walls were made of better materials, more compact, and raised from 5 or 6 ft (1.5-1.8 m) to 6½ ft (2 m) high. The light-slot in the wall was replaced by a glass window, though it rarely had more than four panes. The rooms of the house continued to be divided by its furniture. In the best of the improved houses, iron grates were introduced into the fireplace in the best room, over which a loft was built to hold lumber. In the living or kitchen end, the old style continued, and the bare cabers formed the only ceiling. The fuel, peat or broom, burned on a hearth by the gable wall, and the smoke escaped through a smoke hole in the roof, or through the door. The midden remained near the house door. The technique of keeping the cattle in a court with shelter sheds developed only later. The stable was in the same range as the house, and had then no stalls. The dung was cleared through a muck-hole in the back wall. The barn, in a separate range, was always the best building, since it held the corn that was the life blood of the farm. The roofs of all the houses were of thin sods spread on uneven timbers. Such farm buildings could still be found in 1813, and for a farm of 100 acres, would cost £40 to £50 sterling.[389]

Fig. 113.   Typical cobbled floor in a byre. Many of these floors were covered in concrete to comply with dairy regulations but many still survive in feeding byres where the dairy regulations do not apply. (NMAS: 32.27.33)

The houses of smaller tenants, about 1813, were about 32 to 40 ft (9.8-12.2 m) long by 14 ft (4.3 m) wide internally, with walls 7 ft (2.1 m) high. The door was placed centrally, with a single window to right and left. The kitchen had a floor of clay or earth, and no grate. The small room for the master at the other end usually had a grate, and often a deal floor. It contained two box beds, one or two presses, an oaken table, a small mirror, a chest of drawers, three or four chairs, and an eight-day clock. The kitchen had some plain wooden beds, a few stools or chairs, and a long fir table. A narrow stair between these two rooms, led to a garret above the master's end, holding the meal ark, cheeses, and lumber, and serving as an occasional spare bedroom. The room for milk was behind the stair in a small room lit by a single central window with perhaps no more than one pane of glass.

Stables and byres were only 12 to 14 ft (3.7-4.3 m) wide, with walls about 5 ft (1.5 m) high. The floors were generally well paved, with a drainage channel. There was little order in the layout of the units, which could lie intermixed, pointing in all directions.

The larger farms were better arranged. The houses were nearly always of two storeys.

Fig. 114.   Cairnfield, Rathven, Banffshire. Neat oval cobbles forming the floor to the tackroom. This is an early steading possibly from the end of the eighteenth or early nineteenth century and obviously of some quality. (NMAS: 32.18.32)

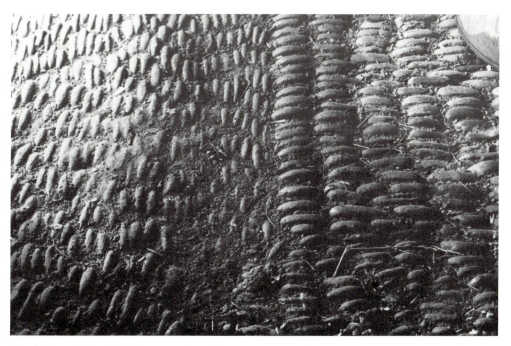

Fig. 115.   Cairnfield, Rathven, Banffshire. Change of cobble pattern at the end of the stable stalls. (NMAS: 33.22.9)

Fig. 116. Waterstone, Ecclesmachan, West Lothian. Henhouse with outside steps to high-level entry. Note the change in character between the lower and upper parts of the wall pointing to a re-building on the former wall base. (IM: 3.7)

They were about 40 to 50 ft (12.2-15.2 m) long by 16 to 20 ft (4.9-6.1 m) wide inside. The ground floor had two rooms for the family and for receiving guests, and the bedrooms were upstairs. The kitchen, pantry, cellars, milk house and brewhouse were in a separate range, at right angles. The cost was £400 to £800. The offices were a little distance apart, and arranged round a square court with the cattle yard in the centre. On one side was the barn with its threshing mill; on another, a stable divided into single horse stalls; on the third, feeding houses for cattle; and on the fourth, implement sheds and a bothy for the unmarried servants. Grain lofts overlay much of the whole range. The average cost was £500 to £1,500 for farms of 150 to 300 acres or £250 to £1,200 of

Fig. 117.   Corstorphine Bank Farm, Edinburgh, Midlothian.
Interior of henhouse, showing nesting boxes and the high-level
entry. Note the plastered interior. (NMAS: A Fenton, 1961)

rent. A good example of such an up-to-date farm was the Stone of Morphy, St. Cyrus, four miles north-west of Montrose. This cost £1,200, and the rent was £400.[390]

In Aberdeenshire, eighteenth century buildings had walls about 5 ft (1.5 m) high, and measured 30 to 60 ft (9.1-18.3 m) in length by 12 ft (3.7 m) wide internally, and were frequently divided by an internal stone wall known as a stone couple, as a support to the roof. A door in this partition, opposite the lobby, gave access from one end of the house to the other. Divisions could also be by means of box beds, presses and wooden doors.

The house was of one storey, usually in three parts, unceiled. Master and men ate in the kitchen. The farmer sat on the *lang seat* to the back of which was a hinged board measuring three feet (91 cm) by one foot (30 cm), let down at meal times, and held back by a wooden sneck when not in use. In the other end of the house, there was a small table of Scotch fir and a few chairs of fir or ash, with one or sometimes two beds. The middle section was a cellar for milk and ale, and also served as a bedroom for the children. Floors were of clay, or sometimes of natural-faced stones. The hearth lay against a backstone, about 5 ft (1.5 m) long, 1 ft (30 cm) thick and 3 ft (91 cm) high, built into the gable wall. It consisted of a few stones laid with clay and sand. The wooden smoke opening was 2 ft (61 cm) square. If the wind was in a bad direction, the smoke could be driven the full length of the house and come out at the opening at the other end. The

K

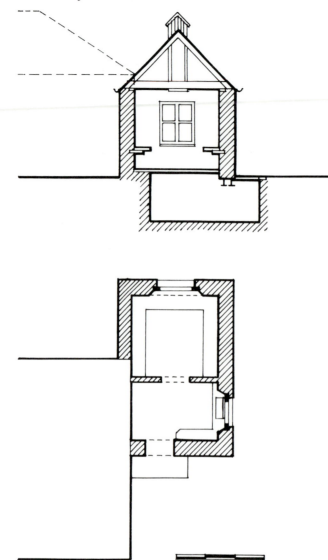

Fig. 118.   Scone Palace Estates, Perthshire. Plan of a
standard milk house with ice well under the floor, dated
27/3/(19)05. As redrawn by Bruce Walker from the original
blueprint.

doors were rarely over 5 ft 6 in (1.7 m) high, and if a window measured 2 ft 6 in (76 cm) high by 1 ft 6 in (45 cm) wide, it was reckoned a fair size. The top part had two or three small panes of glass, and the lower part had two wooden leaves.

Barns, stables and byres were of drystone, with loose earth poured into the heart of the wall, for the first 3 feet (91 cm), and above this was 2 or 3 feet (61-91 cm) of turf. The roof was the same as for the house, but with weaker timbers. There were no windows.[391]

In Banffshire, improved farm houses built by the tenants of Lord Findlater about 1759, between Cullen and Banff, were of two storeys, with a steading on three sides of a

Fig. 119.   Home Farm, Kinfauns Castle, Perthshire. A dairy and scullery in the steading. The dairy is under the octagonal ogee roof and is shaded all round, the scullery is under the square roof and is linked to the dairy by an open but roofed, passageway. (NMAS: 41.6.7.) Designed by Sir Robert Lorimer. The original drawings are in the National Monuments Record, Edinburgh.

Fig. 120.   Drumsleed, Fordoun, Kincardineshire. Drawing of the house and steading, probably showing the original buildings of 1796. (NMAS: C673; from Robertson 1813. Facing 184)

Fig. 121. Drumsleed, Fordoun, Kincardineshire. The steading drawn from a photograph taken in 1969 by R Scott-Morton. The central arch of the 1796 steading appears to have been retained, and four additional arches added to provide a five-bay cart shed under the granary. The original bay has had a sliding door added on the face of the arched opening to provide a lockable unit.

square. On poorer farms, in the 1790s, a two-pane window was beginning to replace an opening closed by a board.[392]

For this area, the layout and contents of the house have been documented in considerable detail. There were, basically, three parts. The *but* end contained a *bun breist* (bound breast), consisting of a box bed and a press, with panelled doors, an eight-day clock, a table, a few chairs, a looking glass, and a cupboard or two. The floor was of earth, and there was a four-paned window which was sometimes boarded. The *ben* end, where the business of everyday living went on, had a similar box bed, a plate rack on the wall, called a *bench,* with a dresser below it holding bowls and dishes, with pails, pots and milking vessels in the space underneath. Opposite the dresser was the standard settle or *lang seat,* with a table hinged to the wall. Between the but- and ben-ends was a sleeping closet with a small window, and the entrance passage or *trance.* The open fireplace had raised sides, *binks,* and two recesses or openings in the wall above for holding the Bible, tobacco and tinder, flint and *fleerish,* and a *candle gullie* or knife for splitting off resinous pieces of fir to give light. The alternative was an oil-burning *eely* (oil) *lamp, dollie,* or *crusie.* The smoke escaped through a smoke-hole in the roof, and the crook hung from the *rantle-tree* above. Canopy chimneys came in only in the course of the nineteenth century in Banffshire, though in areas like Glamis in Angus they were to be found from the early eighteenth century. In the byres, the cattle were bound to stakes, the youngest with *tyave* ropes round their necks. Similar ropes were also used for tethers, for traces, and for horse harness. They were made of bog fir peeled into

Fig. 122.   Drumsleed, Fordoun, Kincardineshire. The steading as rebuilt in 1970, after a fire, with altered arches and now used as living accommodation. (NMAS: 39.27.22)

strands and twisted. The older cows were tied with *sells* or bindings made of a bent piece of birch or rowan.[393]

By 1812, freestone was being got from the Portsoy quarries for building, and for the sides of grates and hearths, because it was little affected by fire. Most farms remained of one storey, with three rooms of medium size and a closet. Floors were still of earth, and the midden was in front of the dwelling-house doors.[394]

Before 1760 in Moray and Nairn, farm houses had no chimneys, and timber floors were rare. There was usually only one hearth. Some had a small glass window. Poorer tenants had turf-built houses, especially in the more highland areas, 'without order or connexion with each other'. There were some also in the lower-lying districts, with no windows, or only a light closed by a hinged board. Such buildings were often one-roomed, with a box bed. In the more stormy districts, houses and offices were often arranged in two lines so as to shelter each others' doors.[395]

By 1811, farm buildings were in general good, usually of two storeys, with a parlour, drawing room, and two or three bedrooms. The one-storey kitchen, as farther south in Scotland, was in an adjoining wing, with a similar thatched store room or cellar on the opposite side.[396]

In the early 1800s, Caithness had a number of farm houses with five to nine 'fire-rooms' in each, and squares of office houses. A farm of 100 to 150 acres needed one stable 24 ft (7.3 m) long by 16 ft (4.9 m) wide, for six horses, with a hay-loft above, and another 15 ft (4.6 m) long by 12 ft (3.7 m) wide for four garrons kept for harrowing or for working a threshing machine in winter; a byre 60 ft (18.3 m) long by 16 ft (4.9 m) wide for about 40 head of small black cattle, and one 18 ft (5.5 m) long by 15 ft (4.6 m) wide for six cart oxen; a threshing barn 50 ft (15.2 m) long by 14 ft (4.3 m) wide and a kiln barn 30 ft (9.1 m) long by 14 ft (4.3 m) wide, with a kiln 14 ft (4.3 m) in diameter and a loft for grain; and a cart shed 40 ft (12.2 m) long by 13 ft (4 m) wide with a grain loft above. This would cost about £1,500, or less if thatch was used. Smaller tenants in farms of from £5 to £20 or £30 rent had low, thatched houses, with horses and cattle at one end. The living room had a central hearth.[397]

In the 1840s, chimneys remained few in areas like Olrig.[398] In Halkirk, the minister complained that the peasant houses ignored the rules of architecture, for they were built in a continuous line, with the barn and kiln on one end, then the house with its three rooms, and then the byre and stable.[399]

Orkney, though separated from Caithness by the Pentland Firth, nevertheless shares many of the same building characteristics, especially where these are affected by the nature of the flagstone that is available in both areas. All the farms were at one time longhouses, said in 1773 to have been built half underground—probably into the slope of a hill—'where people and cattle all sleep under the same roof, and sometimes the calf has a better apartment than the heir of a family that can boast of twenty-four generations of uninterrupted lineal succession'.[400]

In 1808 there was no regular court of farm offices in Orkney, though by 1814 a number had appeared in several islands. The small size of the farms, few exceeding 40 acres arable,[401] did not encourage lavish buildings, so change was slower than in Mainland Scotland. In the 1840s, central hearths with freestanding stone-built backs were common. The animals still often shared the same roof. Windows were rare.[402]

In the Highland area, in Argyll, a stable, barn and byre under one roof were noted in 1794, the barn overlying the other two. Hay was dried in the barn and to facilitate this there were in it branders of wood.[403] By this decade, many of the more substantial tenants and storemasters had good houses, but the poorer tenants, who were in the majority, had long, low houses. In Islay in 1772, the houses were of stone, chimneyless, and with no doors other than a 'heap of faggots', and in Jura there were both oblong and conical houses made of sod-covered branches, again with doors consisting of a faggot of birch twigs.[404] Between 1789 and 1793 in Gigha and Cara, two new public houses with two storeys and garrets had been built, along with a malt kiln and granary, all slated. The tacksman's house also had two storeys, with garrets. The houses of the ordinary folk in Tiree were of the blackhouse form, with walls 4 to 6 ft (1.2-1.8 m) thick, consisting of an outer and an inner face with a core of sandy earth.[405]

In the 1840s, groups of three or four families could still be found in one farm, living in longhouses often built of drystone. The township of Auchindrain, now preserved as the Museum of Argyll Farming Life, is a surviving example. In Kilfinan there were still the 'old black huts'.[406]

In Inverness-shire, there are surprises from the seventeenth century, for even then St. Kilda had a kind of street running between the houses of its farming village. The walls of the houses had bed spaces built into their thickness.[407] On the mainland however, the houses in the villages were often irregularly placed, with a few huts, and barns and stables of smaller size. These houses had peat fires in the middle of the floor, with a smoke-hole in the roof. Floors were of earth, damp and uneven. The buildings were in general longhouses, with a living end containing a central hearth with no chimney, and with or without a smoke-hole, separated from the byre by a slight partition. People made use of the byre end, according to an account in 1750, at weddings, when the partition was removed and a floor of boards, propped up on sods laid over the byre floor, was strewn with rushes or heather tops.[408] In the houses of the lower classes, trees or branches were laid around the central hearth, 'behind which they lay heath for beds, where the family sleep promiscuously, few of them having any other covering than their body clothes'. This information, in a report to the Board of Manufactures, related to the area of Lochcarron, Lochbroom, and Glenmoriston.[409]

In the Hebrides in 1775, Samuel Johnson saw gentlemen's houses with glass windows, boarded floors and chimneys. The ordinary folk, however, had huts of loose stones, sometimes of blackhouse form with an inner and an outer skin. There were two rooms, the first getting its light from the door, the second from the smoke-hole.[410] In the 1790s, it was said of Moy and Dalarossie that the central fire was still used, with the family sitting round it in a circle,[411] and in fact the central hearth survived in use well into the twentieth century in the Hebrides.

The difference in quality between the houses of the poorer folk and those of the gentlemen and wealthier tenants became increasingly marked at this period. Towards the east coast, in parts of Strathspey, Badenoch, Urquhart, on some estates in the Aird, on the Rivers Lochy and Spean, etc, farm houses were of a better style. Good farm houses were mostly of two storeys, covered with blue or grey slate, with separate rooms, sometimes painted timber work, and plastered walls and glazed windows. The offices were arranged in a square.[412]

The early nineteenth century situation in the Hebrides was similar. Tacksmen's houses had improved much in the later 1700s. They were of two storeys, and included a kitchen. The houses of the gentlemen had up to three storeys, with windows in the roofs and garrets. They tended to face west or south-west, which was the wrong direction for the weather. Porches had to be built before the main doors. Tenants and sub-tenants lived in poorer buildings, with walls of stone cemented with clay. A type of house recommended in 1811 was 30 × 15 ft (9.1 × 4.6 m) internally, by 10 ft (3 m) high, with windows in the gables and side walls, each 2 ft (61 cm) high and 3 or 4 ft (91 cm-1.2 m) broad. The fact that this was recommended, however, implies that there were few such places.[413]

In the 1840s in Harris, families, horses and cows lived for seven months of each year in their houses of unhewn stone with clay mortar, and straw thatch. The rest of the time they were at their shieling huts in the hills.[414] Houses in North Uist were better than in some areas. Many had chimneys, glass windows and box beds. The women swept and sanded their earthern floors daily.[415] In Barra, the blackhouses had no windows or chimneys, though round openings in the roofing thatch admitted light. There were one or more at each side of the house, which could be opened or shut according to the way the wind was blowing. There was a smoke-hole in the roof. Horses and cattle were in the same building during winter and spring, and possessions were few: 'they have seldom much furniture to boast of; sometimes not a chair to sit upon, a bed to sleep on, or bedclothes to cover them from the severity of the night air'.[416] In the parish of Kilmuir in Skye, lotters and small tenants lived in stone buildings, many of which still also held the cattle. There were usually three units in them, separated by stone walls or partitions of wattle-work, straw or reeds. The middle unit was the main living area, with a central fire, and the crook and links hanging from the rafters. The furnishings consisted of a wooden bench that could hold six to eight people. Across from it was the wife's armchair of plaited straw, with the cradle, spinning wheel, cupboard, and large, covered dye pot. The inner room could serve either as a barn or as a bedroom. The outer room was the byre. The thatch was removed annually for use as top dressing on the potato ground.[417] In Portree, the houses of the poorer tenants had no chimneys, and there were no divisions between people and cattle.[418] In Snizort, the houses were as in Kilmuir, sometimes with a separate place for threshing the corn. The long wooden bench was said to be a mark of the more respectable houses, whereas poorer folk might have no more than a row of turf-covered stones. In a few cases, there were panes of glass in the thatch, to serve as windows.[419] In Strath, the internal partition of stone or wattle, the *hallan*, was only a few feet high.[420] In Duirinish, it was noted that the single door was next to the byre end of the house. The cattle were sometimes fastened by a straw rope to the rafters, whilst the young animals roamed free. Cleaning out took place twice a year, at the beginning of winter and the beginning of spring, when the potatoes were planted. Anyone entering the house had to cross over the manure. In some cases, a small space was railed off for stowing potatoes and fish. There were usually a couple of bedsteads with straw, heather or ferns to sleep on, though some simply slept on the floor. There could be a table and a few chairs, or no chairs at all, but one or two stools instead. Walls were 6 to 7 ft (1.8-2.1 m) thick, with earthen cores 18 in to 2 ft (46-61 cm) thick, and green sods growing on the outer wall-ledge. There was seldom more than one window at the edge of the roof, and this could be stuffed with straw or rags in windy weather.[421]

In Ross and Cromarty, the Black Isle had longhouses in the eighteenth century, with a common door for men and animals, and no internal partitions.[422] By about 1810, the main farmers in the Lochcarron and Applecross area had good buildings. The smaller farms, however, remained as longhouses. Beds were said to be sometimes slung above the cattle, and dung was cleared out once a year.[423]

By the 1840s, longhouses in Gairloch parish still had a common door for men and beasts, but some farmers were building byres near the houses. In Lochcarron there were still some turf houses, but most were of stone, and frequently built with lime. The fire was kindled alongside the wall, or on a stone in the centre of the floor, which was of clay or mud. Chimneys were rare. Though there was only one door for men and animals, there was a partition of boards, wattle or stone between the byre and the house, with a door in the middle of it. The windows were often only wooden shutters. In Glenshiel, there was usually a division into three compartments: a living and sleeping room, a store room for potatoes, and a byre for the cows and stirks. There was one window, of which the upper part was sometimes glazed, the lower part having wooden shutters. The fire was set against a backstone, and had a smoke-hole above. Pots and pans were supported by a wooden crook. In Stornoway in Lewis, all the houses were said to be bad except those of the tacksmen. They were longhouses. If stones were available, the walls were built 4 to 6 ft (1.2-1.8 m) thick with a central core of earth or pounded moss. The house doors were very low. Few houses had windows with even a single pane of glass. There was a smoke-hole to clear excess smoke from the central fire, and another opening for light near the wall-top, which was stuffed with straw at night. The laird and his lady had ordered the erection of a partition between men and animals, as well as one window at least, but the tenants were not keen and though these innovations were sometimes carried out, it was 'sorely against the will of the people'. In Lochs, there were no partitions to separate people and cattle.[424] Pressure from the lairds continued, for in 1872 the crofters in Barvas, Lewis, were made to improve their houses, with two doors and a division between house and byre. The doors, windows and woodwork were supplied to them.[425]

In Sutherland in 1800, the two-storey manse at Kildonan had two low buildings stretching out in front of it from each end of the manse. On the west was a nursery, a kitchen, and a byre, divided by cat-and-clay partitions; on the east side was a barn and stable. To the north-east of the stackyard a flimsy stone and clay building was fitted up as a kiln.[426] In the Highland straths towards Assynt, the houses had smoke-holes, and another hole in the roof, closed when it was windy by a sod or a bunch of straw. At one end of the building, cattle were tied to wall-stakes by means of birch withies round their necks.[427] The houses were built on a downhill slope, with the byre at the lower end. There was one door, and a central fire, which was paved around with stones, but otherwise the floor was of earth. On new lots, however, houses were of stone, and the byre no longer formed part of the dwelling.[428]

By the 1840s, in Dornoch, the old turf houses had been largely replaced by neat cottages of stone and clay, harled with lime. Chimneys replaced the former smoke-holes and the central hearth had vanished. Of Rogart parish, it was said that 'in no part of the North Highlands are there so many well built neat looking cottages as in . . . Sutherland'. In Durness, some longhouses with central fires were still to be found.[429]

Although in the 1820s it was becoming more common for byre and house to be separated by a partition, in Tongue such division walls were still only being put up in the 1880s.[430]

In Shetland, sources of the 1790s are unusually quiet about the nature of the houses, though the majority evidently occurred in township groups, apart from the many small farms established as new *outsets* in former grazing areas to provide homes for fishermen. However, according to a writer of 1809, the houses were nearly the same everywhere. Chimneys were beginning to appear especially in the best room, though the living room often retained its central fire and smoke-hole.[431] The houses were generally erected as longhouses at the proprietors' expense,[432] though the very much poorer quality outhouses were often left to the tenants.[433]

In Quendale, the houses were said to be better than elsewhere in Shetland. By 1824, windows were becoming more general, though the smoke-hole still served to admit light too. A common door to house and byre was usual, and most houses had a turf partition across the room, carried up to the height of the house to make a store for food as well as a bedroom at one end. But in Quendale this old style was passing, and slate roofs, regular windows and separate byres had become the norm.

Elsewhere, older traditions remained. At the house of the farmer at the Hill of Aithsness, Vementry, some stepping stones led to the byre door, through which the visitor entered. A door led into a room with a central fire, a clay floor and soot-covered walls. There were too long wooden forms for the servants of each sex, and a high and separate chair for the mistress of the house. A rough division divided this main room from a small, private room, containing two or three box-beds. The guest climbed a ladder—on each side of which were stored barrels of meal and oats, ropes, fishing nets and rods, and fishing lines—to reach a loft room with a bed. The same arrangement of two rows of servants, separated by sex, with the laird on a high seat at the end, was also found at the small laird's house at Burrafirth in Aithsting.[434] At Vailey Sound, the blacksmith's house was also entered through the byre. Around the central fire were soft turf seats for the family. The smithy was at the far end.[435]

By the 1840s, many farm houses had been rebuilt on an improved plan in Bressay, Burra and Quarff.

In Walls, the byre usually still lay in front of the house, which could only be entered through the byre. In Sandsting and Aithsting, the proprietor sometimes built the houses and charged rent from the time of entry, or else the tenant built his own and sat rent-free for seven to nine years. Once erected, the houses were not much looked after, however. Chimneys were rare, but some houses had two to six holes in the roof for letting out smoke and letting in light. The smoke-hole had a movable board on top to adjust the draught. Window openings were sometimes filled with a bladder, or untanned sheepskin cleaned of wool and stretched on a frame.[436]

The standard cottage in the late nineteenth century was 28 to 30 ft (8.5-9.1 m) long by 8 to 10 ft (2.4-3 m) broad. Side walls were 4 to 6 ft high (1.2-1.8 m), with fairly steeply pitched gables. The roof was of turf and roped thatch. A wooden partition about a third of the way along separated the living room and ben-end. The living room also served as a bedroom for family and servants. It had an 18 in to 2 ft (46-61 cm) square window, and two or three large roof openings to let out smoke and admit light. Proper chimneys were still rare. There was a long wooden settle at each side of the fire, a table, a spinning-wheel, and a few kitchen chairs. The floor was of earth. The ben-end served as a bedroom for the parents, and best room for receiving visitors of standing, such as the minister. It was ceiled with lath and plaster, and floored with wood. There was a proper chimney in the thickness of the gable at this end. There was a window, and the walls were plastered and whitewashed.[437] There were sometimes one or two lofts above, and the byre was now usually separate.[438]

8

The Housing of Farm Workers

IN reviewing the evidence for the century up to 1850, one of the gaps that becomes evident is that of improved housing for the farm workers. Until the latter half of the nineteenth century, relatively little attention was paid to this matter, and in general, accommodation for stock on the improving farms took priority over that for workers. Before this period, unmarried male and female servants lived for the most part in the farm house or in the attached buildings. Other workers, often married, had cot-houses, or cottar-houses, sometimes in groups which have left the place name 'Cottown' on the map. 'Cot' originally had the sense of a small house, a shelter for a shepherd or the like, but by the sixteenth century the compounds 'cot house', 'coitter house' occur in sources which relate them clearly to farm workers.[439] Such houses were often to be found in groups of four or more, sometimes in clusters, and sometimes in a row near the farm steading. Sometimes they were single. This was also true of Berwickshire.[440]

In 1661, it was observed by a traveller passing through East Lothian to Edinburgh that the houses for farm workers were 'pitiful Cots, built of Stone, and covered with Turves, having in them but one Room, many of them no Chimneys, the Windows very small Holes, and not glazed'.[441] By the 1790s, most such cot-houses had been pulled down in the parish of Whittinghame in East Lothian.[442] Yester had some two-roomed houses in 1792, each room being occupied by a separate family.[443] At this period in the South-East, the married occupant of a cottar house generally paid for its rent through the work of his wife in reaping, carting stacks into the barn for threshing, and winnowing. Summer grass and winter fodder for the worker's cow were supplied by the master. Single workers remained part of the farmer's household.[444]

By the 1840s, the social conscience of the country was beginning to start pricking. The minister of Saltoun parish was complaining of immorality due to the one-roomed dwellings of the peasantry,[445] which could contain families of eight to ten persons, as in Morham. Two-roomed cottar houses were being built at Morham Mains, however,[446] and in Aberlady there was 'ground to hope, that the cottages on every farm will, at no very distant period, have two apartments instead of one'.[447] In Pencaitland, Lady Ruthven was pursuing a particularly enlightened policy by building three-roomed houses containing a kitchen-cum-sleeping room, a bedroom, and one for dairy produce and household necessities, all with the walls plastered internally.[448]

The picture was not everywhere so rosy. At the same period, the houses of day-labourers in Tranent and Haddington had fowls roosting in the rafters and pig sties under the window. The walls were unplastered and the floors were of earth. Bedding might be no more than a pile of straw.[449] But such descriptions in reports often have a bias towards the worst, though it is not to be doubted that workers at the day-labourer level, multitudes of whom worked at least part-time on the farms, were for the most part poorly housed.

Alexander Somerville, for example, was brought up in a house in a row in

Craigton farmhouse

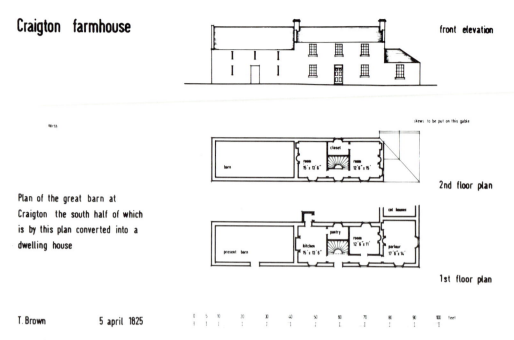

front elevation

2nd floor plan

Plan of the great barn at
Craigton the south half of which
is by this plan converted into a
dwelling house

1st floor plan

T. Brown   5 april 1825

Fig. 123. Craigton, Abercorn, West Lothian. A farmhouse and barn converted from the former great barn in 1825. Barns of this size are most unusual on Scottish farms. The house provided is typical of many farmhouses built at that date on medium to large farms. Drawn by Ingval Maxwell from T. Brown's original drawing. (NMAS: C2412)

Berwickshire, as one of eight children. The living space was about 12 ft by 14 ft (3.7 × 4.3 m), and not quite high enough at the walls for a man to stand upright. The room was not ceiled, and had a clay floor. Cupboards were totally lacking. The grate was made by the iron bars the tenants brought with them, and took away again when they left. The only divisions were made by the beds. The window consisted of four small panes at one side, and even this might be carried from house to house by the tenants.[450]

The advantage of cot-houses and cot-towns was that they served as reservoirs for manpower at times like harvest, when a plentiful supply of labour was needed to get the ripe crops in safely. Even as late as the 1840s, the farms of Coates and Hairlaw in Gladsmuir parish, East Lothian, kept labour forces of 76 and 87 respectively.[451]

The next twenty years saw considerable improvements, as George Hope of Fenton Barns pointed out at a public meeting on labourers' dwellings in 1861: 'Instead of being four bare walls covered with thatch, having a small hole twelve or fifteen inches (30-38 cm) square, with a fixed piece of glass, for a window, and a door covered with key-holes, made to suit the size of the lock of each successive occupant, on many estates they had been rebuilt in a commodious and comfortable manner.'[452] Even then, a great deal remained to do, and credit must be given to the Highland and Agricultural Society of Scotland which, as early as 1832, was offering premiums for essays on the construction of improved dwellings for the labouring classes. The prize-winner was an Edinburgh architect, George Smith, and houses of the types illustrated in his plans

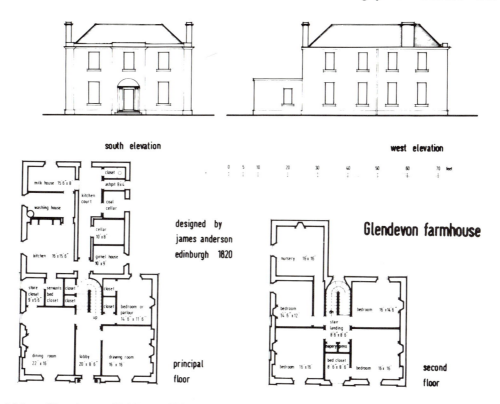

Fig. 124.   Glendevon, Kirkliston, West Lothian. Farmhouse designed by James Anderson of Edinburgh in 1820 and typical of large farmhouses of that period. Note the double-bank plan and piend roof behind a low parapet and the Georgian style detailing of the facade. Drawn from the original by Ingval Maxwell. (NMAS: C2416)

remain in the Lothians to this day.[453] The influence of the Society may be seen in buildings like those erected at Yorkstone by Mr Dundas of Arniston. They were for four families, arranged two by two in line with spaces between for the outside coal houses, privies, and ashpits. At Cauldcoats nearby there was a double house, each unit having a rear annex containing a sink, a privy and a space for coal, in this case accessible from inside.[454] Though standards in the South-East were higher than in many other areas, matching the scale of the farms, nevertheless this pattern of improvement was general, and cottar houses, usually in paired units for two families, spread throughout the country in the second half of the nineteenth century.

But the picture often remained black. In 1871, the *Fourth Report of the Royal Commission on the Employment of Children, Young Persons, and Women in Agriculture (Scotland)* spoke of stables, byres, cowsheds, dilapidated farmhouses and dog kennels being converted into labourers' cottages.[455] In the same year, according to *Fraser's Magazine* (May), the agricultural labourer lived in disgraceful conditions, in a one-roomed house divided in two by box-beds placed crossways, and behind these the cow with her tail to the door. Forty per cent of the houses in Berwick and Roxburgh had only one window or none at all. Some of the one-roomed houses between Ailsa and Girvan

Fig. 125.   Duntarvie, Abercorn, West Lothian. Typical late nineteenth-century large farmhouse unusually linked to the farm steading but standing in its own ornamental garden. (IM: 8.4)

had up to ten or eleven occupants. The same was true of farmworkers' houses on the Queensberry Estates.[456] The pattern of improvements, therefore, was patchy.

Accommodation for unmarried workers was for the most part poor. In the South-East, and in Fife and Angus from the late 1700s, single men and seasonal migrant workers were housed in bothies, which were either rooms in the farm-steading or sometimes a separate building near the steading. Here the men slept and ate, usually making their own food. Angus and the Mearns took the lead in the development of bothies, which became common there and in parts of Fife, the Lothians, Berwickshire, Easter Ross and Caithness. When William Cobbett travelled into Scotland in 1832, he noted a bothy for four men near Edinburgh, and another near Dunfermline, with three wooden beds for six men in a room measuring 16 by 18 ft (4.8-5.4 m), one window and

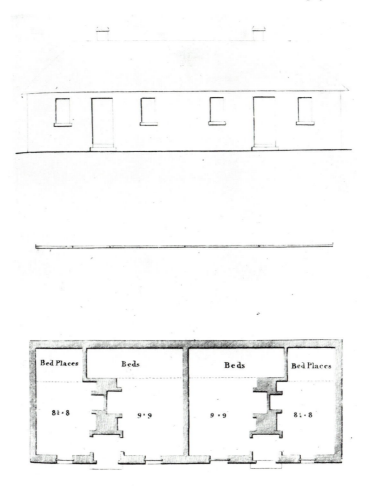

Fig. 126.   Farm Cottages, West Lothian. Semi-detached two-room cottages with central fireplace. Cottages of this type appear in various parts of the country in the early nineteenth-century but their popularity appears to be limited to the first half of the century. Beds sited along the north wall were very common at this time. (NMAS: C3988)

an earthen floor.[457] A Wick minister wrote in *The Scotsman* of 23 October 1860 that Caithness bothies were sinks of physical and moral filth and pollution, where well-grown lads and unmarried men and women lived together.[458] In Cromarty, Hugh Miller lived as an apprentice stonemason in an old corn-kiln used as a bothy for 24 men. It was no more than 30 ft (9.1 m) long, with a row of beds formed of undressed slab along each side, filled with hay.[459]

Bothies lasted in places like Angus till the coming of the tractor, during and following the First World War.[460] The same was true of another kind of accommodation, on small and medium-sized farms in North-East and East Central Scotland. It was described as *kitchying* in the North-East, from the fact that the men slept in a room known as the *chaumer,* but took their meals in the farm kitchen. In Morayshire the room was called a *berrick* (barrack). Such men's rooms were still being included in the steadings of farms

Fig. 127. Double Cottages, Midlothian: 1795. Semi-detached double-bank plan cottages with gabled thatched roof. Although designs of this type were produced and published, they appear to have had little effect on the country as a whole—the single-bank plan being more generally adopted even towards the end of the nineteenth century. (NMAS: C3924; from Robertson 1795. Facing 166)

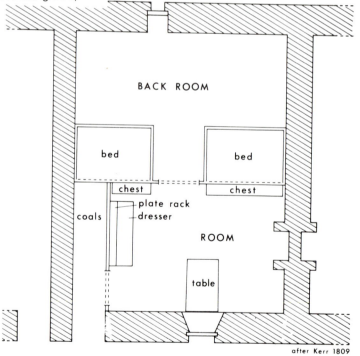

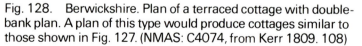

Fig. 128. Berwickshire. Plan of a terraced cottage with double-bank plan. A plan of this type would produce cottages similar to those shown in Fig. 127. (NMAS: C4074, from Kerr 1809. 108)

Fig. 129.   Monzie, Crieff, Perthshire. A group of cottages for estate workers forming a square in front of the factor's house—the two-storey house in the centre. The caption claims that the factor and workers resided there in the sixteenth and seventeenth centuries but it is unlikely that these buildings are earlier than the late eighteenth century and could be much later. (NMAS: C3009)

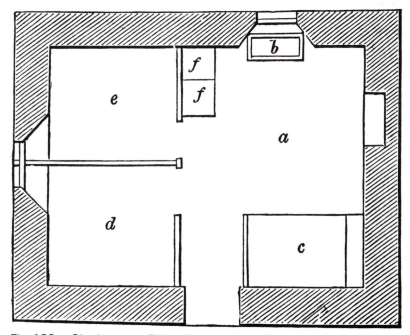

Fig. 130.   Single-storey Bothy, Berwickshire. Shows the floor plan of an improved form of bothy. The spartan nature of the accommodation is clearly shown: a. The kitchen or living space; b. sink; c. double bed; d, e. bed closets; f. cupboard. (NMAS: C 7705; from Kerr 1809. 108)

L

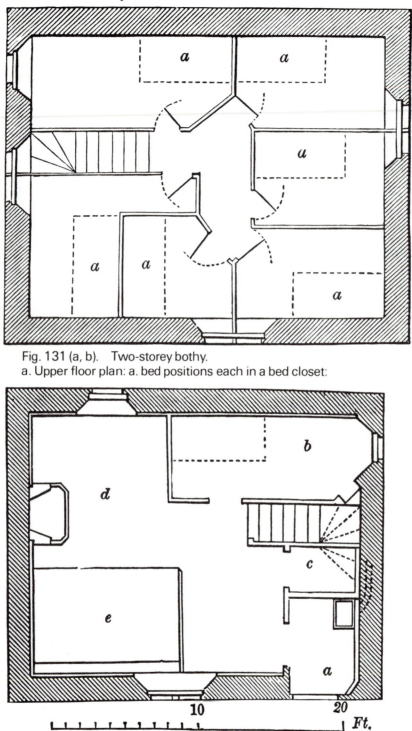

Fig. 131 (a, b). Two-storey bothy.
a. Upper floor plan: a. bed positions each in a bed closet:

b. Ground floor plan: a. scullery; b. bed closet; c. cupboard under stair; d. kitchen or living area; e. bed. (NMAS: C7703 & C7704; from Stephens and Burn 1861. 119)

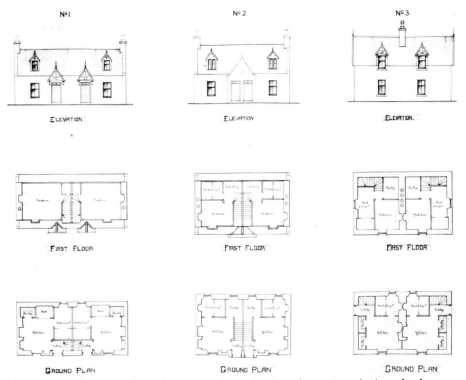

Fig. 132.   Farm Cottages, Aberdeenshire. Late nineteenth-century designs for farm cottages by James Duncan, Architect, Turriff and now in the archive of Alan Keir & Smith, Architects, Turriff. Note the bed closets off the principal bedroom and kitchen.
(NMAS: C4101)

built in the early 1900s and later. Improved versions of these rooms continued to be built into the 1930s.

If in the nineteenth century it was the ministers who repeatedly expressed concern about farmworkers' housing, in this present century the overtones have been of a more political nature. Throughout the centuries, farmworkers' cottages have been tied. They belonged to the farmer, and undoubtedly maintenance was minimal in many cases. This lack of regard was encouraged by the fact that up till the time of the Second World War, it was customary for cottars to move annually to another farm. There was, therefore, little continuity of occupation. And the men who lived in chaumers, the unmarried workers, were even more peripatetic, often moving every six months. Nevertheless, though Joseph Duncan, writing in 1926, said that nothing more cheerless than an Aberdeenshire chaumer can be imagined, this was not so in the memory of one of the present writers, who knew chaumers within the last 30 years that, with their beds and kists and fireplace, were pleasant places indeed. As in other things, standards are relative, and there were good and bad chaumers of which different people had different kinds of experience. By the 1950s, chaumers and bothies alike had become things of the past. Tied cottar houses remain, but usually improved, harled, with water and electricity laid on and sometimes with two units knocked into one to make a commodious dwelling.[461]

Fig. 133.   Foula, Shetland: 1902. Cottage interior with central
hearth, without backstone, with the kettle suspended on the crook
and links, and fish drying on a rectangular brander centred over the
hearth. Note the simple nature of the furniture and of the partition.
(H. B. Curwen: OE144)

Fig. 134.   Aird, Benbecula, Inverness-shire: 1934. Blackhouse interior with central hearth, without backstone. Note the adjustable crook on a strap hanger supporting the griddle. The occupant is Angus MacEachen. (Göteborgs Historiska Museet: B5188)

Fig. 135.   North Uist, Inverness-shire. Welsh dressers on the north wall of a cottage interior. (NMAS: 7.13.3)

Fig. 136.   Bridge of Brown, Tomintoul, Banffshire.
Cottage interior with timber lum and wood-lined ceiling.
(NMAS: 29.9.5)

Fig. 137.   Brockan, Stromness, Orkney, 1920s–30s.
Cottage interior with timber lum. Note the hangings and
wallpaper and the large pot set in the fireplace. (W. Hourston,
per P. Leith)

Fig. 138.   Hubie, Fetlar, Shetland: 1963. A neat cottage interior, perhaps with flush canopy chimney (see Fig. 140—items 9 and 10). Note the frieze of magazine pages under the mantelpiece and the waxcloth hanging. (NMAS: 2.5.12A)

Fig. 139.   Caithness. Fireplace with cast iron range by "D. R. Simpson & Son, Ironmongers, Wick". Note the settee to one side of the fireplace and the brass ornaments on the mantelpiece. (NMAS: x.3.3)

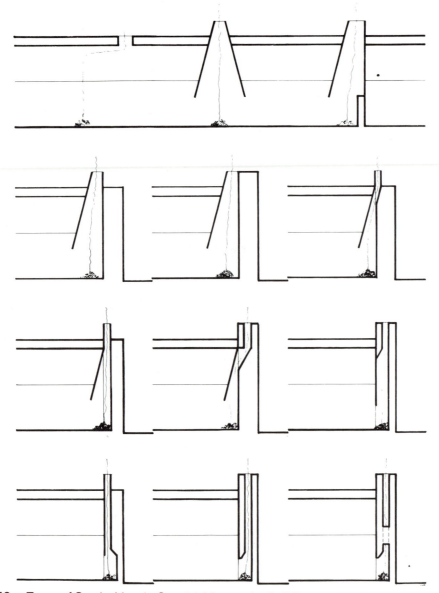

Fig. 140.   Types of Smoke Vent in Scottish Vernacular Buildings.
1. Central hearth with or without a backstone and vented through a hole in the roof or in the apex of the gable. 2. Central hearth with suspended canopy chimney. 3. Central hearth with backstone supporting a canopy chimney. 4. Gable hearth with canopy chimney. This may also have a backstone. 5. Gable hearth with canopy chimney carried up the inside face of false stone chimney heads. This may also have a backstone. 6. Gable hearth with reduced canopy chimney let into gable and capped with a chimney pot on the ridge of the gable. 7. Gable hearth and smoke channel both let into the gable and combined with a reduced canopy chimney and leading to a chimney pot on the ridge of the gable. 8. Gable hearth with reduced canopy chimney let into top of gable and terminating in a stone-built chimney head. 9. Gable hearth and smoke channel both let into the gable and combined with a "flush" canopy leading to a stone-built chimney head. 10. Gable hearth deeply recessed into gable with recessed smoke channel combined with flush "canopy" leading to a chimney pot on the ridge of the gable. 11. Deeply recessed hearth with straight gable flue leading to stone chimney head. 12. Deeply recessed hearth with gable flue incorporating offset to prevent downdraught and leading to stone chimney head.
In each case where "stone" chimney head is mentioned "brick" is equally valid and perhaps is the more common material. (Top line: 1—3; 2nd line: 4—6; 3rd line; 7—9; bottom line; 10—12) (all left to right)

Fig. 141. Newton of Glamis, Glamis, Angus. Fireplace with cast iron cheeks, swey, smoke/draught control and mantelpiece. (NMAS: C6562)

Fig. 142. Strathmiglo, Strathmiglo, Fife. Dining room of upper middle class house at the end of the nineteenth century. (NMAS: C2469; Miss Sherratt, Auchtermuchty, Fife)

Fig. 143.   Churchyard, Banff, Banffshire. Gravestone with carving of fourposter bed with hangings. (NMAS: 33.9.27)

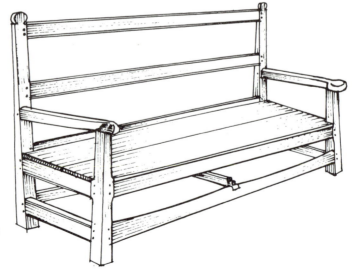

Fig. 144.   Long Settle. Drawing of a simple "long settle", a type of furniture common throughout Scotland in the nineteenth century. From Shetland. (NMAS: C5806)

Fig. 145. North Lodge of Rossie Priory, Abernyte, Perthshire. Steps to the attic showing one method of achieving a reasonable tread with a very steep rise. (NMAS: xv.35.6)

Fig. 146 (a, b). Latches & Locks. a. Various types of common latches and locks. Locally made timber locks were also common on buildings up to the mid-nineteenth century. (NMAS: C7706; from Stephens and Burn 1861. 404) b. Angus door latch with snib. BW

A

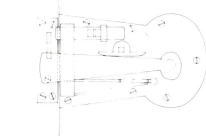

Door Latch with Snib.

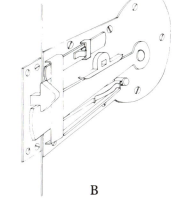

B

9

The Influence of Technology on Farm Buildings

OF all the technological innovations of the late eighteenth century, none had as profound an influence on farm buildings as the threshing mill, of which the world's first fully practical example was made in Scotland by Andrew Meikle in 1786. The main influence, however, came not so much from the machine itself, but from its motive power whether horses, water, or, less often, wind. Even before 1786, the simple, ubiquitous, hand-operated flail played its part in barn design, for the roof had to be high enough to allow for the overhead swinging movement of the 'souple' or beating end of the flail, and normally a special clay floor was prepared on which the threshing took place. These floors were normally laid across the barn adjoining the space between the doors on which the winnowing was done.[462]

The threshing-mill machinery fitted easily into the standard width of farm buildings—a width developed to fulfil the requirements of stables, byres, cart sheds etc, whilst being an economic span for simple A-frame coupled roofs.

It was mainly in terms of its position that it influenced the layout of the steading. The threshing barn was central to the working of the farm. Unthreshed sheaves were kept in the stackyard as was excess straw. A close relationship between stackyard and barn was therefore desirable to minimise handling. After threshing, both grain and straw had to be stored until required. This was done in the granary and straw barn respectively. The granary had to be capable of storing the following year's seed, the surplus grain for sale, and the grain prepared on a weekly or fortnightly basis for feeding to the livestock. The granary therefore had to be sited to allow easy access to carts, for the transporting of grain to the fields or market. Easy access to the bruiser and subsequently to the stable, byre and poultry houses was also important. The straw barn, for the storage of straw for day-to-day use, also required to be close to both the threshing mill and to the stables, byres, cattle courts or yards etc. where it was used.

These requirements, together with the need for a power source to drive the mill, created a planning problem to which certain standard solutions were developed, depending on the type of farm and the acreage involved. This problem could be further complicated by an obvious wish to use the engine to power other smaller machines such as cereal bruisers, turnip and hay cutters, saws, grindstones, and, on some of the larger dairy farms, power churns. Site conditions and the power source also modified these standard layouts.

There was no further basic change in the principles used for threshing until the advent of the combine harvester, although many different power sources were utilised. The mills were modified and improved, and mobile mills were developed in the latter half of the nineteenth century.

With the invention of the threshing mill existing sources of power were employed to drive the machinery. By 1814, Andrew Gray, the Engineer, had published plans for threshing machines to be driven by two horses, by water or by four horses and by wind

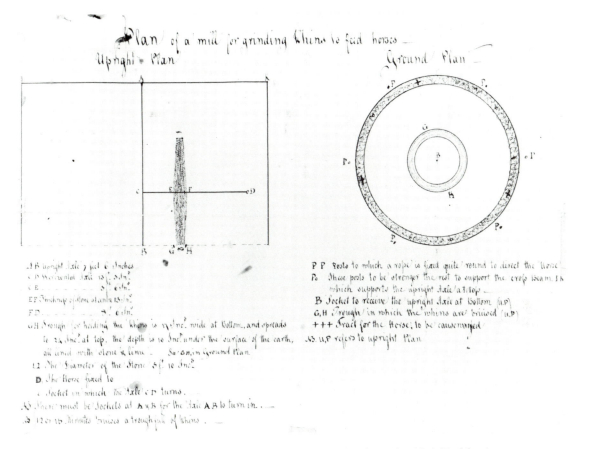

Fig. 147.   Melville, **Monimail**, Fife. Manuscript drawing from the Melville Muniments showing diagrammatic dimensions for a Whin Mill. These were used to bruise whins for horse fodder in winter. Fife Folk Museum. (NMAS: C210)

or by six horses.[463] All three machines incorporated a new system of yoking, invented by Walter Samuel, blacksmith at Niddry, Linlithgow. This system of yoking was designed to ensure that each horse pulled its weight, and the advantages listed include 'a real saving of labour; for it is no exaggeration to affirm, that five horses, yoked by this apparatus to a threshing machine will perform with equal ease the labour of six horses, of equal strength and weight, yoked in the common way, each horse being independent of the rest'.[464] It also saved wear and tear on the machine by providing a regular and uniform movement eliminating the sudden jerks and strains with which horse machinery had previously been troubled—'the machinery moving with that kind of uniformity as if driven by water'. Very few farms could afford this belt as well as braces approach to the power source and most threshing mills surviving today were built originally with a single engine, normally utilising either water or horses.

Wind-power was the most expensive to harness. Accidents could happen because the sails could not be shifted if a brisk gale arose, until an invention by Meikle allowed the sails to be taken in by a rope worked from inside the mill.[465] Gray described a means of

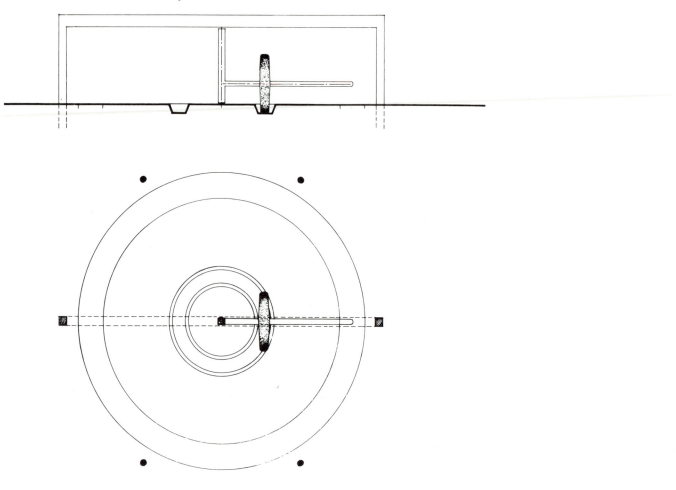

Fig. 148.   Melville, Monimail, Fife. Scale drawing made from the diagram and measurements given in Fig. 147. (BW: xii. 79)

controlling the vanes automatically at an earlier date, but though too cumbersome for general adoption then, it became standard on all 19th century windmills.[466]

A wind-powered machine cost at least twice as much to construct as a similar machine using water or horses and it was not every farm that could afford this expense or that was ideally situated to utilise the available wind. This in some ways explains the relatively few remains of wind-powered threshing mills in Scotland, though by 1813 they were said to have been numerous and preferred to horse threshing mills because they did not interrupt the ordinary work of the farm to the same degree. Nevertheless horse mills remained most numerous. In a circle of three miles round the home of the writer of the Report on the Agriculture of Berwickshire, there were four driven by water, four by wind, and ten by horses.[467]

Fig. 149.   Whitelums, Gartly, Aberdeenshire. Sketch of a simple whin mill from an old photograph. The stone from this mill can still be seen on the east side of the road as one passes the farm. A similar stone but with a cogged circumference is at the Agricultural Museum, Ingliston. (BW: 1.80)

Fig. 150.   The Cock, Strathdon, Aberdeenshire. Old farm limekiln built into side of small hillock to south of farm. (NMAS: 32.23.18)

Fig. 151.   Holland Farm, Papa Westray, Orkney. Corn kiln attached to gable of barn, with large stone-slated conical-roofed horse-engine house in background. (NMAS: xviii. 28.29A)

Fig. 152.   Hillhead, Wick, Caithness. Bottle-shaped corn kiln attached to gable of barn. Barn kilns of any type are rare on farms outside Orkney and Caithness. (NMAS: vi.53.17)

Fig. 153. Denmill, Fordoun, Kincardineshire. A mill building with attached corn kiln. This kiln has a permanent louvred kiln vent of a type more normally associated with the kilns in whisky distilleries.

Three threshing windmills are known to survive in Angus, each of the farms being situated on an exposed ridge. These farms are Bankhead, Forfar; Dumbarrow, Dunnichen; and Bolsham, Kinnell. None of these structures have sails or machinery. The windmill tower at Bolsham was later used as a chimney for a steam engine and now serves as a water tower, a large tank having been fitted in the upper section. The

M

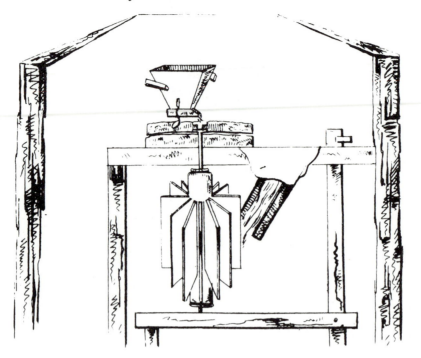

Fig. 154.   Shetland: 1822. Print of a horizontal water mill of the type found mainly in the Islands and Western Highlands. From S. Hibbert, *Description of the Shetland Islands* Edinburgh 1822. Plate 6, Fig 21. (NMAS: C1596)

windmill tower was normally about 12 ft (3.6 m) in diameter internally and the tower about 33 ft (9.9 m) high to the base of the cap.[468] Four sails appear to have been the norm, fitted with wind vanes.

Steam power for threshing purposes appeared shortly after the invention of Meikle's threshing machine with steam-powered mills operating in 1799 in the West Riding of Yorkshire;[469] in 1800 in Norfolk;[470] and in 1803 in East Lothian.[471] These were single examples, however, and although a few steam-powered threshing mills were built, and a high pressure steam engine was produced by 1832,[472] steam power can be considered as experimental until the second half of the nineteenth century when these early ideas were consolidated and developed on entirely practical lines. The early distribution pattern of steam-engine sites appears to be closely related to coal mines or ports where cheap fuel could be obtained.

Expense was again the main restriction on the use of steam-powered mills and they are found only on larger farms, as the steam engine cost about the same as a windmill to install.

Water and horse power were the popular power sources and the rate of spread of threshing mills using these power sources was dramatic, testifying to the urgent need that was felt for them at the time. The first was set up for Mr Stein, a distiller at Kilbagie in Clackmannanshire, in 1786. In the same year, Francis Trells, a Hungarian, erected one in Midlothian.[473] George Patterson had one by 1787 at Castle Huntly in the Carse of

Fig. 155.   Mill of Minnes, Foveran, Aberdeenshire. Overshot water wheel attached to a small meal mill. Note the cowl to the corn kiln at the other end of mill building. (NMAS: 32.7.32)

Gowrie, and by 1794 there were already 61 mills in this small area.[474] John Nichol of Stonehaven built eight mills in six months in 1795; John Gladstone of Castle Douglas built 200 between 1794 and 1810. One was erected at Castle-Hill in Caithness in 1790, but in general they took longer to reach the more northerly areas. Sutherland had one in 1807, and ten by 1811. By 1811, the large farms in the Hebrides had them.[475]

By the 1840s there was hardly a farm over 50 acres that did not have a threshing mill. In 1845, for example, East Lothian had 386 mills, of which seven were driven by wind, 30 by water, 80 by steam and 269 by horses. Other less fertile areas had proportionately greater numbers of horse- and water-operated mills, and the adoption of cast-iron gearing from about 1840-50 reduced the cost of the threshing mill, so that it spread to small farms, pendicles and crofts. The circular, uncovered walk alongside the barn still marks the use of horse-power, with cast-iron gearing on crofts and small farms in the crofting counties, North-East and Borders of Scotland.[476]

It was the covered horse gang or horse engine house that created the biggest visual impact on the appearance of farm buildings.

The surmise that the large timber engine enclosed in a building disappeared with the introduction of the cast-iron horse gear appears to be entirely unfounded. The distribution of horse-engine houses appears to be directly related to the distribution of farms large enough to afford this type of structure, but this general rule must be tempered by the availability of water, wind or steam as alternative sources of power. Similarly the distribution of cast-iron horse gear used in open walks appears to relate

Fig. 156.   Pease Mill, Cockburnspath, Berwickshire. A group of mill buildings comprising (from back to front) an outhouse, a single-storey pantiled dwelling, a square corn kiln with pantiled pyramidical roof surmounted by a kiln vent, a slated mill building with forestair to the upper storey and a very fine lade serving an overshot water wheel in a timber wheel ark. (GWW: E2618)

directly to the distribution of farms under fifty acres of arable land, which were not large enough to afford the large timber engine and house or to farms which were not improved substantially until after 1850, i.e. the bulk of the farms in the Grampian Region, especially in Aberdeenshire and Banffshire.

The timber horse-engine normally had a central vertical shaft or axle, pivoted top and bottom, and supporting arms which carried the 'limbers' or hanging pieces, at their outer ends, on which the animals drew when operating the machine. These arms were normally stiffened by struts supported off the base of the axle and meeting the arms just short of the inner 'limber'. Over the arms was placed the great timber cogged wheel which engaged the drive shaft. Both engine and drive shaft were restrained by the engine frame comprising normally a large timber beam lying parallel to the wall of the barn and linked to the barn wall by two lesser beams, the drive shaft being supported between these lesser beams on heavy transverse struts or dwangs. Diagonal braces between the engine beam and the drive shaft beams were usually incorporated in larger mills as was a tie beam to the outer wall of the engine house. Another type of engine frame comprised two parallel beams lying tangentially to the barn and linked at intervals

Fig. 157.   Typical mill-stone casings in a large corn mill. The corn is fed into the hoppers above the stones by means of the enclosed elevators shown, and is then shaken into the eye of the stone through the movable part under the hopper.

Fig. 158.   Gullane, Dirleton, East Lothian. A typical lowland smiddy with a pantiled roof. Pantiles were popular for smiddies even outside the normal pantile-using areas as they formed a cheap alternative to thatch which was vulnerable to fire. Note the brick extension to the stone chimney head, the slightly raised skews and the cement fill where the roof over the doorway changes pitch. (GWW: A1566)

Fig. 159.   Smiddy Interior: 1898. This painting by A. W. Hogg captures the internal atmosphere of the rural smiddy. Note the bellows to the left of the forge, and the metal canopy forming the chimney over the forge. (NMAS: C2323)

by large timber dwangs. These dwangs carried the drive shaft as in the previous type of frame but the central one replaced the engine beam and supported the top pivot of the engine. Only two examples of this type of engine frame have been located to date, at Flatfield, Errol and at Wellbank, Longforgan.

Each horse was yoked to the two limbers of an arm by the ends of a draw-chain or rope, which passed over a pulley at the top and bottom of each limber (a, b, in Fig. 162) and around a pulley (c) in a block. Each block was attached to a rail that allowed limited movement of the block along the arm. Another chain linked all the blocks, circling the engine through pulleys at d, e, f. This allowed the pull of each horse to be equalised, and also ensured the smooth operation of the machine and the elimination of sudden jerks which could be dangerous to the operators and create unnecessary wear on the machine.

The plan form of horse-engine houses varies considerably, considering the basic requirement of enclosing a process that takes place in a circular space. Horse-engine houses have been located with square, diamond, pentagonal, hexagonal, septagonal, octagonal, circular and elliptical plans, some incorporated within the steading structure, a slight projection on either side of the steading being necessary to incorporate the diameter of the walk. Some were attached to the barn, and some completely detached from the barn but close to it. The most common shapes are the circle, hexagon and octagon. The octagonal type sometimes forms a complete octagon with one of the sides being formed by the wall of the barn; another type however uses a geometrically correct octagon with one point cut off forming a figure with six equal sides and one larger side forming the barn wall. Another variation uses a half octagon linked to the barn with two equal sides, the barn wall side being almost equal to these, thus forming an irregular seven-sided figure. The distribution of these plan forms is directly

Fig. 160. Portnalong, Skye, Inverness-shire. Handloom weaver making tweed. The loom was normally sited in a special area within the house or in a weaving shed to the rear of the property. Linen weaving took place mainly on earthen floors as the damp helped keep the thread supple. (NMAS: C619)

linked to the roof covering used. Circular mills are found mainly in Angus, Kincardineshire and Perthshire where slate is the normal roof covering. Segmental roofs are found mainly in Fife and the Lothians where pantiles are commonplace.

Although the mills are usually attached to the barn they normally have an independent roof structure although some do have apsidal roofs linked back to the main barn roof. Structurally there is a very wide range of roof types, almost every roof being unique in some respect.

Circular roofs can be subdivided into three types, according to the main ways of using timber, (a) with roughly squared timber or split poles, roughly tapered at the end to form the apex of the roof; (b) with rectangular section timber of standard size, each rafter running from eaves to apex; (c) with rectangular section timber divided into principal and secondary rafters. The principal rafters are again used between eaves and apex and these support ⅂-shaped purlins made to match the curve of the roof. The secondary rafters span between the purlins, being attached to the purlins by nails through the sole or face into the ends of the rafters.

Fig. 161.   The Square, Errol, Perthshire. The large building behind the fountain provided accommodation for weavers and their families. Most weaving took place at ground level, partly to make use of earthen floors and partly for noise. In Errol and in Kirriemuir, Angus, weaving in galleries was commonplace. The small windows under the eaves of this large building light the weaving galleries, the sill of the window being level with the floor and the upper part of the looms projecting into the large roof space. (GWW: F0449)

The structural form of these conical roofs varies considerably, each being unique in some aspect, but they may be subdivided into certain basic forms as follows:—

a)   No struts, collars or purlins
b)   Purlins on inside face of rafters
c)   Purlins between principal rafters
d)   Cross collars at one level
e)   Cross collars at two levels
f)   Cross collars at three levels
g)   Cross collars at one level plus vertical hangers
h)   Cross collars at two levels plus vertical hangers
i)   Cross collars at three levels plus vertical hangers
j)   Radiating collars at one level
k)   Radiating collars at two levels
l)   Radiating collars at one level plus central pole

m) Radiating collars at two levels plus central pole
n) Inclined radiating collars round central pole
o) Central hanger with tangential collars
p) Metal hangers, plate and radiating collars
q) Cross collars with trimmers forming square supporting radiating rafters
r) Cross collars with trimmers forming octagon supporting radiating rafters
s) Inner structure supporting outer rafters.

The types of structure found in segmental roofs follow the same basic forms as in conical roofs but the segmental roof allows far more variations in collar pattern, a wide range of geometrical permutations being possible. Apsidal roofs follow the same basic forms combined with standard A-frame couples linking back to the barn roof. All roofs were found to have only one single complete couple usually parallel to the barn wall. In segmental roofs this was propped by the hips forming the segments. In conical roofs a second set of rafters was set at right angles to the main couple quartering the roof. Each quadrant was then halved, quartered etc. until an acceptable spacing was achieved. The only exception to this was the purlined roofs mentioned previously.

The main purpose of the engine house was to protect the timber engine from the elements. This conflicted with the needs of the horses as the work was very demanding and any restriction of natural ventilation could cause the beasts unnecessary distress. Horse-engine houses are normally situated on the north side of the barn, possibly in an effort to shade the engine house and thus keep the horses as cool as possible. The ideal solution was to provide a roof without walls giving the maximum cross ventilation to the animals. This resulted in some remarkable structures towards the end of the mill-building period, with large roofs supported on exceptionally slender piers and columns. From the beginning openings were made as large as possible but sizes were restricted by the available technology and openings tended to be spanned by independent lintels normally of timber but in some cases with segmental arches of stone. As the openings grew larger in proportion to the wall surface the lintels were linked by heavy wall plates to form a crude ring beam round the roof. This must have helped considerably to contain the outward thrust of the roof. Most of these ring beams are hidden behind timber facings but one example examined at New Mains, Kinnoull had a laminated timber ring beam. The timbers making up the beam were about twenty millimetres wide and laminated vertically, to the same curve as the wall.

The walls, piers and columns supporting the roof come in a wide range of materials, the most common being local stone. The standard of stonework varies from dressed ashlar on some of the large mains farms to rough whin rubble or field boulders on poorer properties. Brick is found in the Carse of Gowrie at Fala, Errol and on the other side of the Tay in the vicinity of Rhynd at Mains of Kinmonth. Cast-iron columns appear on some of the later mills and timber was used on some of the smaller farms, but none of these timber mills appears to have survived. Openings run from eaves to ground, unlike the examples to be found in north-east England where low stone walls link the supporting piers.

Other openings exist, for example to allow communication between the men in the barn and the one driving the horses. This could take the form of a door, or more often a

Fig. 162 (a, b).   Combined wind and horse-powered threshing mill as illustrated in Gray's *Explanation of the Engravings of the most Important Implements of Husbandry used in Scotland* 1814. 162a—Plate XII 162b—Plate XI.

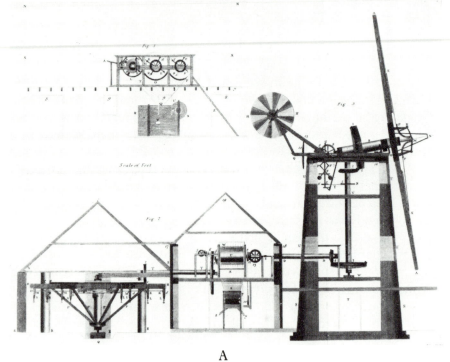

A

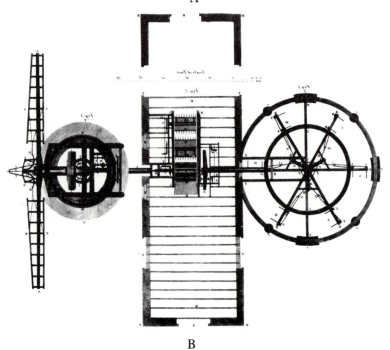

B

Fig. 163.   Montbletton, Gamrie, Banffshire. A large windmill tower situated in the centre of the north range of a large "U" plan steading. The farms had to be large to be able to afford a windmill, 500 acres being the normal limit, and most sat on an exposed ridge where the most use could be made of the wind. Note the access door on the diagonal axis to allow it to open onto the widest part of the square base (NMAS: 33.4.9)

slit window at head level, usually formed of four stones, a lintel, sill, and two jambs. The drive-shaft opening was sometimes left rough, and sometimes the beams supporting the drive shaft formed the cheeks. In some Perthshire examples two large dressed stones, one above the other, are cut to form a circular hole for the drive shaft, and two rectangular slots are also cut to take the ends of the drive-shaft support beams.

Though slate and pantiles are the two most common materials for covering roofs, other materials are also found. In Angus some mills are covered in grey slate—a thick stone slab used as a course slate and pegged to slating battens using timber pegs. Corrugated iron and tarred felt are also to be found but it is unclear whether these materials were the original covering or a later replacement. Both materials were available during the later horse-engine building period. Thatched engine-houses still survive at Wellbank, Longforgan and Flatfield, Errol. One was recently burned down at Murleywell, Glamis but estate drawings show a much wider distribution and it is difficult to say what proportion may have been thatched in the early nineteenth century. All the recently surviving thatched examples have been done in reed thatch but straw-thatched roofs did exist on the Mansfield Estates and in the vicinity of Urquhart, Morayshire, both in the mid-nineteenth century.

Fig. 164. Mayback, Papa Westray, Orkney. Windmills of this type with triangular canvas sails were used for both threshing and grinding corn in Orkney and Shetland into this century. This drawing was made from a photograph taken in 1911. (BW: xi.7)

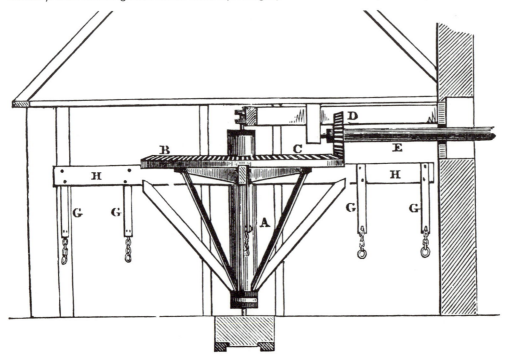

Fig. 165. Detail of Horse Engine: 1840. The horse engine was possibly the most popular power source for threshing machines. Although the machine is referred to as a "horse" engine, these were sometimes driven by oxen, the slowness of pace being offset by yoking the oxen closer to the pivot of the engine. Oxen were also occasionally used as inside partners to horses in these engines. (NMAS: C4000)

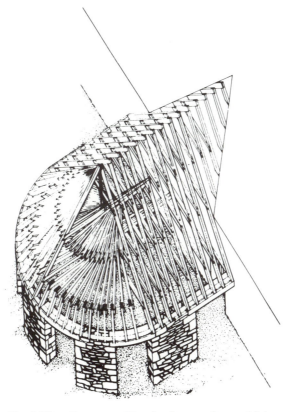

Fig. 166.   Cossans, Glamis, Angus. An apsidal-roofed horse-engine house with three separate layers of collars.

A few horse-engine houses utilised the roof space for other purposes and at Rosebank, Coupar Angus, Sandyhall, Errol and Gortonlee, East Lothian, granaries were incorporated over the engine house. In Kinross-shire some engine houses incorporated doocots in the roof space with dormer-type entries for the birds built into the roof.

Combined horse- and water-mills can still be found in the area, complete buildings surviving at Kildinny, Dunning and Fliskmillan, Fife, and there are ruins of another at Unthank, Brechin.

Weather vanes or finials often embellish the roof, good examples surviving at South Dron, Fife, Grange of Monifieth, Angus, Balado Home Farm, and Wood of Coldrain, Kinross-shire. The last example takes the form of a fish.

Approximately 300 threshing-mill sites have been visited where it has been established that a horse-engine house was standing or had recently been demolished, and yet this is a comparatively small number when compared with the large number that appears on the first and second editions of the large-scale Ordnance Survey sheets. The existence of a large circular shed attached to the steading cannot be taken as conclusive proof of the existence of a horse-engine house, as features known as 'roundy byres' were apparently common in the vicinity of Perth and perhaps elsewhere. One such byre

Fig. 167.   Towmill, Premnay, Aberdeenshire. A start and awe breast-shot water wheel used to drive a threshing machine until recently. (NMAS: 32.17.27)

survives at Elcho on the north wall of the steading close to a horse-engine house. In these byres the cattle stood facing the circular outer wall, and were fed from above and cleaned out from the centre of the floor, thus reducing the cattleman's work. Most surviving horse-engine houses have survived simply because some new use was found for the structure, as implement sheds, storehouses, stock houses, garages, cottar houses etc., but they are being demolished in increasing numbers simply because the new safety cabs on tractors make any use involving entry by a tractor almost impossible to any but the largest mills.

It has been suggested that horse-engine houses date mainly between 1800 and 1830 with 1785 and 1868 as the extreme outside limits.[477] Recent work on the Mansfield Estate Papers together with a list of dated steadings recorded in Angus, Fife and Perthshire suggest that this hypothesis is wrong for eastern Scotland and that horse-engine houses continued to be built until the end of the nineteenth century. A drawing of Bridgeton Farm, Lynedoch dated March 1884 shows a circular horse-engine house coloured as new work. An amended drawing of the same farm, dated July 1884, shows an octagonal horse mill in place of the circular one, also shown as new work. Other farm plans, undated but obviously from the same period as Bridgeton, show proposals for horse-engine houses on other Mansfield farms. Books such as Henry Stephens' *Book of Farm Buildings*, 1861, show horse-engine houses in their proposals for new buildings and illustrate recently built steadings incorporating horse-engine houses. One such example is Drumkilbo, Angus, built in 1856.[478] A series of notices produced for the letting of

Fig. 168.   Waterstone, Ecclesmachan, West Lothian. Steading with steam engine house and factory-type chimney. (IM: 3.1)

farms on the Forneth Estate, Clunie, makes special mention when a threshing mill exists on a farm. These notices date from the 1850s and list threshing mills at Loaning, Wester Tullyneddy and at the Milton of Forneth. No mention of threshing mills is made at Wyndend, Over Forneth, Drumhead and Stars of Forneth but all have the remains of threshing mills today. Water power was used at Over Forneth and horse engines at the other farms, the horse-engine houses surviving at all of the farms except the Stars of Forneth, where the engine house was demolished in the last decade.[479] Thus the Scottish evidence suggests that the building of horse-engine houses carried on, however sporadically, for at least 20 or 30 years after the latest date suggested by the English evidence.

The horse-engine house is known by a number of local names, and even on the same farm different workers may refer to the building using different names. Some of the names recorded in Angus are *horse house, horse mill, horse gin, horse gang, horse course, round house* and *gin case*; in East Perthshire, *roundel* and *round house*; in Fife, *mill rink, wheel rink,* and *gin rink*. Other names encountered during the survey were *wheel shed, gin*

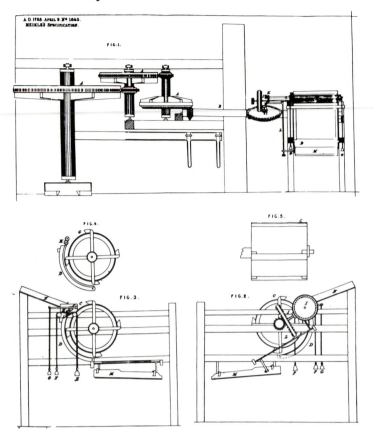

Fig. 169.   Drawings submitted by Meikle to patent his threshing machine. April 9. 1788. The type of horse engine shown in this drawing requires much greater headroom than that shown in Fig. 165. (NMAS: C4012, C4013, C4014; from N. Cartwright *Trans. East Lothian Natural History and Antiquarian Society.* 1968.xi.following p. 80)

house, and *wheel house.* Hutton[480] gives a list of twenty-four names encountered in his survey.[481]

Water power meant the addition of dams, lades and sluices to the scene, and as far as water is concerned an intriguing development was the turbine-driven threshing mill. An entry in the Mansfield Estate Factors' Accounts for 1898-99 reads: '10 May 1899 : Remitted to Gilbert Gilkes & Co. Ltd. Engineers. Railway fare and expenses coming from Kendal to examine water power at Home Farm (Balboughty, Scone) with a view to putting in turbine ——————— £2-17-6.' A drawing in the Mansfield Estates Factors' Office shows a proposal for a turbine and threshing mill at Balboughty by R. G. Morton, Errol Works, Perthshire. This drawing is dated 11 September 1903 and shows the turbine in a pit under the threshing mill. The drive is clearly indicated between the turbine and the mill; but a steam engine and a very large water wheel are also shown on this drawing.[482]

Oil engines of various types and electric motors were utilised to power threshing mills this century until the complete revolution of harvesting techniques brought about by the general acceptance of the combine harvester in the last decade. The threshing mill

Fig. 170. Belton Dodd, Dunbar, East Lothian. A threshing machine similar to that shown in Meikle's patent drawings. (NMAS: C7539; from a colour transparency, A. Fenton)

itself had little effect internally on the form of farm buildings apart from a tendency to increase the height of the barn to 1½ to 2 storeys to allow for larger mills, and for upper floors to be used as granaries and straw barns. Occasionally lean-to sheds against the outside wall of the barn, on the side opposite the power source, are used as chaff houses, but it was the power source and in particular the horse-engine that created the greatest visual impact, as well as the factory-type chimneys that often came to stand alongside them in the areas of high-farming where farmers could afford such expensive aids.

Horse-engine houses are comparatively easy to locate owing to their normally distinctive form but it is only through detailed and systematic study that internal horse-engine houses, open horse walks, water wheels, turbines, steam, oil and electric motors will be located to allow accurate distribution maps to be prepared and related to farm size, type and location.

All too few threshing machines survive and even fewer examples of the early power sources. Modern agricultural methods require the removal of this type of machinery to allow free space within the steading or the complete demolition of the steading to make way for the large multi-purpose shed. Time is short therefore if this type of study is to be completed before the eventual disappearance of these machines and the buildings that housed the machine and its engine.

и

Fig. 171.   Upper Barrack, New Deer,
Aberdeenshire. A small barn threshing
mill of a late nineteenth to early
twentieth-century type which is still
occasionally used. (NMAS: 32.14.6)

10

A Sample Survey : Grampian Region

A survey of farm buildings was carried out by Bruce Walker in 1976-77, having been commissioned by the Countryside Commission for Scotland, on behalf of Grampian Regional Council. The method of approach and of selection of buildings is outlined above (page 42).

It was found that in almost every instance the steadings had been completely or partly gutted and even on those hill farms where the feeding byre was still in use, most of them had been altered considerably during the occupancy of the present tenant. This was normally a move from the cross byre layout to a byre running the length of the steading range and incorporating a turnip store at one end and a hay store at the other. Other alterations could include the incorporation of former stables, barn, implement shed, cart shed, bothy etc into the byres to increase the 'fat cattle' capacity of the steading. On larger farms these alterations normally involved the removal of all internal furnishings and partitions to provide continuous spaces that can be used as stores or cattle sheds and allow access to fork-lift trucks and tractors for depositing and removing materials to be stored or for mechanical 'mucking out' of cattle sheds. This type of alteration often involves the building up of many of the original openings in the walls and the slapping of new openings in the gables of each range to allow easy access for the machines. The degree and rapidity of change in rural buildings was one of the major lessons that was driven home, time and time again.

The evidence collected points to three main divisions within the region, each having distinct architectural features.

The smallest of these districts is the Howe of the Mearns, an extension of the Valley of Strathmore in Angus and closely allied to it in agricultural and architectural terms. Though it has a very distinct form of architectural expression it exerts no apparent influence on the adjoining areas of the Grampian Region apart from those farms in the foothills of the Grampians immediately to the west of the Howe.

The second distinct district is the coastal plain of Moray extending into the Highland Region in the County of Nairn to the west. This district unlike the Howe of the Mearns exerts considerable influence on the glens of the Grampians to the south. The boundaries here are much harder to define but appear to be related to natural routes to the coast. The main core of this district appears to be confined to the west side of the River Spey although its influence can be traced as far east as the River Deveron. To the south its influence can be traced into the west end of Deeside where it appears to meet the main Grampian Region building type spreading west from Buchan.

The Moray district and the east Perthshire district of Tayside Region have similar architectural details which tend to become almost identical when applied to hill farms, for example at the west end of Deeside. Certainly there is a distinct similarity in architectural expression between the glens influenced by the Moray district and Glenshee which contains the only vehicular link between the south-western corner of the Grampian Region and the Tayside Region.

Fig. 172.   Rhinturk, Cabrach, Banffshire. A typical Grampian farmhouse and steading. Note the trees for shelter and the way that the house sits slightly apart from the steading. (NMAS: 32.9.29)

The third district is by far the largest and is centred on Buchan, spreading southwards to Stonehaven and then westwards into Deeside. It also spreads west from Buchan to the River Spey. The Moray district also exerts a limited influence on the area between the Rivers Spey and Deveron.

Within each of these districts, definable in terms of architecture as units, there is a great number of areas distinct in agricultural terms, particularly in the Buchan district. These distinct areas relate to the type of terrain and to the soil quality and these two factors tend to determine the proportion of large farm to small farm or of farm to croft.

The three main differences between the Buchan farms and those of Moray and Mearns are:

1. The average age of the farm buildings.
2. The scale of unit related to acreage.
3. Complexity of plan form.

The majority of farms in the Buchan district appear to have been built between 1860 and 1915 whereas those of the Mearns and Moray appear to date in the main from the late eighteenth and early nineteenth centuries. The Buchan farm steading is very large in relation to the acreage served and to the farm house. This appears to result from a concentration on beef cattle production, and the increased size tends to be the result of larger feeding byres with their associated storage facilities. Units of accommodation such as stables, cart bays, farm house, bothies or chaumers, and cottar houses tend to be in the same proportion in relation to acreage as in the other districts.

The complex plan forms of the average steadings in the Mearns and Moray districts are due partly to larger farming units and partly to improvements following their erection.

Another feature of a number of Buchan farms is a court to the south with the midden to the north, there being a single door in the north wall to allow the byres to be 'mucked

Fig. 173. The Cock, Strathdon, Aberdeenshire. A small farmhouse and steading in a sheltered hollow. Note the group of self-built timber sheds including part of an old railway carriage. (NMAS: 32.23.16)

out' into this midden. This is often found with an L- or U-plan form but more often with a truncated H-plan, which may be unique to the Buchan district.

The architectural detailing of the buildings can also be quite distinctive. The steadings of the Buchan district tend to have gables at the end of each range. Even where two ranges interconnect to form and L- or U-plan, the roof of one range is carried through to form a gable whilst the other abuts the first, forming a valley on either side. These roofs normally have stone or tile ridges. In the Mearns district most of the steading roofs have hipped or piend ends with lead hips and ridges or lead hips with ceramic or stone ridges. In this particular feature the Moray district steadings are similar to those of the Buchan district.

The five-sided dormer tends to be used in all three districts but it is decidedly larger in the Mearns and Moray districts with external lead flashings on the hips. The smaller version used in the Buchan district has either very thin concrete flashings on the hips or, much more commonly, concealed flashings at the hips, giving a much neater appearance. This type of dormer in the Buchan district appears at the end of the nineteenth century. Earlier dormers are extensions of the wall of the building with a stone gable over the window opening. At the beginning of the twentieth century the five-sided dormer was superseded by the gabled dormer, but this time the dormer was set back into the roof and the gable constructed in timber—usually with oversailing roof and decorative barge boards. This detail is found to a limited extent in the cottar houses of the Mearns district.

Fig. 174. Letterfourie Home Farm, Rathven, Banffshire. An eighteenth-century farm steading with well built and well detailed central block surmounted with a bell tower to summon the workers to and from the fields. The rest of the "U" plan steading had been thatched originally and enclosed a large open court.

The Moray district has a high proportion of 'ornamental' farm houses and cottages, often in the Tudor style common in east Perthshire. Harl pointing is also common in the Moray district, the harl often being lime-washed whilst the stones of the wall are left in their natural colour.

Other differences between the buildings of the Buchan, Mearns and Moray districts tend to be much less specific and are often related to scale and proportion rather than to actual differences in construction.

Three clay-building areas occur in the Grampian Region, one centred on Speymouth, the second in Gamrie and King Edward parishes of Banffshire and Aberdeenshire respectively and the third centred on Luthermuir in the Howe of the Mearns.[483]

Archive data in the form of farm house and steading plans dating back to 1860 were located in the keeping of Messrs. Alan Keir and Smith, Turriff. The drawings include all the farms on the estates of Blervie, Eden, Haddo, Hatton, Netherdale, Rothiemay, Towie Barclay, Balthaine, Craigston, Auchry, Carnoustie, Cairnborrow, Delgaty, Elrick, Forbes, Fyvie, Gariochsford, Glasslaw, Leslie, Monkshill, Tollo and others, as well as a number of privately owned farms and farms on lands owned by Inverurie Town Council, Ladybridge Asylum and various Trusts centred in Banff and Aberdeen.

Fig. 175.   Mains of Arbuthnott, Arbuthnott, Kincardineshire. A large square-plan steading with a large house built into the centre of the principal range. This front is built in dressed ashlar with flat voussoir arches to the cart bays on either side of the house.

An analysis of this collection gives a clear view of what is to be found in the area at the present day, in spite of numerous changes and adaptations, often of very recent date.

Single storey cottages are numerous. That of Mountblairy, dated to 1868, has a piend roof with central chimneys, and a milkhouse and coalshed at the rear. It has a kitchen, a room and a small bedroom. More characteristic than Mountblairy are Brownside cottage, dated to 1886, with a kitchen, best room and bedroom, and stairs leading to an attic, and Boggiehead, dated 1885, of similar form but with an attic fireplace.

Oldwood croft on the Hatton Estate still had a thatched roof in 1928. The best room had a gable chimney, whilst the kitchen had a 'hingin' lum', marked by a hollowing of the stonework of the gable, and a wooden chimney set in a little from the edge of the ridge. In that year the roof was raised and re-covered in corrugated iron, a dairy and scullery were added at one end, and the box-beds and wooden presses disappeared. In 1929, Ordley in the parish of Auchterless was altered. Corrugated iron replaced thatch, and a shed with an outdoor privy replaced the office houses built against one gable. The fireplace here had the common feature of protruding stone cheeks, a kind of translation into stone of the wooden sides of the 'hingin' lum'.

Fig. 176. Cassieford, Rafford, Moray. A large late nineteenth-century steading with each range carried through to individual gables, giving the steading a distinctive appearance. (NMAS: 32.25.9)

Fig. 177. Auchachuie, Strathdon, Aberdeenshire. A "U"plan steading on a small hill farm, built jn coursed rubble and roofed in corrugated iron. Note the ferret hutches against the rear gable and the small timber shed.

Single-storey double cottages are numerous. Some have a living room, two bedrooms and a scullery, as at Saphock in 1920, where the total floor space amounted to 700 sq ft (65 sq m); and Upper Oldmill in 1926, with 553 sq ft (51.4 sq m) per house. At Jackston, Fyvie, the cottar houses, each of 550 sq ft (51.2 sq m) in 1924, were in a row of three. A variation with a kitchen and one bed closet was found in a labourer's cottage at Towie.

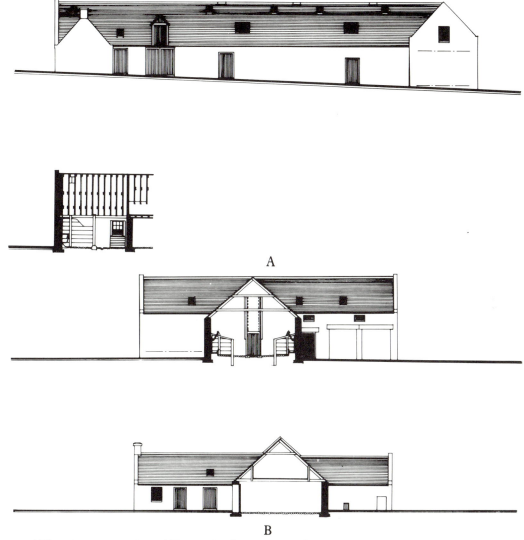

Fig. 178 (a, b).   Brownhill of Pitglassie, Auchterless, Aberdeenshire. Elevations and sections through a typical Grampian steading built in 1902. Note the upward sliding door in the byre.

At Dunlugas in 1867 there was a kitchen, scullery and bed closet, and the cottage had oversailing skews, decorative barge boards, and a rustic timber porch, in the best tradition of estate building. This cost about £150 in 1867. The cattlemen's cottages at Towie in 1873, each with a kitchen and three bed closets, suggest large families.

One and a half storey houses are numerous, for example at Braesterrie, heightened in 1891, and the twin cottages at Burreldales on the Estate of Towie, dated 1900, with dormers in the upper half storey. At Burreldales, the henhouse, sheds, ashpit and privies are in a separate block alongside.

At Ardmiddle, another substantial pair of cottar houses had the attachments at the back, like the leg of the letter R. Back doors opened on to the milk houses; beyond, but

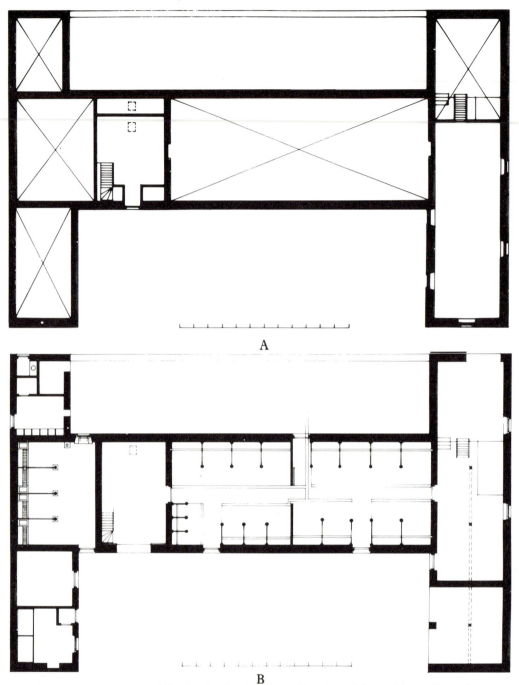

A

B

Fig. 179 (a, b). Brownhill of Pitglassie, Auchterless, Aberdeenshire. a. Upper floor plan—
Note that only two areas of the steading extend into a second floor in the form of a loft over
the turnip shed and the granary over the threshing barn. b. Ground floor plan—"H" plan
(type 3.3) steading comprising threshing barn and two-bay cart shed in east range; double-
sided byre, turnip shed and four-horse stable in the centre range; privy, pig stye and poultry
house to the north of the east range; and chalmer and tack room at the south end.
The midden is situated to the north of the byre.

Fig 180   Fig 181

Fig. 180.   Oldwood Croft, Estate of Hatton, Aberdeenshire. A small croft house surveyed in preparation for alterations, showing layout of fixed furnishings.

Fig. 181. Ordley Croft, Auchterless, Aberdeenshire. A small croft house and office surveyed in preparation for alterations showing layout of fixed furnishings.

separated by a wall, were the coalsheds, henhouses, byres with two stalls each, privies, pigsties, and dunghill between—the ultimate in functional geometry.

A number of one and a half storey double cottages have a kitchen and bed closet on the ground floor, as at Muiresk in 1872, Overhall, Muirs of Fyvie, in 1895, and Ardmiddle Mains in 1908. The ashpits, privies and coalsheds are attached as rear or gable-end units. Some slightly more lavish cottar houses had the additional feature of a fireplace in the bed closet on the ground floor. Examples are Tollo in 1897, Pitglassie in 1898 and Cushnie in 1900.

The majority of cottar houses, which are usually paired, are on a smaller scale, as at Kinbroon. Pitglassie Smithy, in Auchterless, altered in 1930, shows a frequent form of development from a one storey to a one and a half storey building. The walls were raised, and the two skylight windows replaced by two dormers and a skylight. The box bed in the kitchen vanished and the steep, wooden stair gave way to a more elegant stair with banisters and an open landing. Two built-in cupboards were placed across from the landing. One of the two upstairs bedrooms was given a fireplace.

Upper Ashalloch, 1886, had a fireplace in the mid closet, as well as two in the room and kitchen, and two more in the upstair bedrooms. A scullery, milkhouse and bed recess were at right angles to the kitchen at the rear of the house. The dormers were five-sided. The Mill of Towie was similar in 1892, but also had a wooden porch before

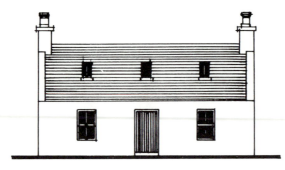

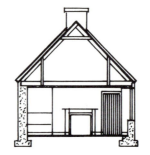

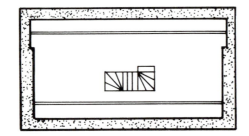

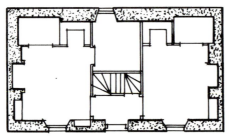

Fig. 182. Muiresk, Turriff, Aberdeenshire. A two-room farmhouse with floored attic showing fixed furnishings comprising bed and pantry on the north wall of both kitchen and room. The mid-press behind the stair may have been used as a bed closet.

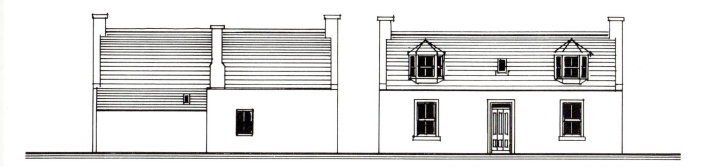

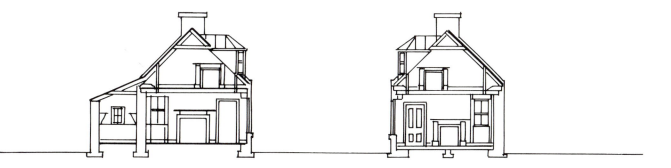

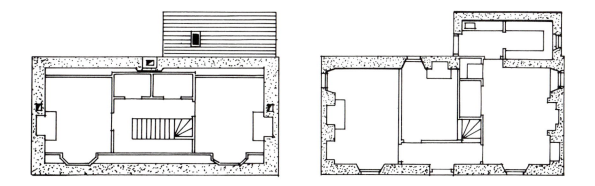

Fig. 183. A 1½-storey north-east farmhouse on a two-room and mid-press plan. Note the scullery and milk house to the north of the kitchen; the built-in bed and pantry off the kitchen; the fireplace in the mid-press; and the pantry and linen closet on the stair landing.

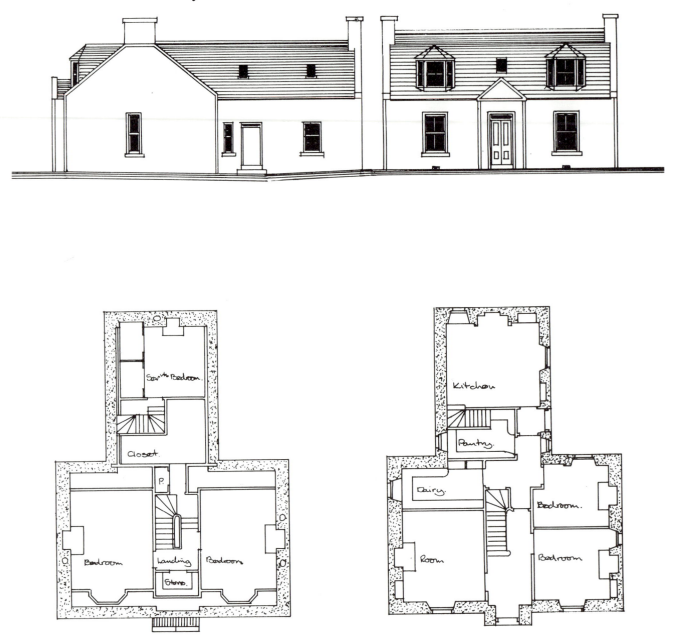

Fig. 184.   Westertown of Forgue, Forgue, Aberdeenshire. A large 1½-storey farmhouse with a two-window frontage, double-bank plan and kitchen wing to rear. Note that the house is split into two sections with a working part to the rear comprising kitchen, pantry, dairy and bedroom on the ground floor and servants' quarters with two double built-in beds and a closet on the upper floor. The front of the house is more formal with a room and bedroom on the ground floor and two bedrooms on the upper floor.

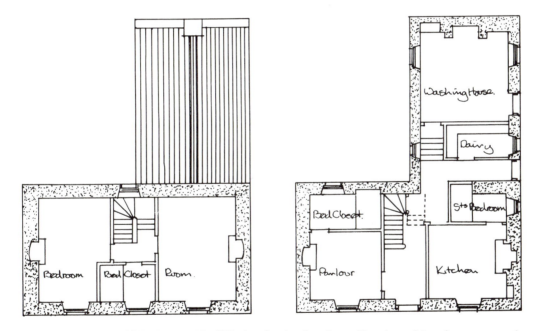

Fig. 185. Uppermill of Pitglassie, Auchterless, Aberdeenshire. A two-storey house with single-bank plan and single-storey wing to rear. Note the bed closets to the north of the room and kitchen and at the head of the stairs. The rear wing comprises a washhouse and milk house.

the front door. In the case of South Mains of Balgaveney, the milkhouse extension had an upper-floor closet.

Rising in the scale of sizes, Conland Mill at Forgue had the additional feature in 1868 of a servant's bed closet in the kitchen. There was another bed closet in the downstairs room. At Mains of Hatton in 1886, the bed closet was to the side of the kitchen. At Carlincraig, 1890, the ground-floor sleeping accommodation occupied three units. In the bulk of examples, the extensions containing the latter two elements are hipped, though the house itself is gable-ended. Middlehill of Seggat had a five-sided dormer window on the upper floor of its extension in 1897. This floor was the chaumer for the men, complete with a fireplace. There was also a servant's bedroom opening off the kitchen on the ground floor.

Bigger one and a half storey farmhouses were built on an L-plan, with a kitchen at the back, a milkhouse in the internal angle, and servants' quarters over the kitchen. Examples of this arrangement are Arnburn in 1886 and Roseburn in 1885. The plan could be adapted so that the entire extension was a kitchen and bedroom wing, sometimes, as at Scotston in 1878, with the chaumer on the extreme end, with its separate door. Bigger scale examples like Garriocksburn, 1888 and Dundee, 1888, had bedrooms or lumber rooms and meal stores in the upper floor of the wing.

A number of houses were built on a T-plan, sometimes with a milkhouse with a sloping roof in one of the internal angles. The leg of the T was the kitchen wing, and the servants' quarters were above it, as at Greenbrae in 1893, and East Pitdoulzie in 1894, both on the Estate of Towie. A few farm houses, such as Fortrie in 1892 and Upper Oldmill in 1896, had a ⊏-plan, of such a kind that the lower element of the ⊏ formed the frontage of the house. Some had a gabled projection on the parlour side of the front, with a kitchen and bedroom wing to the back. Mid Pitglassie in 1912 and Ardmiddle in 1867 exemplify the latter.

A logical development to give more space is the double bank plan. Those at Roberton in 1878, Colyne in 1888, and Backhill of Thomaston have the milkhouse built on at the back. On a slightly grander scale are Little Blackpotts in 1873, and Westerton of Forgue, with kitchen extensions and sleeping accommodation above built out to the back.

In the area covered, the one and a half storey house, with its various forms, is dominant. *Two-storey* farm houses also exist, however, as at Uppermill of Pitglassie, 1902. This is on an L-plan, with a nursery, milkhouse, kitchen and scullery on the ground floor of the back wing and a bedroom above. Seggat had in 1879 a gable projection on the parlour side of the front, and a kitchen-cum-bedroom wing to the back. Pitgair, in 1869, had the double-bank plan with the kitchen extension to the rear, Comisty was similar to Pitgair, but extended in height to *two and a half storeys*.

Glenbuchat and Strathdon Parishes

Surveys were carried out of eighty agricultural buildings in parts of the parishes of Glenbuchat and Strathdon in Aberdeenshire.

As far as farm houses were concerned, the majority were situated to the east or south of the steading. In only two cases was the farm house physically attached to the steading, at the ruinous Coul of Ledmacay and Ryntaing. Only a few of the farms were dated. Peatfold had the date 1902 on the gable of the steading facing the back of the farm house and others had much later dates. A stone cheese-press dated 1853 was noted at Tolduquhill. It is evident, therefore, that architects' plans are an essential back-up to

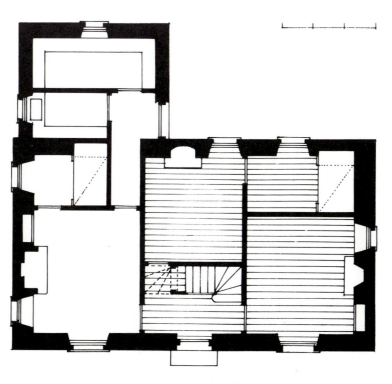

A

Fig. 186 (a, b).   Brownhill of Pitglassie, Auchterless, Aberdeenshire. a. Ground- floor plan
principal elevation of a medium-sized farmhouse built in 1902. Note the servants' bed
closet in the kitchen, the scullery and milk house to the north and the bed closet off the mid-
press. The kitchen area has a concrete floor, the mid-press and room have wooden floors.
b. Upper-floor plan and rear elevation. Note the pantry and linen cupboard on the stair
landing and the closet in the roof space over the milk house.

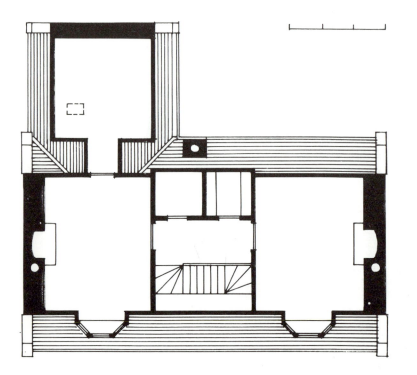

B

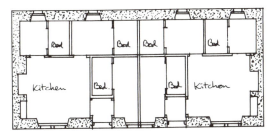

Fig. 187.   Cattlemen's Cottages, Towie, Aberdeenshire. Two semi-detached cottages, each comprising a kitchen and three bed closets.

field surveys, to work out the precise dating of farm buildings. This applies throughout Scotland.

The most widespread farm house size was again the one and a half storey with a two-window façade, with the exceptions of Lynardoch with its one-window façade, and Badenyon with its three-window façade. Twenty-four of the eighty units examined were of this form; nine were of one storey, and three of two storeys. Twelve houses had rough timber porches covering the doors on the principal façade, but only at Roughpark was the porch open and supported on rustic timber columns.

The window patterns of most farm houses were typical of the late nineteenth century. Meikle Tolly, Dulax Cottage and Finnylost had twelve-pane case and sash windows that could date to the early- to mid-nineteenth century. The buildings themselves antedate the first edition of the Ordnance Survey map of 1869. Roughpark had twelve-pane windows in the south gable only, but this is likely to be a re-use of older windows as the house appears to have been rebuilt between 1869 and 1903. The twelve-pane windows at Invernochty are certainly of twentieth century date.

Meikle Tolly and Invernochty were the only farm houses with piend roofs. Meikle Tolly had a roof of blue slate with lead ridge and hips. Invernochty was similar but with blue ceramic ridge and hips. Farm house roofs were normally gabled and covered with blue slate with either a ceramic or stone ridge. Drumanettie and Lost had stone slate roofs, Dulax and Relaquheim had green slate and Badenyon and Lynardoch, corrugated iron roofs. All the roofs examined apart from Brughs and the two piend examples had raised skews. The roof at Brughs was close-cropped at the skews.

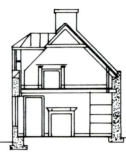

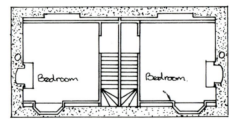

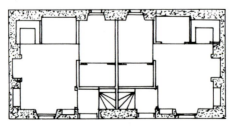

Fig. 188.   Double cottage in north-east, each unit comprising a kitchen, with pantry and built-in bed and bed closet on ground floor and bedroom above.

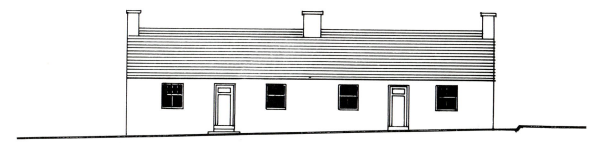

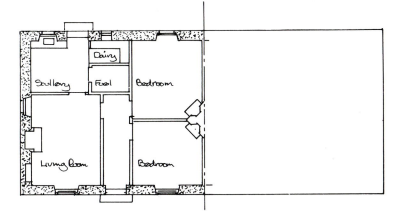

Fig. 189.   Jackston, Fyvie, Aberdeenshire. Single-storey double cottage with double-bank plan comprising living room, scullery, dairy, and two bedrooms.

Waterside was the only example recorded of a gabled roof with lead ridge, and had the only five-sided dormers with lead hip flashings.

Dormer windows of the five-sided and timber-gabled types predominated. Badenyon, Dulax Cottage and the extension to Invernettie were the only examples of stone-gabled dormers. Piend dormers were recorded at Brughs, Invernochty, Ledmacay and Torrandhu.

Harled walls were commonplace on the farm houses in this area, most of the harl being of a lime variety, thinly applied to the walls, with occasional examples of harl pointing in the same material. At Cummerton and Torrancroy only the gables were harled and at Aldachuie only the front. Ledmacay, Relaquheim and Torrancroy were built of coursed rubble and older uncoursed rubble ruins were recorded at Howe and Sloggie. The combination of harl with ashlar chimney heads is also characteristic of the area and at Lost the farm house had stone chimney heads with harl on the gable face only. At Aldachuie, Clasachdhu, Drumanettie, Finnylost and Torrancroy the chimney heads were weathered to take a thatched roof.

Very large fireplace openings were recorded at Badenyon, Drumanettie, Dulax and Howe. These fireplaces were much larger than one would expect in this size of building,

Fig. 190.   Balfeich, Fordoun, Kincardineshire. Concrete
silage tower from the 1930s. (NMAS: 39.19.7)

being of a scale more suitable for the great hall of a tower house or castle. Three of the fireplaces examined had a hearth in a second fireplace within the larger opening and all were fitted with very large sweys.

A cheese-press recessed into the gable of the house was recorded at Dulax and Newseat, a feature also known in the adjoining parish of Cabrach in the neighbourhood of Keith, Banffshire, and in Caithness.

Steadings

In plan type the surviving steadings are mostly L- and U-shaped, with only occasional examples of other categories. Fourteen steadings showed evidence of having had a water-powered threshing mill, and seven of these had dams indicated on the first edition of the Ordnance Survey map in 1869. In contrast to this, of the eighteen examples of horse-engine sites related to threshing mills, only two were indicated on the first edition of the Ordnance Survey map, Netherton (having a covered engine house at that date which had been demolished before the second edition in 1903) and Tornagawn. Apart from Netherton all of the horse-engine sites were open, six being raised above the

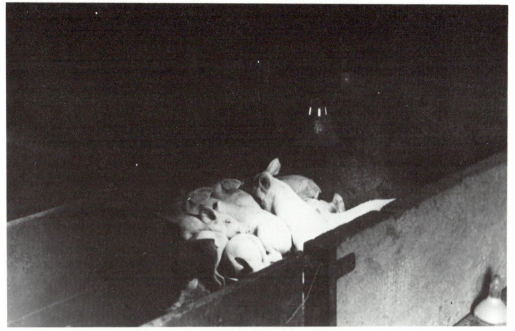

Fig. 191. Meikle Cairnbeg, Fordoun, Kincardineshire. Pig litter under heat lamp.
(NMAS: 40.1.13)

surrounding ground and two sunk into hillsides. In five instances a horse-engine site was indicated on the Ordnance Survey map but had since disappeared. In almost every case the gearing appears to have been mounted over a pit, 47 in (120 cm) square, and kerbed by four large stones. The drive shaft was enclosed in a 26 in (66 cm) square, horizontal duct, buried 10 in (25 cm) below the surface of the horse walk. Seven of these engines appear for the first time on the second edition of the Ordnance Survey map. Broadly speaking the early power source in this area appears to have been water, with a gradual move to horse power towards the end of the century. The only exception to this is Ledmacay where the open horse course was replaced by a water wheel and dam early this century.

Rubble and coursed rubble were the main walling materials with only five harled steadings, three of these having modern harl. Three harl-pointed steadings were recorded at Badenyon, Colquhonnie and Drumallan.

The majority of steadings had a blue slate roof, ceramic ridge and raised skews. At Ledmacay the roof was covered with stone ridge and raised skews. Ryntaing and Drumanettie also had stone ridges but with blue slate roofs and raised skews. Invernettie had a similar roof but with L-shaped timber skews covering the joint between the slate and the gable wall surface, the upper part lapping the slate of the roof and the lower part turning down the wall in the form of a barge board. Brughs and Relaquheim had blue slate roofs, close cropped at the skews and with a ceramic ridge. There were also eight examples of cast-iron roofs with raised skews.

Entry to loft areas was normally through the gable for loading purposes and by internal stair or ladder for personnel. At Aldachuie, Brughs, Crofts, Invernettie,

Fig. 192.   Meikle Cairnbeg, Fordoun, Kincardineshire. Pig shed with pigs in individual cages in which they cannot turn round. These cages have slatted floors with underground drainage to sludge tanks. (NMAS: 40.1.12)

Lynardoch and Roughpark there was an additional dormer entry for loading purposes. At Crofts there was an outside stone stair to a gable entrance. At Colquhonnie and Waterside there were permanent timber stairs to gable entrances, and at Invernochty a semi-permanent ladder standing on a concrete base.

Shallow arched openings to cart bays and turnip sheds were recorded at Drumanettie, Finnylost and Tolduquhill. Lintelled openings were commonplace elsewhere.

Ventilation to byres and stables was normally incorporated in the roof ridge but a number also had tile vents in the walls. Only at Relaquheim were vertical slits in the stonework used for ventilation, and at Peatfold, decorative metal ridge vents.

The midden was normally situated in front of the principal elevation or enclosed in the angle or angles of L- and U-shaped plans. At Lost, Tolduquhill and Torrandhu the midden was situated at the back. The midden at Lost was moved to this position in 1929. Cobbled midden walks were recorded at Aldachuie, Badenyon, Invernochty, and Torrandhu.

Most of the internal fittings were of the same types as shown in the Alan Keir & Smith drawings, including the use of counterbalanced vertically sliding doors in the centre of internal gables. At Roughpark there was an unusual concrete trevis in the stable. Horizontally divided doors were common in stables, barns and byres and quarter opening doors were recorded at Ballochie (North), Ledmacay and Torrancroy. At Colquhonnie and Torrancroy the stable doors were split vertically and hinged in the centre. Tolduquhill had a fuie or gable apex doocot.

Fig. 193. Wairds of Alpitty, Arbuthnott, Kincardineshire. Precast concrete shed for store cattle. (NMAS: 39.14.15)

Rathven Parish, Banffshire

In the parish of Rathven, seventy-nine farms were visited. Of these, twenty-four marked on the map had been demolished, a fact which gives some indication of the rate of disappearance of farms, Two of the farms, Cairnfield and Letterfourie, were the home farms of estates, In these instances the mansion house was situated at some distance from the steading for the grieve or other farm servants and these have here been considered as the farm house.

In this area, the farm house to the south of the steading was slightly more popular than other relationships. Fourteen farm houses faced due south, eight south-east, five south-west, four north, four east, one north-east, one west and one north-west. The farm house of Birkenbush, although having a single bank plan, faces north-west and south-east, with identical windows on opposite sides of each of the principal rooms. The north-west façade, which faces the principal approach, has a decorative Dutch gable as a central feature.

Only two of the farm houses had date stones. Walkerdales was dated 1677 on the skew putt of an apparent extension to the original two-window, central-door façade. Although this farm house has the weight and detailing one might associate with the late seventeenth century, this may be the result of the use of secondhand stone from a former tower house. A decorative dormer stone from such a building has been built into the gable of the porch. Thornybank is dated 1759 on the skew putt, and like Walkerdales and Birkenbush, another farm house, possibly dating from the eighteenth century, was situated on the Letterfourie estate, the Home Farm of which is dated 1776. The farm house at Pressholme belongs to the Roman Catholic Church and is known to have been built in 1830.

The one and a half storey farm house with a two-window façade and central door was the most common type. Eighteen examples were recorded, and four, Bogend, Easter Bogs, Hillfolds and Rannachie, had three-window façades. At Arradoul Mains a standard one and a half storey farm house has been extended to form a treble-gable frontage, the central door being situated in a small single-storey gable between the one and a half storey wings. Cleanhill is also one and a half storey but the principal rooms are contained in an L-shaped plan, the entrance being through a porch in the re-entrant angle. At Letterfourie Home Farm a house attached to the south-west range, but obviously much later than the rest of the steading, has one window and one door at ground floor and two dormer windows at the upper. A one and a half storey double cottage, with a single window and door in each unit, was recorded at Arradoul cottages.

Of nine single-storey farm houses recorded, all except one had a two-window and central-door type façade. The exception was Pressholme Cottage which had an irregular three-window and door façade, possibly the result of combining a double cottage to form a single unit.

Four two-storey farm houses were recorded. Birkenbush and Thornybank had eighteenth century type houses, and Greenbank and Pressholme were early nineteenth century types. The Mill of Buckie was the only two and a half storey farm house and was possibly built in the early nineteenth century but has been altered in the late nineteenth or early twentieth century. All of these larger houses have three-window façades.

The window patterns were mainly types normally associated with the late nineteenth and early twentieth century. Seventeen farm houses had four-pane case and sash windows with panes of equal size, and five had four-pane case and sash windows with a 1/3—2/3 proportion. Seven had two-pane case and sash windows normally arranged in pairs. Only in the centre of the first-floor windows at Mill of Buckie was there a twelve-pane case and sash window. Early nineteenth century pattern windows (normally attributed to the 1830s) were recorded at Arradoul Mains—twelve pane, Cairnfield—ten pane, Cairnfield (dormers), Loanhead, Mill of Buckie (ground floor), and Pressholme Cottage—eight pane, and Birkenbush (upper floor)—six pane. At Walkerdales a circular light over the entrance door was divided into quadrants.

Only Greenbank had a piend roof. The main roof of this house was covered with blue slate with a ceramic ridge and cement flashings at the hips. The single-storey wings on either side were also piend with lead ridge and hips. All of the farm houses had raised skews apart from Pressholme Cottage, where the blue slate roof was close cropped at the skews. This building had a stone ridge. Only Greencraig and Walkerdales had crow steps at the skew. All of the others are smooth and run parallel to the roof surface. Six roofs were covered with stone slate and a stone ridge. Fifteen had blue slate roofs with stone ridges and seven blue slate roofs with ceramic ridges. Castle Grant, Burnside of Letterfourie and Hillhead of Letterfourie have corrugated iron roofs, Pottingbrae has asbestos slate and Hillfolds timber shingles.

The five-sided dormer was the most common pattern, nearly all with lead hips and ridge. Stone-gabled dormers were recorded at six farms and piend-roofed dormers at

A

B

Fig. 194 (a, b). Feddan, Dyke & Moy, Moray. Timber-framed multi-purpose shed.
(NMAS: 32.26.21-22)

five farms. The timber-gabled dormer so popular in other parts of the Grampian Region appeared only at Bogend and Hillfolds.

The most popular wall finish was harl, of which twenty examples were recorded. The new farm house at Smerick, built c. 1907, was constructed of squared sandstone rubble. Coursed rubble was recorded at nine sites, one of which, Arradoul Cottages, had only the façade of rubble, the gables and back being harled. Four examples of uncoursed rubble were recorded, one at Greencraig having harled gables. Clay and bool construction was recorded at Burnside of Letterfourie and Connage (Old House). At Smerick (Old House) the walls were constructed of clay and bool, patched and reinforced in places with mass concrete.

Fourteen farm houses had chimney heads constructed in ashlar and on six farm houses the chimney head was weathered to take a thatched roof. At Arradoul Mains the chimney heads were octagonal and at Burnside of Letterfourie they were finished with a brick cope. Connage and Easter Bogs had decorative skew putts and at Greencraig there were Tudor-type hood mouldings to window and door openings.

Mass concrete was used to construct the milkhouse attached to the east gable at Inkerman and a concrete privy was still intact at Burnside of Letterfourie.

A circular doocot with a slated conical roof stood to the south-east of the farm house at Greenbank.

Most of the surviving steadings in this area tended towards the larger types of plan. The former crofts and small hill farms have for the most part been absorbed into larger units and their steadings left to become ruinous or they have been demolished. Even the larger steadings have, for the most part, been altered or extended, often beyond the point where the observer can recognise the original form. Only the steading of Wester Bogs retains most of its original features. This farm has been incorporated into the adjoining farms of Glasterim and Leitcheston, the three farms now being operated as a single unit from Glasterim.

Seven steadings show evidence of having had a water-powered threshing mill. At Leitcheston the concrete mill dam still survives although the part of the steading which formerly contained the water sheel has been demolished. At Wester Bogs the mill dam has a timber sluice-gate with a short concrete lade onto a breast-shot wheel. Nine steadings show evidence of open horse-engine works to power the threshing mill. Of these Loanhead, Muirycrook and Smerick are shown on the first edition of the six-inch Ordnance Survey map in 1870, but all had disappeared before the second edition in 1905. Hillfolds and Thornybank also had open horse-engine works in 1871 but the Thornybank horse walk was removed about 1960 to improve the curve of the access road to the steading. At Cunningholes and Letterfourie Home Farm, drive wheels on the exterior of the threshing barn wall were used to utilise a mobile power source by means of a belt drive. The majority of threshing barns in the area surveyed have been gutted and only at Cunningholes was the barn threshing mill intact. The manufacturer was Wright Bros., Boyne Mills, Portsoy.

Coursed rubble and random rubble were the main walling materials with clay and bool work appearing in only five examples. At Bogside and Leitcheston mass concrete was used as a base to timber sheds. At Stripeside mass concrete was also used to patch clay and bool walls. Nine examples of harling were recorded and two, at Letterfourie Home Farm and Mill of Buckie, of harl pointing.

Ten steadings had piend roofs against twenty-five with gables and raised skews. Seven had stone slate roofs with stone ridges. At Leitcheston and Letterfourie Home Farm this was combined with lead hips on the piend roofs. Seven steadings had blue slate roofs with stone ridges. Again at Leitcheston this was combined with lead flashings on the hips of the piend roofs. Only Arradoul Mains and Bogend had blue slate roofs with lead ridges. The top seven courses of slate at Arradoul Mains were half slated for ventilation, over the byre areas. Blue slate roofs with ceramic ridges were recorded on seven sites. At Greenbank this was combined with lead flashings on the hips of the piend roof. Corrugated iron roofs were recorded on seven sites and corrugated asbestos on four. At Loanhead the corrugated asbestos roofs stopped against brick skews formed by placing brick on edge on the original stone skew. At Burnside of Rathven, Pottingbrae and Sauchenbush there was a mixture of building materials on the same range of roof. Pantile roofs were recorded at Hillhead of Rannas, Stripeside and Westerbogs. At Stripeside the pantiled roof had a skirt of stone slate which had been repaired with blue slate in some areas. Ceramic ridge vents are found on the roof of Cunningholes and Greenbank. Decorative metal ridge vents were recorded at Bogend, Easter Bogs, Leitcheston and Wester Bogs. A piend louvred ridge vent was recorded at Stripeside.

Eight steadings have arches over larger openings, seven are flat-arched and one, Easter Bogs, has half-round arches. Timber lintels over large openings were recorded on four sites and at Leitcheston, stone lintels with timber safe lintels behind them.

Cobbled yards still survive in only five sites but there are some very fine cobbled floors in some of the unaltered byres, and stables. Cairnfield and Leitcheston are particularly good in this respect.

Tile ventilators were recorded at Arradoul Mains, Leitcheston, Loanhead and Mill of Buckie. At Loanhead there was also a slit ventilator in the stone wall. At Cunningholes the midden was situated to the rear of the steading. Only one gabled loft entry with a forestair was recorded at Easter Bogs where there were also five dormer entries to the same range.

At Burnside of Rathven the stable was still intact. Each stall was fitted with a slatted timber floor to keep the horses off the stonework. Stable windows normally consisted of four or six fixed panes of glass over two timber shutters or a hit and miss ventilator.

Brick jambs normally built in an inband-outband pattern were recorded at Arradoul Mains, Burnside of Rathven and Sauchenbush.

In the ruins of the east range of the steading at Letterfourie Home Farm are a number of interesting features. One is a series of cantilevered steps leading to a small opening high in the wall. This formed the access to the house for the poultry. Another feature of this steading is the two-storey central building dated '1776' and having a central gable feature surmounted by a small bell tower. Also in the east range of this steading is the remains of a 'hingin' lum' which channeled the smoke into a gable flue high in the gable. The only other dated steading is Arradoul Mains which bears the initials 'J—G' and the date '1893'.

At Brankomleys and Cairnfield a fuie was recorded in one of the steading gables.

Most of the byres in this area had been converted internally to comply with regulations for dairy cattle. Concrete floors and trevises were therefore the most common types. Tubular metal trevises were recorded at Birkenbush and Sauchenbush. The only two steadings to retain both the timber trevis and the cobbled floor were Hillhead of Letterfourie and Wester Bogs.

Conclusion

THE material presented in the preceding chapters is very much a digest. From the standard documentary sources available for every parish and county, namely the Agricultural Surveys and the first two Statistical Accounts, information on farm buildings and changes in such buildings, especially for the crucial period between the late 1700s and the mid-1800s, has been brought together in such a way as to form a background guide for future surveys. The mass of material available, though scattered, is such that a highly scientific approach involving computer analysis of data is feasible. The sample surveys that have been undertaken indicate the same need, and have brought to light many factors—for example aspects of architectural detailing—that the historical documentary sources scarcely touch on, but which are nevertheless essential for ascertaining regional patterns of distribution.

Such scientific analysis lies in the future. The authors are very conscious that this digest is only the beginning, and that the task is complicated by the fact that farm buildings combine within their complexes both living and working functions, and that these can vary according to the type of farming carried on in the districts where they stand. To study farm architecture is not only to be an architect: it is also to be a social and economic historian. Besides this, detailed analysis of changes that have taken place within farm buildings from the time of their erection is like working through the stratified layers of an archaeological excavation. The establishment of the dates of major changes is a means of providing a check on the dates of economic change, which, when set against national history, will indicate the relative rates of local change, pointing to areas with advanced or conservative characteristics.

It is, however, far from easy to establish the date of erection of farm buildings, or of subsequent architectural changes. Date stones on buildings, as has been noted, may have been taken from other, older buildings, perhaps of a different kind, where the stone has been re-used. It is a normal, human characteristic to build in a stone with an inscription outwards, rather than conceal it. Date stones may also record an event or change subsequent to the original building. Dates written or gouged into wood or plaster within the building are particularly suspect, for they could be done at any time after the erection of the building. Great care is necessary, and cross-checking if at all possible, before the evidence of a visible date can be accepted.

In this respect, documentary sources are valuable. Over much of Scotland, the main period of erection of farm buildings lies within the period of production of estate plans and plans produced by local architects. A survey of such sources, followed by analysis of the data, would mean a great step forward in the study of farm buildings. Ordnance Survey maps also give visual evidence. But field surveying is a necessary concomitant, if a check is to be made on whether the existing farm is really the one referred to in the documents, especially those of an earlier date. Documentary sources cannot in themselves be accepted as dating evidence, for they merely tell us that there was a building there at the time the document was written or published. Where other evidence is lacking, dating may also be done by the use of judgement in making

211

Fig. 195.   New Technology: Sidlaw Grain Co, Cargill, Perthshire. Grain storage silos and administration unit. (NMAS: 33.17.7)

comparison with buildings of known date, and with their architectural details. However, features that indicate age in one district may not do so in another, and closely localised features should not be used for drawing general conclusions on dates. The accumulation of experience in examining the proportions of buildings, their roofs, window shapes and building materials, allied where possible to ground-plans, types of hearth etc. may often be the only available means of guessing at dates,[484] though even this can be difficult when, as in the case of the farm of Brownhill in Auchterless, Aberdeenshire, a building erected in 1902 retains the style and features of buildings half a century earlier. The age of farm buildings in general is likely to remain a matter of fairly broad interpretation, however, until detailed national surveys have been completed. Even then, however, the problem of relative chronology will remain, for it can happen that designed buildings incorporate features carried over from an older vernacular tradition.[485]

References

1. DAFS 1952. 10; DAFS 1977. 9, 10, 69; Coppock 1977. 170-99.
2. RCAHMS *Kintyre Inventory* 1972; Fisher 1972.
3. NMRS *Report* 1966-71. 1.
4. Stell 1972. 1-2.
5. Walton 1957. 118-20; Stell 1972. 39-48.
6. NMRS *Report* 1966-71. 2-7.
7. Hay 1973. 127-33.
8. Walton 1957. 112-14; NMRS *Report* 1972-74. 2-6.
9. Fenton and Sprott 1975. 4-5.
10. SVBWG *Newsletter* 1975. 6.
11. Cf. Brunskill 1970. 132-57; Brunskill 1976. 115-50.
12. Fenton, Walker and Stell 1976.
13. Walker 1977.
14. Fenton 1970.
15. Fenton 1968. 94-103.
16. Megaw 1962. 6/1. 87-92.
17. Whyte 1975. 55-68.
18. Bartholomew 1950-51. 173-76; Dunbar 1956-57, XC. 81-92; Dunbar 1960. 113-17; Walton 1957. 109-22.
19. McCourt 1967. 75-8.
20. Hay 1973. 127-33.
21. Stell 1972. 39-48.
22. Megaw 1963. 230-34; Dunbar 1965. 61-67; Fenton 1978.
23. Thomas 1857-60. 127-44; 1866-68. 153-95; Mitchell 1880. 48-72; Williams 1900. 73-79.
24. Curwen 1938. 261-89; Gibson 1925. 364-72.
25. Roussell 1934; Greig 1942. 109-48.
26. Kissling 1944. 134-40; Geddes 1955. 78-85; Walton 1957. 155-62; Crawford 1965. 34-63; Fenton 1967. 50-68; Fenton 1978a; Fenton 1978b.
27. MacSween and Gailey 1961. 77-84; Miller 1967. 193-221; Fenton 1976. 134-36.
28. Roussell 1934. 53-4, 56, 59-63; Scott 1951. 197-198; Talve 1960. 372; Fenton 1973; Fenton 1974. 247-58; Fenton 1978b. 376-80.
29. Roussell 1934. 79, 87, 93, 97-8; Scott 1951. 196-208; Fenton 1978b. 380-85.
30. Maxwell 1887-90. 58-9; Marshall 1935. 84-7; Scott 1951. 196-208; Whitaker 1957. 161-70; Scott-Elliott 1960-61. 80-82; Milligan 1963. 53-9; Fenton 1974. 247-58; Fenton 1976. 95-99.
31. Mitchell 1880. 39-43; Goudie 1885-86. 257-97; Dickinson and Straker 1932-33. 89-94; Id. 1933; Curwen 1944. 130-46; Cruden 1946-47. 43-47; Cruden 1949; Maxwell 1954-55. 185-96; Maxwell 1954-56. 231-32; Fenton 1976. 102-05; Fenton 1978b. 396-410.
32. Clouston 1924-25. 49-54, 65-72.
33. Gregor 1892-95. 125-59.

34. Jespersen 1950; Jespersen 1963-64. 237-44.

35. Tindall 1970.

36. Donnachie 1971. 30-40.

37. Skinner 1966. 188-90.

38. McLaren 1944-45. 6-14; Greenhill 1945-46. 144; Greenhill 1950-51. 165; Donnachie and Stewart 1967. 176-299; Donnachie 1971. 40-42; Fenton 1978b. 399, 409.

39. Hutton 1976. 30-35; Walker 1977. 52-74.

40. Whitaker 1934-38. 1-22; Waddell 1937-40. 189-94; Robertson 1945. 146-203; Robertson 1949. 169-70; Robertson 1958; Whitaker 1952. 59-66; Barley 1963. 23-52; Dunbar 1966. 88-92; Beaton 1978.

41. Walker 1977; Walker 1979.

42. Skinner 1969. 20-21.

43. Stephen 1967. 248-54.

44. Hall 1972.

45. Pride 1975.

46. Cf. Brunskill 1976. 115-50.

47. Maxwell 1974.

48. Maxwell 1976. 5.

49. Maxwell 1974.

50. Payne 1976. 6-7.

51. OSA 1975. XIV. 55-59.

52. OSA 1795. XVI. 349, 495.

53. OSA 1798. XX. 274.

54. Kerr 1809. 93.

55. Beatson 1794. 19.

56. Headrick 1813. 127-29.

57. Henderson 1812. 30 : Caithness.

58. Donaldson 1794. 21-22 : Banff

59. Whyte 1975. 57-59.

60. Anderson 1794. 96-98 : Aberdeen.

61. Whyte 1975. 57-59.

62. Milne 1912. XXIV. 150-52.

63. Erskine 1795. 28-32.

64. Donaldson 1794. 23; Donaldson 1794. 20-21; OSA 1792. IV. 107.

65. Henderson 1812. 45-47.

66. *Seafield Papers* 1762. Box 37, Bundle 4.

67. Sinclair 1795. 130.

68. Barron 1892. 113, 116, 168-69.

69. *Seafield Papers c.* 1762. Box 37, Bundle 4(3) 23; 1763. Box 38, Bundle 1, 107-08; Box 25, Bundle 1, 8.

70. Buchanan 1793. 93-95.

71. NSA 1845. XIV. 268.

72. Graham 1812. 77.

73. Headrick 1807. 312.
74. Graham 1812. 77-78
75. Smith 1810. 56-72.
76. Thomson 1800. 74-77.
77. OSA. 1795. XIV. 7.
78. Fenton 1978b. 161-62.
79. Dunbar 1960. 113-17.
80. Pennecuik 1815. 58 note.
81. Aiton 1811. I. 114-15.
82. Marshall 1794. 19-21.
83. Roger 1794. 3; Headrick 1813. 33-34, 127-29.
84. Keith 1811. 129-30; Dinnie 1865. 15-17.
85. Grant 1901-02. 8-10.
86. Sinclair 1795. 211; Henderson 1812. 152-53, 200.
87. Smith 1798. 15.
88. Robertson 1808. 56-59.
89. NSA 1845. XIV. 96, 111, 128, 164, 196 : Glenshiel.
90. Henderson 1812. 45-47; Loch 1820. 52-53, 86-88, 120, 154.
91. Whyte 1975. 60-62.
92. Fenton 1970. 46-50.
93. Whyte 1975. 54-60.
94. Pennant (1759) 1776. I. 131.
95. OSA. 1795. XIV. 23 : Chirnside.
96. Douglas 1798. 245.
97. Findlater 1802. 46.
98. Aiton 1811. I. 115-117, 123-24.
99. Headrick 1807. 312-14.
100. Wilson 1812. 63-64.
101. Ure 1794. 18-19.
102. Whyte & Macfarlane 1811. 28-29.
103. NSA 1845. VI. 474, 831-32.
104. Singer 1812. 90-91, 93-95.
105. Smith 1810. 57-62.
106. Graham 1814. 32.
107. *Seafield Papers* 1762. Box 37, Bundle 4.
108. Marshall 1794. 19-21.
109. Robertson 1799. 51-52, 59.
110. Wight 1778. II. 59-60.
111. Gibson 1959. 39.
112. NSA 1845. X. 392.
113. Robertson 1813. 177-79.
114. Anderson 1794. 96-99.
115. Hamilton 1946. 75-6, 111-12.
116. OSA 1794. X. 242.

117. Keith 1811. 129-30; Dinnie 1865. 15-17.
118. OSA 1791. II. 534.
119. Leslie 1811. 60-61, 64-65.
120. Pococke 1760. 159-60.
121. Sinclair 1795. 211, 277-78.
122. Henderson 1812. 27-30.
123. NSA 1845. V. 143, 146, 148.
124. Smith 1798. 15-18.
125. NSA 1845. VIII. 30, 44.
126. *Ib*. 99.
127. Martin 1884. 291.
128. Campbell 1752. 20-21.
129. Robertson 1768. II. Folio 40.
130. Buchanan 1793. 93-95.
131. Heron 1794. 32-3.
132. OSA 1794. X. 464; 1797. XIX. 266.
133. Mackenzie 1813. 232, 234, 246, 258.
134. NSA 1845. XIV. 96, 111, 128, 164, 196.
135. *Ib*.
136. NSA 1845. XV. 7, 44, 57, 73, 94, 203-04.
137. OSA 1793. VI. 299.
138. Sage 1889. 56-7, 60, 180-81, 197.
139. Fenton 1978b. 175-90.
140. OSA 1792. II. 105.
141. Fenton 1970. 40-50.
142. Collier 1831. 190-95; Gailey 1960. 68-70.
143. Cf. Robertson 1795. 40-41 : Midlothian; Trotter 1794. 28, Trotter 1811. 18 : West Lothian.
144. OSA 1792. III. 327.
145. OSA 1794. XII. 370.
146. Aiton 1811. I. 115-17, 123-24; NSA 1845. V. 112, 163, 229, 341, 531, 568, 688, 713, 766-67.
147. NSA 1845. V. 25, 76.
148. Aiton 1816. 41.
149. OSA 1791. I. 321.
150. NSA 1845. VII. 39, 50, 100, 127, 257, 375.
151. OSA 1796. XVII. 271; Graham 1812. 77-82.
152. OSA 1793. VIII. 483.
153. NSA 1845. VI. 474, 831-32.
154. Smith 1810. 57-62.
155. OSA 1799. XXI. 444, 451, 460.
156. Singer 1812. 90-91, 93-95.
157. Erskine 1795. 28-32.
158. Thomson 1800. 74-77.

159. OSA 1793. VI. 491 : Kincardine; 1796. XVII. 50 : Lecropt; 1797. XIX. 467, 473 : Longforgan; 1798. XX. 72 : Kilmadock.

160. Robertson 1799. 51-52, 59.

161. Headrick 1813. 41-42, 130-31.

162. Robertson 1813. 180-82.

163. OSA 1794. XII. 283; 1799. XXI. 142.

164. Donaldson 1794. 21-23.

165. Souter 1812. 57-8, 89-91, 99, 120, 211.

166. Leslie 1811. 60-61, 64-65.

167. OSA 1795. XIV. 137 : Firth & Stenness; 1795. XIV. 317 : Birsay & Harray; 1795. XVI. 467 : Sandwick & Stromness.

168. Fenton 1978b. 188-190.

169. OSA 1792. IV. 569.

170. OSA 1794. XI. 301.

171. OSA 1798. XX. 293.

172. OSA 1793. VIII. 44, 59.

173. NSA 1845. VII. 404.

174. Macdonald 1811. 665-67.

175. Heron 1794. 32-3.

176. OSA 1794. XIII. 325.

177. Robertson 1808. 40.

178. OSA 1794. X. 464; 1797. XIX. 266.

179. Sinclair 1795. 50-51, 103.

180. Mackenzie 1813. 232, 234, 246, 258.

181. NSA 1845. XIV. 96, 111, 128, 164, 196.

182. Sage 1849. 56-7, 60, 180-81, 197.

183. Loch 1820. 52-3, 86-8, 120, 154, App. II. 5-6, 9, 14, 17, 24, 27, 30, 33.

184. *Report* 1884. App. A, LXIV. 302-03.

185. NSA 1845. XV. 14-15, 21, 117, 122, 138-39.

186. Fenton 1978b. 180-81.

187. Graham 1812. 77-82.

188. Lowther etc. 1894. 12.

189. E.g. Keith 1811. 129; Henderson 1812. 200; OSA 1794. XI. 269 : Watten; NSA 1845. V. 27; Canisbay 143 : Wick.

190. OSA 1795. XVI. 58.

191. Robertson 1829. 78-80.

192. Douglas 1813. 29.

193. OSA 1799. XXI. 451.

194. Headrick 1813. 127-29, 138.

195. Robertson 1813. 184-87.

196. Souter 1812. 97.

197. Sinclair 1795. 50.

198. Sage 1889. 60.

199. Aiton 1816. 98-100.

200. Fenton 1968. 100-101.
201. Fenton 1978a. 34, 37.
202. Marshall 1794. 19-21.
203. *Seafield Papers* 1762. Box 37, Bundle 4.
204. Pennant 1776. 128; OSA 1792. IV. 154; NSA 1845. 37.
205. Leslie 1811. 61, 67.
206. NSA 1845. V. 143, 146, 148.
207. OSA 1791. I. 289.
208. Sinclair 1795. 130.
209. Hutcheson 1927.
210. Douglas 1934. 450.
211. Fenton 1970. 28.
212. MacGill 1909. 196.
213. Grant and Leslie 1798. 95-6; OSA 1795. XIV. 390; Leslie 1811. 513;
Lauder 1830. 299.
214. Walker 1977. 16.
215. Fenton 1970. 30; Walker 1977. 20-26.
216. Souter 1812. App. 9-11.
217. Fenton 1970. 30-35; Walker 1977. 28-32.
218. Gardenstone 1795. III. 244-45; Headrick 1813. 129-30.
219. Robertson 1813. 186-87.
220. Walker 1977. 40-43.
221. Walker 1977. 46-48.
222. Walker 1977. 49-51.
223. Walker 1977. 51-57.
224. Belsches 1796. 21-22.
225. Roy 1792. 521-22; OSA 1793. VI. 548.
226. Fenton 1970. 38.
227. Douglas 1798. 24-25.
228. OSA 1792. III. 343.
229. Brunskill 1962. 65.
230. NSA 1845. IV. 551.
231. OSA 1792. II 22-23.
232. Pennant 1776. II. 87.
233. Lauder 1873. 156.
234. Walker 1977. 55.
235. Fenton 1970. 40.
236. SWRI. 1966. 9, 13.
237. Walker 1977. 7.
238. Walker 1977. 6-7.
239. Cf. Donaldson 1794. 20-21; Walker 1977. 6.
240. OSA 1793. VI. 491.
241. Buchan-Hepburn 1783-87.
242. Walker 1977. 10-12, 39, 53-59.

243. Walker 1977. 10, 16, 59.
244. ABC 1699. 30.
245. Buchan-Hepburn 1783-87.
246. Somerville 1805. 33, 36-47.
247. OSA 1795. XIV. 363.
248. Aiton 1811. I. 115-17, 123-24.
249. Whyte & Macfarlane 1811. 28-29.
250. OSA 1795. XIV. 768.
251. Singer 1812. 90-91, 93-95.
252. Milne 1912. XXIV. 150-52.
253. Smith 1810. 57-62.
254. Erskine 1795. 28-32.
255. Thomson 1800. 74-77.
256. Wight 1778. I. 10, 19, 21.
257. Robertson 1799. 51-52, 59.
258. OSA 1792. III. 272-73.
259. OSA 1793. VI. 380.
260. Headrick 1813. 33-34, 127-29.
261. OSA 1791. I. 426-27.
262. Headrick 1813. 41-42, 130-31.
263. Robertson 1813. 180-82.
264. OSA 1791. II. 534.
265. Taylor 1972. Indexed under Anchorage and Syseboll, and Lime.
266. Donaldson 1794. 21-23.
267. OSA 1793. VIII. 260.
268. Leslie 1811. 60-61, 64-65.
269. Fenton 1978b. 136, 143-44.
270. Burt 1754 (1974 reprint) II. 204-05.
271. OSA 1792. IV. 569.
272. OSA 1795. XIV. 176.
273. OSA 1798. XX. 293.
274. Johnson 1775. 232.
275. Heron 1794. 32-3.
276. Macdonald 1811. 82-89.
277. Sinclair 1795. 50-1, 103.
278. Sage 1849. 56-7, 60, 180-81, 197.
279. Henderson 1812. 45-47.
280. NSA 1845. XV. 7, 44, 57, 73, 94, 203-04.
281. *Report* 1884. App. A, LXIV. 302-03.
282. Cowie 1871. 92.
283. OSA 1794. X. 242.
284. NSA 1845. XV. 7, 44, 57, 73, 94, 203-04.
285. *Report* 1884. App. A, LIX. 270-80.
286. II. 144.

287. Buchan-Hepburn 1783-87.
288. Headrick 1807. 312-14.
289. Whyte & Macfarlane 1811. 28-29.
290. Belsches 1796. 21-22.
291. Sinclair 1795. 50-1, 103; Robertson 1808. 56-59.
292. Cowie 1871. 92.
293. Cf. Beveridge 1911. 325.
294. Fenton 1978b. 143-44.
295. OSA 1791. II 534.
296. Headrick 1813. 33-34, 127-29.
297. Burt 1754. I. 56.
298. DOST s.v. Harl, Harling.
299. Paul 1922. 335.
300. Sinclair 1795. 29.
301. Somerville 1805. 33, 36-47.
302. OSA 1793. V. 367.
303. Fenton 1978b. 155.
304. Burnett-Stuart 1978. 1-2.
305. Lowther etc. 1894. 11.
306. Lucas 1956. 16-35.
307. Pennant 1776. 216, 246, 261.
308. Aiton 1811. I. 114.
309. Robertson 1768. Folio 22-3.
310. Burt 1754, II. 60.
311. Millar 1909. 115.
312. Johnson 1775, 74ff., 232.
313. MacWilliam 1973. 85.
314. Robertson 1808. 58.
315. NSA 1845. XIV. 268, 308.
316. Robertson MS 1768 Folio 48.
317. Dunbar 1966. Fig. 182 facing 238.
318. Mackenzie 1813, 232.
319. Mackenzie 1813. 232, 246.
320. Sage 1889. 4.
321. MacCulloch 1824. II. 271-72.
322. Henderson 1812. 45-47.
323. Whyte 1975. 64-5.
324. Belhaven 1699. 29-33.
325. Whyte 1975. 64-5.
326. Wight 1778-84.
327. OSA 1791. I. 83 : Ayton; 1794. XII. 47-8, 50 : Coldingham; 1794. XIII. 226 :
Cockburnspath; 1795. XIV. 7-8, 23 : Chirnside; 1795. XIV. 588-89 : Mertoun; 1795.
XIV. 577-8 : Langton; 1795. XVI. 352 : Whitson and Hilton; XVI. 495 : Legerwood;
1798. XX. 274-75 : Fogo.

328. Lowe 1794. 62.
329. Kerr 1809. 93-7.
330. NSA 1845. II. 76.
331. Buchan-Hepburn 1783-87.
332. Somerville 1805. 33, 36-47.
333. Ure 1794. 17; Douglas 1798. 23-25.
334. OSA 1792. I. 307.
335. Johnston 1794. 17-18.
336. Findlater 1802. 38-40.
337. Wight 1783. Survey VI. 372, 379, 384, 426, 430.
338. Robertson 1795. 40-41.
339. Robertson 1795. 40.
340. Trotter 1794. 28; Trotter 1811. 18.
341. Aiton 1811. I. 115-17, 123-24.
342. OSA. 1791. II. 105; 1797. XIX. 455; 1798. XX. 148.
343. Aiton 1811. I. 114-15.
344. Headrick 1807. 312-14.
345. Aiton 1816. 92-3, 98-9.
346. Ure 1794. 18-19.
347. Whyte & Macfarlane 1811. 28-29.
348. Belsches 1796. 21-22.
349. OSA. 1795. XV. 385; 1796. XVIII. 104.
350. Graham 1812. 77-82.
351. NSA 1845. VI. 474, 831-32.
352. Pococke (1760) 1887. 34.
353. Johnston 1794. 74-75.
354. OSA. 1791. I. 206; 1792. IV, 218, 225.
355. OSA. 1794. X. 446.
356. OSA. 1792. II. 341.
357. OSA. 1794. XIII. 260.
358. Singer 1812. 90-91, 93-95.
359. Webster 1794. 10-11, 15.
360. Smith 1810. 39.
361. Harper 1896. 1.
362. OSA. 1792. IV. 141.
363. OSA. 1796. XVII. 562.
364. OSA. 1795. XIV. 474.
365. Smith 1810. 57-62.
366. Erskine 1795. 28-32.
367. Graham 1814. 32.
368. Thomson 1800. 74-75; Beatson 1794. 19.
369. OSA. 1791. I. 371.
370. Thomson 1800. 74-77.
371. Wight 1778. (Survey 1773) I. 10, 19, 21.

372. Marshall 1794. 19-21.
373. Robertson 1799. 51-52, 59.
374. OSA. 1792. IV. 194.
375. OSA. 1792. III. 272-73.
376. OSA. 1797. XIX. 467, 473-74.
377. OSA. 1793. VI. 380.
378. OSA. 1793. VI. 491.
379. OSA. 1795. XV. 606.
380. OSA. 1796. XVII. 50.
381. OSA. 1796. XVII. 555.
382. OSA. 1797. XIX. 474.
383. OSA. 1797. XIX. 347.
384. OSA. 1796. XIX. 467, 473.
385. OSA. 1798. XX. 72.
386. Roger 1794. 3; Headrick 1813. 33-34, 127-29.
387. Roger 1794. 4.
388. Wight 1778. II. 21-22.
389. Robertson 1813. 177-79.
390. Robertson 1813. 180-82.
391. Keith 1811. 129-30; Dinnie 1865. 15-17.
391. Donaldson 1794. 21-23.
393. Grant 1901-2. 8-10
394. Souter 1812. 57-8, 89-91, 99, 120, 211.
395. *Seafield Papers* 1762. Box 37, Bundle 4; Leslie 1811. 58-59.
396. Leslie 1811. 60-61, 64-65.
397. Henderson 1812. 27-30.
398. NSA. 1845. V. 65.
399. NSA. 1845. V. 75-6.
400. Low. 1923-24. 52.
401. Barry 1805. 337.
402. NSA. 1845. XV. 19 : Orphir; 107 : North Ronaldsay; 129 : Westray; 179, 181 : St. Andrews.
403. Robson 1794. 18; Smith 1798. 15.
404. Pennant 1776. 246, 261.
405. OSA. 1793. VIII. 44, 59 : Gigha and Cara; 1794. X. 403 : Tiree.
406. NSA. 1845. VII. 368; Fenton 1979b.
407. Martin (1695) 1884. 291.
408. Ray 1753. 353.
409. Warden 1864. 453.
410. Johnson 1775. 232.
411. OSA. 1793. VIII. 510.
412. Robertson 1808. 56-59.
413. MacDonald 1811. 82-89.
414. NSA. 1845. XIV. 157.

415. NSA. 1845. XIV. 172.
416. NSA. 1845. XIV. 212.
417. NSA. 1845. XIV. 268.
418. NSA. 1845. XIV. 226.
419. NSA. 1845. XIV. 292.
420. NSA. 1845. XIV. 308.
421. NSA. 1845. XIV. 345-46.
422. Sinclair 1795. 50-51, 103.
423. Mackenzie 1813. 232, 234, 246, 258.
424. NSA. 1845. XIV, 96, 111, 128, 164, 196.
425. *Report* 1884 App. A. XLI. 157-174.
426. Sage 1849. 56-7, 60, 180-81, 197.
427. Henderson 1812. 45-47.
428. Loch 1820. 52-3, 86-8, 120, App. II. 5-6, 9, 14, 17, 24, 27, 30, 33.
429. NSA. 1845. XV. 7, 44, 57, 73, 94, 203-04.
430. MacCulloch 1824. III. 15; *Report* 1884. App. A, LXIV, 302-03.
431. Edmondston 1809. II. 48.
432. Shirreff 1814. 19.
433. Laing 1818. 36.
434. Hibbert 1822, 114-16, 537, 545.
435. Charlton (1834) 1935-46, 61-2.
436. NSA. 1845. XV.14-15, 21, 117, 122, 138-39.
437. Cowie 1871, 92.
438. Tudor 1883, 157.
439. DOST s.v. Cot, Cotar, Cotehouse, Cothouse, Cottar, Cot-toun.
440. Hume 1797. 78-79.
441. Derham 1760.187-8
442. OSA. 1792. II. 358.
443. OSA. 1792. I. 344-45.
444. Hume 1797. 99-102, 149.
445. NSA. 1845. II. 129.
446. NSA. 1845. II. 351-52.
447. NSA. 1845. II. 255.
448. NSA. 1845. II. 351-52.
449. Alison in Gauldie 1974. 22.
450. Somerville 1848. 10.
451. NSA. 1845. II. 188.
452. Hope 1881. 231.
453. Smith 1834.
454. *Plans* 1851. 245-80.
455. Quoted in Johnston 1974. 349.
456. *Ib*. 354.
457. Cole 1930. III. 783.
458. Quoted in Johnston 1974. 349.

459. Miller 1856. 177, 215-16.
460. Mitchell 1921. 36-40.
461. Smith 1973. 121-45.
462. Fenton 1976. 80-89.
463. Gray 1814. Plates IX, X, XI, XII, XIII.
464. Gray 1814. 50-52.
465. Brewster 1830. 280.
466. Gray 1814. 56-57.
467. Kerr 1809. 161.
468. Gray 1814. 55, 61.
469. Brown 1799, 61.
470. Young 1804, 73.
471. Curtler 1909. 236-7.
472. Burstall 1832. 233-5.
473. Robertson 1813. 238.
474. Donaldson 1794. 19-20.
475. Fenton 1977. 84-87.
476. Walker 1977. 56-57.
477. Hutton 1976. 32.
478. Stephens 1861, plate XII.
479. *Forneth Papers*, in National Museum of Antiquities of Scotland.
480. Hutton 1976, 35.
481. Walker 1977. 52-74.
482. Walker 1977. 57.
483. Walker 1979.
484. Cf., for Denmark, Michelsen 1979.
485. Walker 1979. 46.

Bibliography

ABC (Lord Belhaven). *The Country-Man's Rudiments : or Advice to the Farmers in East-Lothian how to Labour and Improve their Ground*. Edinburgh 1699.

Aiton, W. *General View of the Agriculture of the County of Ayr*. 2V. Glasgow 1811.

Aiton, W. *General View of the Agriculture of the County of Bute*. Glasgow 1816.

Alison, S. Scott. Report on the Sanitary Condition and General Economy of the Labouring Population in the Town of Tranent and Neighbouring District in Haddington. In *Reports on the Sanitary Condition of the Labouring Population of Scotland, in Consequence of an Inquiry Directed to be made by the Poor Law Commissioners*. London 1842.

Anderson, J. *General View of the Agriculture of the County of Aberdeen*. Edinburgh 1794.

Barley, D.C. Dovecotes of East Lothian. In *Transactions of the Ancient Monuments Society* 1963. New Series Vol. 11, 23-52.

Barron, D.G., ed. *Court Book of the Barony of Urie* (Scottish History Society). Edinburgh 1892.

Barry, G. *The History of the Orkney Islands*. Edinburgh 1805.

Bartholomew, G. The Paton Cottage, Torthorwald. In *Transactions of the Dumfriesshire and Galloway Natural History and Antiquarian Society* 1950-1. XXIX. 173-6.

Beaton, E. *The Doocots of Moray* (Moray Field Club) n.p. 1978.

Beaton, E. and Moran, M. A cottar house with a hingin' lum. In *Vernacular Architecture* 1977. Vol. 8.

Beatson, R. *General View of the Agriculture of the County of Fife*. Edinburgh 1794.

Belhaven 1699. See ABC.

Belsches, R. *General View of the Agriculture of the County of Stirling*. Edinburgh 1796.

Beveridge, E. *North Uist, its Archaeology and Topography*. Edinburgh 1911.

Brewster, D. *The Edinburgh Encyclopaedia*. 1830.

Brown, R. *General View of the Agriculture of the West Riding of Yorkshire*. Edinburgh 1799.

Brunskill, R.W. The Clay Houses of Cumberland. In *Transactions of the Ancient Monuments Society* 1962. Vol. 10. 57-80.

Brunskill, R.W. *Illustrated Handbook of Vernacular Architecture*. London 1970.

Brunskill, R.W. Recording the Buildings of the Farmstead. In *Transactions of the Ancient Monuments Society* 1976. Vol. 21. 115-150.

Buchanan, J.L. *Travels in the Western Hebrides, 1782-90*. London 1793.

Buchan-Hepburn, G. *Buchan-Hepburn MS Account Book, No VI. Cash Book*. 1783-87.

Burnett-Stuart, T. Modern Harling for 18th Century Buildings—Do We Want It? In *Newsletter* (SVBWG) 1978. No. 4. 1-3.

Burstall, Mr. Description of a New Mode of applying High Pressure Steam Engines to Threshing Mills. In *Transactions of the Highland and Agricultural Society*. 1832. IX. 233-35.

Burt, Captain. *Letters from A Gentleman in the North of Scotland to His Friend in London*. 1754 (reprint Edinburgh 1974). 2V.

Campbell, J. *A full Description of the Highlands of Scotland*. London 1752.

Charlton, E. Journal of an Expedition to Shetland in 1834. In *Old-Lore Miscellany* 1935-46. X. 55-71.

Childe, V.G. Another Late Viking House at Freswick, Caithness. In *Proceedings of the Society of Antiquaries of Scotland* 1942-3 LXXVII. 5-17.

Clouston, J.S. The Old Orkney Mills. In *Proceedings of the Orkney Antiquarian Society* 1924-5. III. 49-54, 65-71.

Cole, G.D.H. and M. *W. Cobbett, Rural Rides—together with Tours of Scotland—* London 1930.

Collier, J. On Thatching with Heath. In *Prize Essays and Transactions of the Highland Society of Scotland* 1831, New Series 2, 190-195.

Coppock, J.T. *An Agricultural Atlas of Scotland*. Edinburgh 1976.

Cowie, R. *Shetland and its Inhabitants*. Lerwick 1871.

Cramond, W., ed. *The Records of Elgin*. 2V. (New Spalding Club) 1903.

Crawford, I.A. Contributions to a History of Domestic Settlement in North Uist. In *Scottish Studies* 1965. 9/1. 34-63.

Cruden, S. The Horizontal Water-Mill at Dounby. In *Proceedings of the Society of Antiquaries of Scotland* 1946-7. LXXXI. 43-47.

Cruden, S. *Click Mill, Dounby, Orkney*. (HMSO) 1949.

Cruden, S. Excavations at Birsay, Orkney. In Small, A., ed. *The Fourth Viking Congress*. Edinburgh and London 1965. 22-31.

Curle, A.O. An Account of the Excavation of a Dwelling of the Viking Period at 'Jarlshof', Sumburgh, Shetland. In *Proceedings of the Society of Antiquaries of Scotland* 1934-5. LXIX. 265-321.

Curle, A.O. A Viking Settlement at Freswick, Caithness. In *Proceedings of the Society of Antiquaries of Scotland* 1938-9. LXXIII. 71-110.

Curtler, W.H.R. *A Short History of English Agriculture*. Oxford 1909.

Curwen, E.C. The Hebrides : a Cultural Backwater. In *Antiquity* 1938. Vol. 12. 261-89.

Curwen, E.C. The Problem of Early Water-mills. In *Antiquity* 1944. XVIII. 130-146.

DAFS. Department of Agriculture and Fisheries for Scotland.

DAFS. *Types of Farming in Scotland*. HMSO Edinburgh 1952.

DAFS. *Agricultural Statistics 1976 Scotland*. HMSO Edinburgh 1977.

Dent, J.S. Building materials and methods of construction, the evidence from the archaeological excavations at Broad Street, Aberdeen. In Fenton, A., Walker, B. and Stell, G., edd. *Building Construction in Scotland. Some Historical and Regional Aspects* (SVBWG) 1976. 65-71.

Derham, W., ed. *Select Remains of the Learned John Ray*. London 1760.

Dickinson, H.W. and Straker, E. The Shetland Watermill. In *Transactions of the Newcomen Society* 1932-3. XIII. 89-94.

Dickinson, H.W. and Straker, E. The Shetland Watermill. In *The Engineer,* 24 March 1933.

Dinnie, R. *An Account of the Parish of Birse.* Aberdeen 1865.

Donaldson, J. *General View of the Agriculture of the County of Banff.* Edinburgh 1794.

Donaldson, J. *General View of the Agriculture of the County of Elgin or Moray.* London 1794.

Donaldson, J. *General View of the Agriculture of the County of Nairn.* London 1794.

Donaldson, J. *General View of the Agriculture of the Carse of Gowrie, Perthshire.* London 1794.

Donnachie, I. *The Industrial Archaeology of Galloway.* Newton Abbot 1971.

Donnachie, I.L. and Stewart, N.K. Scottish Windmills—An Outline and Inventory. In *Proceedings of the Society of Antiquaries of Scotland* 1967. XCVIII. 176-299.

DOST. Dictionary of the Older Scottish Tongue.

Douglas, R. *General View of the Agriculture of Roxburgh.* Edinburgh 1798.

Douglas, R. *General View of the Agriculture of Selkirk.* Edinburgh 1798.

Douglas, R. *General View of the Agriculture of Roxburgh and Selkirk.* London 1813.

Douglas, R. *Annals of the Royal Burgh of Forres.* Elgin 1934.

Dunbar, J.G. Some Cruck-framed Buildings in the Aberfeldy District of Perthshire. In *Proceedings of the Society of Antiquaries of Scotland* 1956-7. XC. 81-92.

Dunbar, J.G. Pitcastle, a Cruck-Framed House in Northern Perthshire. In *Scottish Studies* 1960. Vol. 4. 113-17.

Dunbar, J.G. Auchindrain : a mid-Argyll township. In *Folk Life* 1965. Vol. 3. 61-7.

Dunbar, J.G. *The Historic Architecture of Scotland.* London 1966.

Dunbar, J.G. The organisation of the building industry in Scotland during the 17th century. In Fenton, A., Walker, B. and Stell, G., edd. *Building Construction in Scotland. Some Historical and Regional Aspects* (SVBWG) 1976. 7-15.

Edmonston, A. *A View of the Ancient and Present State of the Zetland Islands.* Edinburgh 2V. 1809.

Erskine, J.F. *General View of the Agriculture of the County of Clackmannan.* Edinburgh 1795.

Fairweather, B. *A Short History of Ballachulish Slate Quarry* (The Glencoe & North Lorn Folk Museum) n.d.

Fenton, A. Das Bauernhaus auf Orkney und Shetland. In *Deutsches Jahrbuch für Volkskunde* 1967. Vol. 13. 50-68.

Fenton, A. Alternating Stone and Turf—An Obsolete Building Practice. In *Folk Life* 1968. Vol. 6. 94-103.

Fenton, A. Clay Building and Clay Thatch in Scotland. In *Ulster Folklife* 1970. 15/16. 28-51.

Fenton, A. Corn Drying Kilns in Shetland. In *Shetland News,* 25 January 1973.

Fenton, A. The Scottish Vernacular Buildings Working Group. In *Scottish Studies* 1973. 7/2. 165-7.

Fenton, A. Lexicography and Historical Interpretation. In G.W.S. Barrow, ed. *The Scottish Tradition.* Edinburgh 1974. 243-258.

Fenton, A. Thatch and thatching. In Fenton, A., Walker, B. and Stell, G., edd. *Building Construction in Scotland. Some Historical and Regional Aspects* (SVBWG) 1976. 39-51.

Fenton, A. *Scottish Country Life*. Edinburgh 1976. Reprinted 1977.

Fenton, A. *The Island Blackhouse*. HMSO Edinburgh 1978a.

Fenton, A. *The Northern Isles : Orkney and Shetland*. Edinburgh 1978b

Fenton, A. *Continuity and Change in the Building Tradition of Northern Scotland* (The Ása G. Wright Memorial Lectures). Reykjavík 1979a.

Fenton, A. *A Farming Township. Auchindrain. Argyll*. Perth 1979b.

Fenton, A. and Sprott, G.C. The Vernacular Buildings Section of the Scottish Country Life Archive, National Museum of Antiquities of Scotland. In *Newsletter* (SVBWG) 1975. No. 1. 4-5.

Fenton, A., Walker, B. and Stell, G. *Building Construction in Scotland. Some Historical and Regional Aspects* (SVBWG) 1976.

Findlater, C. *General View of the Agriculture of the County of Peebles*. Edinburgh 1802.

Fisher, I. *Survey Work on Vernacular Buildings in Argyll* (paper read at SVBWG Conference, 1972).

Fisher, I. Building—stone and slate; some regional aspects of Scottish quarrying. In Fenton, A., Walker, B. and Stell, G., edd. *Building Construction in Scotland. Some Historical and Regional Aspects* (SVBWG) 1976. 16-27.

Forneth Papers. In National Museum of Antiquities of Scotland.

Fullarton, W. *General View of the Agriculture of the County of Ayr*. Edinburgh 1793.

Gailey, A. The Use of Mud in Thatching : Scotland. In *Ulster Folklife* 1960. Vol. 6. 68-70.

Gailey, A. The Peasant Houses of the South-west Highlands of Scotland : Distribution, Parallels and Evolution. In *Gwerin* 1962. III/5. 227-242.

Gardenstone, Lord. *Travelling Memorandums*. Edinburgh 1795.

Gauldie, E. *Cruel Habitations. A History of Working-Class Housing 1780-1918*. London 1974.

Gauldie, E. The Middle Class and Working-class Housing in the Nineteenth Century. In A.A. MacLaren, ed. *Social Class in Scotland : Past and Present*. Edinburgh 1976. 12-35.

Geddes, A. *The Isle of Lewis and Harris. A study in British Community*. Edinburgh 1955.

Gibson, C. *Folklore of Tayside* (Dundee Museum and Art Gallery) 1959.

Gibson, G. The Black Houses of the Outer Isles. In *Caledonian Medical Journal* 1925. Vol. 12. 364-72.

Goudie, G. On the Horizontal Water-mills of Shetland. In *Proceedings of the Society of Antiquaries of Scotland* 1885-6. XX. 257-297.

Graham, P. *General View of the Agriculture of Stirlingshire*. Edinburgh 1812.

Graham, P. *General View of the Agriculture of Kinross*. Edinburgh 1814.

Grant, J. Agriculture 150 Years Ago, in *Transactions of the Banff Field Club* 1901-2.

Grant, J. and Leslie, W. *A Survey of the Province of Moray*. Aberdeen 1798.

Gray, A. *Explanation of the Engravings of the most important Implements of Husbandry used in Scotland*. Edinburgh 1814.

Greenhill, F.A. Old Windmill at Whithorn, Wigtownshire. In *Proceedings of the Society of Antiquaries of Scotland* 1945-6. LXXX. 144.

Greenhill, F.A. Old Windmill at Broughty Ferry. In *Proceedings of the Society of Antiquaries of Scotland* 1950-1 LXXXV. 165.

Gregor, W. Kilns, Mills, Millers, Meal, and Bread. In *Transactions of the Buchan Field Club* 1892-5. III. 125-159.

Greig, S. Norrøne Hus på Vesthavsøyene. In *Viking* 1942. Vol.6. 109-48.

Hall, R. de Zouche. *A Bibliography on Vernacular Architecture* (Vernacular Architecture Group) 1972.

Hamilton, H., ed. *Life and Labour on an Aberdeenshire Estate 1735-1750.* (Third Spalding Club). 1946.

Hamilton, J.R.C. *Excavations at Jarlshof, Shetland.* (HMSO) 1956.

Harper, M. McL. *Rambles in Galloway.* Dalbeattie 1896.

Hay, G.D. The Cruck-Building at Corrimony, Inverness-shire. In *Scottish Studies* 1973. 17/2. 127-133.

Hay, G.D. Some aspects of timber construction in Scotland. In Fenton, A., Walker, B. and Stell, G., edd. *Building Construction in Scotland. Some Historical and Regional Aspects* (SVBWG) 1976. 28-38.

Headrick, J. *View of the Mineralogy, Agriculture, Manufactures and Fisheries of the Island of Arran.* Edinburgh 1807.

Headrick, J. *General View of the Agriculture of Angus.* Edinburgh 1813.

Henderson, J. *General View of the Agriculture of Caithness.* London 1812.

Heron, R. *General View of the Agriculture of the Hebrides.* Edinburgh 1794.

Hibbert, S. *A Description of the Shetland Islands.* Edinburgh 1822.

(Hope.) *George Hope of Fenton Barns. A Sketch of his Life.* Compiled by his daughter. Edinburgh 1881.

Hume, J. *General View of the Agriculture of Berwickshire.* Berwick 1797.

Hutcheson, A. *Old Stories in Stone and other Papers.* Dundee 1927.

Hutton, K. The Distribution of Wheelhouses in the British Isles. In *The Agricultural History Review* 1976. 24/1. 30-35.

Jespersen, A. River Eden Watermills 4V. (typescript, National Museum of Antiquities of Scotland) 1950.

Jespersen, A. Watermills of the River Eden. In *Proceedings of the Society of Antiquaries of Scotland* 1963-4. XCVII. 237-44.

Johnson, S. *A Journey to the Western Islands of Scotland.* London 1775.

Johnston, B. *General View of the Agriculture of Dumfries.* London 1794.

Johnston, T. *General View of the Agriculture of Tweeddale.* London 1794.

Johnston, T. *The History of the Working Classes in Scotland* (1946). Trowbridge 1974.

Keith, G. S. *General View of the Agriculture of Aberdeenshire.* Aberdeen 1811.

Kerr, R. *General View of the Agriculture of Berwick.* London 1809.

Kissling, W. The Character and Purpose of the Hebridean Black House. In *Journal of the Royal Anthropological Institute* 1943. Vol. 73. 75-99.

Kissling, W. House Traditions in the Outer Hebrides : the Black House and the Beehive Hut. In *Man*, 1944. Vol. 44, No. 73. 134-40.

Laing, J. *Voyage to Spitzbergen.* Edinburgh 1818.

R

Lauder, Sir T.D. *An Account of the Great Floods of August 1829, in the Province of Moray* (1830). Elgin 1873.

Leslie, W. *General View of the Agriculture of Nairn and Moray.* London 1811.

Loch, J. *An Account of the Improvements on the Estates of the Marquess of Stafford, in the Counties of Stafford and Salop, and on the estate of Sutherland.* London 1820.

Low, G. A Description of Orkney, 1733. In *Proceedings of the Orkney Antiquarian Society* 1923-4. II. 49-58.

Lowe, A. *General View of the Agriculture of Berwick.* London 1794.

Lowther, C., Fallow, R. and Mauson, P. *Our Journall into Scotland 1629.* Edinburgh 1894.

Lucas, A.T. Wattle and Straw Mat Doors in Ireland. In *Arctica* (Studia Ethnographica Upsaliensia XI) 1956. 16-35.

McCourt, D. Two cruck-framed buildings in Wester Ross, Scotland. In *Ulster Folklife* 1967. Vol. 13. 75-8.

MacCulloch, J. *The Highlands and Western Isles of Scotland* 4V. London 1824.

MacDonald, J. *General View of the Agriculture of the Hebrides.* Edinburgh 1811.

MacGill, W. *Old Ross-shire and Scotland* 2V. Inverness 1909.

MacKenzie, Sir G. *General View of the Agriculture of Ross and Cromarty.* London 1813.

MacLaren, A. A Norse House on Drimore Machair, South Uist. In *Glasgow Archaeological Journal* 1974. Vol. 3. 9-18.

McLaren, T. Old Windmills in Scotland, with special reference to the Windmill tower at Dunbarney, Perthshire. In *Proceedings of the Society of Antiquaries of Scotland* 1944-5. LXXIX. 6-14.

MacSween. M.D. and Gailey, A. Some Shielings in North Skye. In *Scottish Geographical Magazine* 1961. Vol. 5. 77-84.

MacWilliam, Very Revd. Alex. Canon. A Highland Mission : Strathglass, 1671-1777. In *Innes Review* 1973. XXIV/2. 75-102.

Marshall, J.N. Old Kiln at Kilwhinleck. *Transactions of the Buteshire Natural History Society* 1935. Vol. 11. 84-7.

Marshall, W. *General View of the Agriculture of the Central Highlands.* London 1794.

Martin, M. *Description of the Western Islands of Scotland* (1695). Glasgow 1884.

Master of Works Accounts 1529-1679. (MS) 30V. (HM Register House).

Maxwell, I. *Functional Architecture, Hopetoun Estate, West Lothian. A Study of Estate Farm Buildings* (typescript, 2 volumes). 1974.

Maxwell, I. Farm Buildings—Information Sources and Method of Study. In *Newsletter* (SVBWG) 1976. No. 2. 5-6.

Maxwell, S. Paddles from Horizontal Mills. In *Proceedings of the Society of Antiquaries of Scotland* 1954-6 LXXXVIII. 231-2.

Maxwell, S. A Horizontal Water Mill Paddle from Dalswinton. In *Transactions of the Dumfriesshire and Galloway Natural History and Antiquarian Society.* 1954-5. XXXIII. 185-196.

Maxwell, W.J. Old Cornkilns at Barclosh. In *Transactions of the Dumfriesshire and Galloway Natural History and Antiquarian Society* 1887-90. Vol. 6. 58-9.

Megaw, B.R.S. The 'Moss Houses' of Kincardine, Perthshire, 1792. In *Scottish Studies* 1962. 6/1. 87-93.

Megaw, B.R.S. Auchindrain, a multiple tenancy farm in mid-Argyll. In *Scottish Studies* 1963. 7. 230-4.

Michelsen, P. *Bondehuses alder.* Copenhagen 1979.

Millar, A.A. ed. *A Selection of Scottish Forfeited Estate Papers 1715; 1745* (Scottish History Society) Edinburgh 1909.

Miller, H. *My Schools and Schoolmasters.* Edinburgh 1856.

Miller, R. Land Use by Summer Shieldings. In *Scottish Studies* 1967. 11/2. 193-221.

Milligan, I.D. Corn Kilns in Bute. In *Transactions of the Buteshire Natural History Society* 1963. Vol. 15. 53-9.

Milne, R.W. Some Notes on Estate Management in the Eighteenth Century. In *Transactions of the Dumfriesshire and Galloway Natural History and Antiquarian Society 1911-12.* XXIV. 146-55.

Mitchell, A. *The Past in the Present : What is Civilisation?* Edinburgh 1880.

Mitchell, E.B. *Today and To-morrow in Rural Scotland* (United Free Church of Scotland Federation of Young People's Societies). Edinburgh 1921.

Morton, R.S. *Traditional Farm Architecture in Scotland.* Edinburgh 1976.

NMRS. National Monuments Record of Scotland.

NMRS. *Report* 1966-71; 1972-74.

NSA. *New (Second) Statistical Account.*

OSA. Old (First) Statistical Account.

Paul, Sir J. Balfour, ed. *Diary of George Ridpath, Minister of Stitchel 1755-1761* (Scottish History Society) Edinburgh 1922.

Payne, J. Mackintosh School of Architecture, University of Glasgow. In *Newsletter* (SVBWG) 1976. No. 2. 6-7.

Pennant, T. *A Tour in Scotland 1769.* 3V. London 1776.

Pennecuik, A. *Works.* Leith 1815.

Plans. Plans and Specifications of Cottages. In *Transactions of the Highland and Agricultural Society of Scotland* 1851. 245-80.

Pococke, R *Tours in Scotland 1747, 1750, 1760* (Scottish History Society) 1887.

Pride, G.L. *Glossary of Scottish Building.* n.p. 1975.

Radford, C.A. Ralegh. *The Early Christian and Norse Settlements at Birsay, Orkney.* (HMSO) 1959.

Ray, J. *A Compleat History of the Rebellion, From its first Rise, in 1745, To its total Suppression at the glorious Battle of Culloden, in April, 1746.* n.p. 1753.

RCAHMS. Royal Commission on the Ancient and Historical Monuments of Scotland.

RCAHMS. *Inventory of Kintyre* (HMSO) 1972.

Report 1884. *Report of Her Majesty's Commissioners of Inquiry into the condition of the Crofters and Cottars in the Highlands and Islands of Scotland.* Edinburgh 1884.

Ritchie, A. Pict and Norseman in Northern Scotland. In *Scottish Archaeological Forum* 1974. 6. 23-36.

Robertson, A.N. Old Dovecotes in and around Edinburgh. In *Book of the Old Edinburgh Club* 1945. XXV. 146-203; 1949. XXVI. 169-170.

Robertson, A.N. *The Old Dovecotes of Scotland* (illustrated typescript, National Museum of Antiquities of Scotland) 1958.

Robertson, G. *General View of the Agriculture of the County of Mid-Lothian*. Edinburgh 1795.

Robertson, G. *General View of the Agriculture of Kincardineshire or, The Mearns*. London 1813.

Robertson, G. *Rural Recollections*. Irvine 1829.

Robertson, J. *Tour through the Western Isles* (unpublished communications to the Society of Antiquaries of Scotland) 1768. II.

Robertson, J. *General View of the Agriculture of Inverness*. London 1808.

Robertson, J. *General View of the Agriculture of Perth*. Perth 1799.

Robson, J. *General View of the Agriculture of Argyll*. London 1794.

Roger, Mr. *General View of the Agriculture of the County of Angus or Forfar*. Edinburgh 1794.

Roussell, A. *Norse Building Customs in the Scottish Isles*. Copenhagen & London 1934.

Roy, N. Topographical Description of the Parish of Aberlady. In *Archaeologia Scotica* 1792. I. 511-22.

Sage. D.F. *Memorabilia Domestica*. Edinburgh 1889.

Scott, L. Corn-drying Kilns. In *Antiquity* 1951. XXV. 196-208.

Scott-Elliott, J. A Grain Drying Kiln in Dumfriesshire. In *Transaction of the Dumfriesshire and Galloway Natural History and Antiquarian Society* 1960-1. 39. 80-2.

Seafield Papers (Scottish Record Office).

Shirreff, J. *General View of the Agriculture of the Shetland Islands*. Edinburgh 1814.

Sinclair, C. *The Thatched Houses of the Old Highlands*. Edinburgh & London 1953.

Sinclair, J. *General View of the Agriculture of the Northern Counties and Islands of Scotland*. London 1795.

Singer, W. *General View of the Agriculture of Dumfries*. Edinburgh 1812.

Skinner, B. The Heugh Mills at Dunfermline, In *Scottish Studies* 1966. 10/2 188-190.

Skinner, B. *The Lime Industry in the Lothians*. Edinburgh 1969.

Slezer, J. *Theatrum Scotiae*. London 1693.

Small, A. Preliminary Notes on Excavations at Underhoull, Westing, Unst. In *The Aberdeen University Review* 1963. XL. No. 130, 138-144.

Small, A. Excavations at Underhoull, Unst, Shetland. In *Proceedings of the Society of Antiquaries of Scotland* 1964-6. XCVIII. 225-48.

Small, A. *Excavations in Unst*. Lerwick 1966.

Small, A. A Viking Longhouse in Unst, Shetland. In Niclasen, B., ed. *The Fifth Viking Congress*. Tórshavn 1968. 62-70.

Smith, G. *Essay on the Construction of Cottages suited for the Dwellings of the Labouring Classes*. Glasgow 1834.

Smith, J. *General View of the Agriculture of the County of Argyll*. Edinburgh 1798.

Smith J.H. *Joe Duncan. The Scottish Farm Servants and British Agriculture*. Edinburgh 1793.

Smith, S. *General View of the Agriculture of Galloway.* London 1810.

Somerville, A. *The Autobiography of a Working Man.* London 1848.

Somerville, R. *General View of the Agriculture of East Lothian.* London 1805.

Souter, D. *General View of the Agriculture of Banff.* Edinburgh 1812.

Stell, G. Two Cruck-framed Buildings in Dumfriesshire. In *Transactions of the Dumfriesshire and Galloway Natural History and Antiquarian Society 1972.* XLIX. 39-48.

Stell, G. *Some Small Farms and Cottages in Latheron Parish, Caithness* (typescript: publication forthcoming).

Stephen, W.M. Toll Houses of the Greater Fife Area. In *Industrial Archaeology* 1967. IV/3. 248-254.

Stephens, H. and Burn, R.S. *The Book of Farm Buildings.* 1861.

SVBWG. Scottish Vernacular Buildings Working Group.

SVBWG. *Newsletter* 1975. No. 1; 1976. No. 2; 1977. No. 3.

SWRI. Scottish Women's Rural Institutes.

SWRI. *Village History : Nigg* (typescript). 1966.

SWRI. *History of Latheron District.* (typescript). 1966.

Talve, I. *Bastu och Torkhus i Nordeuropa* (Nordiska Museets Handlingar : 53). 1960.

Taylor, L.B., ed. *Aberdeen Shore Work Accounts 1596-1670.* Aberdeen 1972.

Thomas, Captain F.W.L. Notice of Beehive Houses in Harris and Lewis. In *Proceedings of the Society of Antiquaries of Scotland* 1857-60. III. 127-44.

Thomas, Captain F.W.L. On the Primitive Dwellings and Hypogea of the Outer Hebrides. In *Proceedings of the Society of Antiquaries of Scotland* 1866-68. VII. 153-95.

Thomson, J. *General View of the Agriculture of the County of Fife.* Edinburgh 1800.

Tindall, F.P. *East Lothian Water Mills.* 1970.

Trotter, J. *General View of the Agriculture of West Lothian.* Edinburgh 1794 and 1811.

Tudor, J.R. *The Orkneys and Shetland.* London 1883.

Ure, D. *General View of the Agriculture in the County of Dumbarton.* London 1794.

Ure, D. *General View of the Agriculture of Roxburgh.* London 1794.

Ure, D. *General View of the Agriculture of Kinross.* London 1797.

Waddell, J.J. Some Old Stone Dove Cots, Mainly in Lanarkshire. In *Transactions of the Glasgow Archaeological Society* 1937-40. 9. 189-194.

Walker, B. Some regional variations in building techniques in Angus, Fife and Perthshire. In Fenton, A., Walker, B. and Stell, G., edd. *Building Construction in Scotland. Some Historical and Regional Aspects* (SVBWG) 1976. 52-64.

Walker, B. Keeping it Cool (Scottish Ice Houses). *Scots Magazine,* New Series 105.6 1976. 563-572

Walker, B. *Clay Buildings in North East Scotland* (SVBWG) 1977.

Walker, B. The Influence of Fixed Farm Machinery on Farm Building Design in Eastern Scotland in the late 18th and 19th Centuries. In *The Archaeology of Industrial Scotland* (Scottish Archaeological Forum 8) 1977. 52-74.

Walker, B. *List of Farm Plans in the Scone Palace Estate Office.* National Register of Archives (Scotland) 1979.

Walker, B. The Vernacular Buildings of North East Scotland : an Exploration. In *The Scottish Geographical Magazine* 1979. Vol. 95. 45-60.

Walker, B. *Farm Buildings in the Grampian Region : An Historical Exploration* (Grampian Regional Council, Countryside Commission for Scotland) 1979.

Walton, J. The Skye House. In *Antiquity* 1957. XXXI. 155-162.

Walton, J. Cruck-Framed Buildings in Scotland. In *Gwerin* 1957. I/3. 109-122.

Warden, A.J. *History of the Linen Trade*. London 1864.

Webster, J. *General View of the Agriculture of Galloway*. Edinburgh 1794.

Webster, L.E. and Cherry, J. Medieval Britain in 1971. In *Medieval Archaeology* 1972. XVI. 147-212.

Whitaker, I. Two Hebridean Corn-kilns. In *Gwerin* 1957. I/4. 161-170.

Whitaker, J. Ancient Dovecots of East Lothian : a Survey. In *Transactions of the East Lothian Antiquarian and Field Naturalists' Society* 1934-38. Vol. 3. 1-22; 1952. Vol. 5. 59-66.

Whyte, A. and Macfarlane, D. *General View of the Agriculture of the County of Dumbarton*. Glasgow 1811.

Whyte, I.D. Rural Housing in Lowland Scotland in the Seventeenth Century : The Evidence of Estate Papers. In *Scottish Studies* 1975. 19. 55-68.

Whyte, I.D. *Agriculture and Society in Seventeenth-Century Scotland*. Edinburgh 1979.

Wight, A. *The Present State of Husbandry in Scotland*. 4V. Edinburgh 1778-84.

Williams, H.W. The 'Clachans' of Lewis. In *The Reliquary and Illustrated Archaeologist* 1900. VI. 73-79.

Wilson, D.M. and Moorhouse, S. Medieval Britain in 1970. In *Medieval Archaeology* 1971. XV. 124-179.

Wilson, J. *General View of the Agriculture of Renfrew*. Paisley 1812.

Young, A. *General View of the Agriculture of Norfolk* (1804). Newton Abbot 1969.

Index and Glossary